The Entrepreneurial Connection

East meets West in the Silicon Valley

Gurmeet Naroola

Special TiE Edition
California, USA

www.indusbrainpower.com

A version of this book to be published by
Tata-McGraw Hill in India

You can contact the author at E-mail: gsnaroola@yahoo.com

First published in USA, 2001

Copyright © by *Gurmeet Naroola 2001*

ISBN 0971119600

Current Printing (last digit):
10 9 8 7 6 5 4 3 2 1

Printed and bound in the United States of America

The Publishers' policy is to use paper manufacturing for sustainable forests

Edited by Diana Cooper
Formatted by Bill Berry
Cover Design by Patricia Andersson

Praise for The Entrepreneurial Connection

John Chambers - President and CEO, Cisco Systems

"This book captures the essence of one of the key drivers in the Silicon Valley phenomenon...the Indus entrepreneurial spirit. It is a road map to success for companies and individuals competing in the networking economy."

Jim Clark - Founder of Silicon Graphics & Netscape

"Indus entrepreneurs are some of the best educated scientific and engineering minds in the world. It has been my good fortune to work with several of them featured in this book. They fit a perfect profile for success: good business instincts, a commitment to hard work, high integrity, and a team spirit."

Pramod Mahajan - IT Minister, India

"Over the years, Silicon Valley has blossomed as an IT nerve centre, due in part to the enterprise and zeal of brilliant Indian minds. These bright minds have combined hard work, efficient pricing and an invincible entrepreneurial spirit that has made India's present-day image one of a tech-savvy nation that can deliver cutting edge technologies."

"This book will help our young scholars road map their vision of an ideal entrepreneurial role model."

Nara Chandrababu Naidu - Chief Minister, Andhra Pradesh

"This book is an inspiration to all those striving to achieve excellence. Gurmeet Naroola has provided a glimpse of India's true potential as represented in the achievements of some of the most outstanding individuals from this country."

Jerome S. Engel - Executive Director Lester Center for Entrepreneurship & Innovation, Haas School of Business, UC Berkeley

"Entrepreneurship is learned through mentors. In the Entrepreneurial Connection author Gurmeet Naroola has assembled the best Indus Entrepreneurs in the Valley to be our mentors and guides. In a series of intimate interviews the author has assembled their individual and collective wisdom in a way that can be easily understood and acted upon."

Kailash Joshi, Ph.D - President, TiE

"This book captures the phenomenal achievements of twenty four of the most noteworthy achievers with origins in India. This book is a must read for parents in search of role models for their aspiring children, students who want to explore contemporary success stories in business, teachers who seek satisfaction from examples of educational successes, and above all, the entrepreneurs who wish to be inspired from these extraordinary profiles of determination and hard work . "

Ratan N. Tata – Chairman of Tata Enterprises, India

"The book offers very interesting insights into the contribution of Indian entrepreneurs to the revolution in information technology in Silicon Valley."

Rajan Nanda - Chairman of Escorts Group, India

"The foundation of growth has come from entrepreneurs who have the vision with which they have mustered capital to create new discoveries and inventions for the world. Documenting current generation entrepreneurs in the same effort should be an inspiration for all who read this well assembled book for its research and contents."

Dedication

To Mother Teresa and Mahatma Gandhi who represent the entrepreneurial spirit at its best.

Acknowledgements

Several individuals played a vital role in bringing this book to life and I am extremely grateful to each one of them.

Dr. Kailash Joshi, I thank you for playing an instrumental role in this book. You challenged me by raising the bar of quality and excellence. Your mentoring has played a vital role. Kanwal Rekhi and Dr. Suhas Patil, I am grateful to you for agreeing to participate in the book and giving me the jump-start I needed.

Dad, thank you for your guidance and brilliant ideas. Aparna, my dear wife without your love, support and encouragement this book would never have become a reality. My sister Minni, without your help the book would have taken a good six months longer. To the little one on his way, the thought of you kept me going when I could have easily given-up.

Raghu Batta, your knowledge and effort were instrumental in making this book a reality. Your team-work brought a third dimension to this book. I value our friendship and am grateful to you. Amar Chauhan, I appreciate your assistance in taking the extra weight off my shoulders when this project seemed almost impossible.

Dr. Gupta and Dr. Dossani, I am grateful to you for providing valuable guidance and encouragement throughout the project. I would also like to thank Lata Krishnan, Ajay Shah, Satjiv Chahil, A.J. Patel, Dr. Kappany, Raj Desai, Parveen Gupta, Romesh Mathur and Veena Birla for their valuable input and guidance.

Behind every successful entrepreneur there is an extremely resourceful executive administrative assistant. Special thanks to Tibby, CeCe, Cecilia, Leah, Crystal, Sandi, Anilyn, Rayleen, Marlene, Caryl, Carolyn, Pandu, Rafeal, Lisa, Carrie for coordinating the interviews with these phenomenal individuals.

Diana Cooper I thank you for your patience and diligence in editing this book. Bill Berry I am sure the readers will appreciate your design for the layout of the book.

Thank you all! It was fun all the way.

Foreword

This book captures the phenomenal success stories of twenty four of the most noteworthy achievers of Indian origin. It brings to life their thought processes and values driving their success. India plays a central role in these achievements, but the U.S. is the land where most of their stories came to fruition.

Their collective thoughts represent *"The Entrepreneurial Connection."*

What make these stories most interesting are combined elements of excellence, which India inculcates and the U.S. brings to the fore. Together they represent the shared values of India and the U.S. and the very best that each country has to offer. This is not a mere compilation of success stories, but a narrative of a quiet India-U.S. phenomenon of the last three decades. These profiles of significant success represent the aspirations of tens of thousands of professionals who share, in varying degrees, the same aspirations and perspectives. These success stories do have a great deal to do with the U.S. tradition of innovation, risk-taking and rewarding of successful entrepreneurs.

From the numerous Indo-American success stories, one can easily see how the equitable and meritocratic immigration policies adopted by the United States in the 1960's brought these prodigious economic value creators to its shores. Common themes across the success profiles are apparent. These include an upbringing in India's environment, excellence in technical education, an early grasp of meritocracy, hard work, and an ability to take advantage of available opportunities.

The twenty four individuals described in this book come by and large from middle class backgrounds but represent the diversity of India in geography, religion, language, and traditions. However, the biggest equalizer for them was the high quality of education India could offer, one that instilled in them a strong sense of academic competitiveness. Their accomplishments allowed them to avail of the opportunities for higher education found in the U.S. They also enjoyed a facility with the English language and a healthy understanding of the democratic system that makes the assimilation of Indians so natural in the U.S. As they stepped into their professional domains, this same competitive spirit gave them an edge in their search for new ideas and the confidence to plunge into ventures of their own. Success came to them in gradual steps and most of them were in their forties before they truly made their names in business. Above all, they enjoyed the traditional, deep-rooted support of their families in all their endeavors. This is an integral component of "Indianness".

Gurmeet Naroola a young determined Silicon Valley engineer has accomplished an amazing task by bringing out the knowledge behind these vibrant minds. I commend him for this achievement.

This book is a must read for parents in search of role models for their aspiring children, students who want to explore contemporary success stories in business, teachers who seek satisfaction from examples of educational successes, and above all, the entrepreneurs who wish to be inspired from these extraordinary profiles of determination and hard work. Finally, the architects of government policies in India and the U.S. can draw their own conclusions about the value of educational and economic cooperation between the two countries. Hopefully this book will also help with the ongoing introspection in India about how it can help the future generations of its children in achieving many such successes at home.

Kailash Joshi, Ph.D.
President, The IndUS Entrepreneurs (TiE)

Preface

This book represents an amazing journey into the entrepreneurial world. It is my education in hands-on entrepreneurship; the teachers were amongst the best in the world, the classrooms were Silicon Valley, Route 128 (Boston) and Bangalore.

Here is how it started. I had a great corporate American job, worked 8 to 5, had a corner office with a great view, attended beer bashes every other Friday and even traveled the world twice a year. Life was good. Then one fine, sunny Californian day I got hit by the "Silicon Valley Bug" and all hell broke loose. I began searching for the answers to the infinite number of questions I suddenly had.

Why are these immigrants so successful? What attributes fuel their success? How do they build great companies? Is it hard work, timing, education, dedication, or is it just plain luck? How does one establish a startup? How do the ideas germinate? What are the first few steps? What makes the Silicon Valley so innovative and unique? How do they build and lead their teams? Where does the money come from? What are their pathways to success and the roadblocks they encounter? What sacrifices do they make and is it all worth it?

And so I decided to embark on this rather ambitious project. The answers to these questions is what this book is about. The book brings the brainpower of visionaries and startup gurus under one umbrella and provides their roadmaps to success. It explains the "nuts & bolts" of the entrepreneurial world and gives an insight into the innovative and successful management skills utilized by them. The book highlights the strengths and thought processes of each entrepreneur as applied to their success. In addition it showcases the effective habits of these successful people. This is a book about entrepreneurial management.

We interviewed the top twenty-four Indus entrepreneurs from around the globe. Many of the interviews required several meetings, and in some cases, took over a month to complete. Some interviews were conducted face-to-face, others over conference calls across the globe, a few during rides to the airport, and one during an early morning walk. This was a mind-expanding experience. All those interviewed were engaging, cooperative and willing to their share knowledge. The book was edited to preserve and accentuate their personality.

The focus of the questions for each entrepreneur was dependent upon several factors – their background, their expertise, their strengths, and their current challenges. Entrepreneurs featured in this book were selected based on several criteria: domain expertise, availability and location. Several entrepreneurs interviewed could not be included in this work due to timing, deadlines, and publishing limitations. I am grateful to all of them for giving me their time, advice and kind words of encouragement.

The interviews are organized according to the various phases of a company's life: conception, company building, market penetration, growth and globalization, morphing and transformation, diversification, mentoring, angel and VC investing, and finally the synergy of eastern and western values.

This book is intended for anyone with a hunger for knowledge. Entrepreneurs who have a desire to build great companies, executives who want to benchmark against the best, managers who want to break through the glass ceiling, students who want to learn from the gurus, and consultants will all find this book extremely useful. It is a book for all levels of interest and experience.

The book was developed with an entrepreneurial mindset. Use it to fuel your entrepreneurial journey.

Gurmeet

Table of Contents

AnnaLee Saxenian

University of California - Berkeley

Culture and Competition in the Silicon Valley

Dr. AnnaLee Saxenian is a Professor of City and Regional Planning at the University of California at Berkeley and an internationally recognized expert on regional economies and the information technology sector. Her current research examines the contributions of skilled immigrants to Silicon Valley and their growing ties to regions in Asia. Her recent publications include *Silicon Valley's New Immigrant Entrepreneurs* and *Regional Advantage: Culture and Competition in Silicon Valley and Route 128*. She has written extensively about innovation and regional development, urbanization, and the organization of labor markets in Silicon Valley.

Dr. Saxenian was the Gordon Cain Senior Fellow at the Stanford Institute for Economic Policy Research in 1999-2000. She is currently an Adjunct Fellow at the Institute for the Future. She holds a doctorate in political science from MIT, a master's in regional planning from the University of California at Berkeley, and a BA in economics from Williams College in Massachusetts.

Raghu Batta and I met with Dr. Saxenian at her residence in Berkeley. We had a very interesting discussion around her dining table that was covered with her son's toys. We started off the conversation by looking at the core ingredients that make Silicon Valley a center of entrepreneurship. She shed light on the culture capital, venture capital, support capital, and intellectual capital that fuels the chemical reaction making Silicon Valley the most fertile area for entrepreneurs. We then discussed, through examples, what it would take to emulate the Silicon Valley in different parts of the world.

"Silicon Valley has always been unusually open and meritocratic."

Your research indicates that 29% of the technology companies begun in Silicon Valley since 1980 are run by Indian and Chinese entrepreneurs, and that they have generated jobs and wealth for the California economy. What are the characteristics that make Silicon Valley a center for entrepreneurship?

Silicon Valley is an environment that is unusually open, allowing skilled professionals to experiment freely. It allows them to experiment with new technologies, new products, new markets, and new applications in a relatively unfettered fashion. This is a radical departure from the way business has been done in the rest of the U.S. and probably in the rest of the world in the postwar period. One of the region's most important innovations is the institutionalization of venture capital as a mechanism for financing high-risk, high return ventures. The other critical element in this environment is a set of attitudes and relationships between individuals and companies, a very open attitude towards sharing ideas and information.

Silicon Valley is notable for its dense social networks that grow out of a high rate of mobility. Professionals move between companies at a very high rate. As a result, ideas and know-how are transferred very quickly between individuals and firms within the regional economy. People maintain their social networks when they move between jobs, so when they decide to start another company they draw on a much broader network. And engineers frequently move between industries and sectors - from university to industry, from semiconductors to telecommunications, and from industry to finance (venture capital). This contributes to the cross-fertilization of ideas and know-how and leads to unanticipated technological recombinations.

These cross-cutting social networks, when combined with the venture capital which allows for the seeding of multiple experiments and the presence of intellectual resources in universities such as Stanford and Berkeley, create an environment that supports repeated parallel experiments - far more experiments than would be tolerated within a large corporation. Finally, risk-taking is part of the culture in Silicon Valley, and failure is not a stigma. Instead, there is recognition that learning can only happen through failure. So a very different cultural environment emerged in Silicon Valley in the post war period than that which existed in most other industrial regions.

Can you elaborate on what you mean by "open attitude"? Is it open in the sense that ideas flow much more freely?

Information and know-how circulate faster and more freely in Silicon Valley than anywhere else I've seen. The traditional business attitude has been one of secrecy and pursuit of corporate self-sufficiency. This involved protecting corporate resources and technology by building boundaries around the company. Silicon Valley's pioneers broke away from this model by opening up the boundaries both between firms and other local institutions like universities and venture capitalists.

For example, let's go back a few years and compare Silicon Valley with its counterpart, the Route 128 area in Boston. This is the story I told in my book, *Regional Advantage*. Although Boston had a strong pool of technical talent, outstanding educational institutions (M.I.T. and Harvard), was a nice place to live, had a fledgling venture capital industry and a long industrial history, the Boston corridor failed in the 1980s to keep pace with technological change in Silicon Valley. The region's leading minicomputer companies, such as DEC and Data General, pursued vertical integration and built hierarchies as they grew large. They also became very autarkic; they built corporate boundaries that made it difficult for people to leave or to share information outside of the firm. As a result, the skills and technology in the region were trapped within the boundaries of a small number of very big companies, while in Silicon Valley they were being continually recombined. Moreover, vertical integration made it very difficult for companies like DEC to adapt as markets shifted. This problem intensified as the pace of technological change accelerated in the 1990s and the big, integrated East Coast companies could not keep up with the more flexible and entrepreneurial startups in California. Geography is also important. The geography certainly both reinforces and reflects these corporate differences. The Route 128 companies actively pursued geographic isolation in the 1980s while Silicon Valley firms and other institutions are very densely clustered within a small area. This proximity supports the continuous exchange and face-to-face communications that characterize the region.

Do you see the Boston area becoming more like the Silicon Valley these days?

Absolutely. The Boston area fell into crisis in the early 1990s because its leading producers failed to keep up with the pace of technology and market change. But as companies like DEC and Wang declined, they freed up thousands of engineers and managers who went out and started new companies. These entrepreneurs learned from the mistakes of their predecessors; the new generation of firms is more focused and integrated into a more open and horizontal network business model. As a result the Route 128 corridor today looks more and more like Silicon Valley.

Of course it takes time for individuals and institutions to change. It is not just the technology companies that have been changing. The region's universities, professional service firms, and the financial community are all adapting to support a faster-paced, more decentralized and entrepreneurial industrial system. This helps explain why the Boston area remains the second largest center of entrepreneurship in the U.S.

What attracts immigrants from all over the world to Silicon Valley?

Silicon Valley has always been unusually open and meritocratic. People of different backgrounds, including first-generation immigrants, feel comfortable here and can progress in the region in a way that is not possible in many other parts of the world. In the 70s and 80s, large numbers of immigrants came to the U.S. to study engineering and sciences. This influx of immigrant engineers coincided with the boom of Silicon Valley and these newly-minted graduates got pulled into the Silicon Valley economy. Immigrants went to graduate schools all over the country, from Iowa to New York State to Texas, but they eventually migrated to the Valley in huge numbers because the jobs were here.

These people were primarily Indian and Chinese, the best and the brightest from their countries, graduates of the elite technical institutions like I.I.Ts in India, National Taiwan University in Taiwan and Beijing University in China. They were also risk-takers by nature, having left their homes to come to the U.S. When they came to Silicon Valley, one of two things happened; they either succeeded in a big company or they faced a glass ceiling. Some of those pioneers faced barriers or were forced out of the leading positions in the companies that they founded. But the thing about the Silicon Valley environment is that if you face a glass ceiling in one environment you have a very easy run-around; you simply leave and start your own company. And that's essentially what happened; the response to such limits has been successive waves of entrepreneurship. The openness of the environment and the opportunities for entrepreneurship go a long way toward explaining the tremendous success of immigrant entrepreneurs in the Silicon Valley today.

> *Silicon Valley has always been unusually open and meritocratic.*

Why are the entrepreneurs mainly from India and China? Does it have any-thing to do with the society back there and their desire for knowledge?

I think it has to do with the desire for knowledge and the desire for economic success. The Indians and Chinese came from developing countries with tre-mendous ambition, with no pressures or immediate reason to return. Most Indians and Chinese would say, "What would I do? I have a Ph.D from Illi-nois Institute of Technology but there is nothing that I could do back in India or China." The best opportunities are in the U.S.

Immigrants from other countries typically feel pressure to go back home after completing their studies. A lot of Koreans and Japanese who came to the U.S. to study could return home to stable, high paying jobs in their coun-tries' biggest, most successful companies. Europeans often felt a similar pressure. If you were a French student, you could go back home to France and get one of the most elite jobs in the country.

So the immigrants who have stayed and worked here in large numbers are the ones from the poorest countries; initially Taiwan, then India and then China. The Mainland Chinese are the most recent arrivals in the U.S., but they also represent the biggest group of immigrant engineers. They haven't proven themselves yet, but I am certain that they will.

Why are there so many more entrepreneurs in Silicon Valley than elsewhere in the U.S., even though there are engineers all over the country?

When you work in the Silicon Valley environment you become part of it and you learn how it works; you learn how to network, how to find venture capi-tal, how to start a company, you learn what the support infrastructure looks like, how to deal with the venture capitalists, the lawyers, all the things that make it easy to start a company very fast and succeed. It's very hard to learn that outside the Valley. In the Valley you kind of marinate in it, you learn it almost by osmosis. But if you are an equally good engineer who takes a job in Chicago, I'm not sure that you're going to understand how to do it.

Take a look at The Indus Entrepreneurial group (TiE). The fact that Kanwal Rekhi has started an institution like TiE that helps other Indus entrepreneurs is very much a reflection of the Valley culture of helping one another, of net-working, of trying to build a set of horizontal networks that help. You will find that there are dozens of associations like that for different ethnic groups.

Moving to educational systems, how have Stanford and Berkeley become top-notch educational institutions?

The most interesting thing about Stanford is not simply that it is an excellent institution but that it has overcome the Ivory Tower syndrome. It's deeply integrated into the industrial economy that surrounds it. People move quite freely from Stanford to various corporations. Stanford University is a critical part of the open culture of Silicon Valley.

In fact, Stanford itself played a key role in developing this culture. Fredrick Terman, the former dean of engineering, is often referred to as "the father of Silicon Valley" because he envisioned "a community of technical scholars" in Northern California. He sought to create a technical community where there was, in his words, "continuous ferment of new ideas

Stanford University is a critical part of the open culture of Silicon Valley.

and stimulating new challenges." And perhaps most importantly, he collaborated closely with local industry and entrepreneurs in achieving this goal. So he not only amassed resources aggressively and hired top-notch people but he created a new model of a university, one with much more open boundaries to the surrounding industrial community.

Of course other educational institutions have been central to Silicon Valley's success, including not just the University of California at Berkeley, but also San Jose State University and DeAnza and Foothill Community Colleges. All of these institutions are part of the state-funded California education system that excelled in the postwar period and which contributes to the supply of skill and intellectual capital that are central to Silicon Valley's continued dynamism.

Is education a common platform between India, China and Taiwan?

Absolutely. If you look at India, Taiwan and China, they have all created first-rate science and engineering universities, even if in small numbers, and have all developed unusually meritocratic processes for entrance in spite of the corruption elsewhere in the society. This allows middle class families to push their kids to obtain higher education, and in each of these societies, engineering is regarded as one of the most desirable pursuits. The kids that excel at home in India and China and Taiwan are the ones who go on to study in the U.S. and ultimately become part of the skilled labor force in places like Silicon Valley and the Boston area.

> *The interesting thing about the new technology economy is that it is a middle class phenomenon.*

The interesting thing about the new technology economy is that it is a middle class phenomenon. It's being spearheaded by young engineers from the middle classes of their societies. Silicon Valley is not the home of the established American corporate or political elites, nor is it attracting the older elites from places like India and China. These are the hard-working kids of the middle class.

Would it be correct to say that to replicate or emulate the Silicon Valley success story, universities and corporations have to work side by side?

Collaboration between universities and companies is at the core of the Silicon Valley experience. My sense is that in most of the world, educational institutions remain separate from the world of industry and there is little knowledge flow between them. This is the legacy of the Ivory Tower. Take India, for example. I visited the Indian Institute of Science in Bangalore. It's beautiful, but it is like a separate world from the local software industry. There are people trying to build links, but as elsewhere in the world, the tradition is to maintain distance from the industry. These institutional habits are often slow to change.

Shifting gears to the venture capital community, isn't it the case that venture capital in Silicon Valley and the Boston corridor comes primarily from people who've "been there, done that" rather than bankers or traditional financiers?

Venture capital grows right out of the environment. The most successful venture capitalists are individuals who understand the industry first-hand, who know how to start a company, who have networks of relationships that they turn to help build teams. Unlike traditional bankers, the U.S. venture capitalists are very much part of the local industrial infrastructure and it's essential that they are part of it. In Silicon Valley it is like an evolutionary process; first you start a company, then if you succeed and make lots of money you become an angel and invest small amounts in companies run by friends and acquaintances. Later in life, when you're ready to leave management, you might become a venture capitalist. Very few people in Silicon Valley actually retire; rather, they become angels and venture capitalists in their old age, sharing their knowledge, experience, and networking skills with the next generation of entrepreneurs.

How could we create the Silicon Valley phenomenon in India?

There are many elements to the Silicon Valley phenomenon, some of which cannot be reproduced anywhere else by virtue of the simple fact that Silicon Valley already exists in California. However the dynamism of Silicon Valley is fundamentally a product of an open environment that supports continual experimentation with new technologies, products, markets and applications, and one that encourages learning from failure.

Rather than making a checklist of factors such as university, venture capital, science park, and so on, that contribute to the "high tech recipe", I think that the first step in a place like India is to begin to create a more open environment. It should be one that encourages horizontal flows of information and joint problem-solving across traditional boundaries. This means bringing together traditionally separate communities: university researchers and corporate managers and aspiring entrepreneurs and financiers and policymakers to address shared problems. This could include everything from problems of the physical infrastructure and telecommunications system to the availability of venture capital and skilled labor.

The key is to create a context where people come together repeatedly and start to build relationships with one another. They start to recognize that they have shared interests and shared problems. In India they might get together first and say, "Damn it, we need to fix the roads because they are driving us all crazy." Later it might involve providing training in management or marketing or it might involve supporting research in a particular area. Over time, as these relationships mature and evolve, they can provide the foundation for entrepreneurship as well. It's interesting that many of the most promising startups you see in a place like Bangalore come out of WIPRO. WIPRO is a big technology company that has served as an important training ground for many Indian engineers. These individuals were able to build a set of relationships and gain managerial skills and knowledge within the big company. These skills and relationships become an invaluable resource when they start new businesses. It's no different in a region. You just have to create opportunities for people to get to know one another, build up the cross-cutting social networks and the process of collective learning in the region

There are important aspects of the institutional context that matter, and one of the things that is interesting about India is that the non-resident Indians like Kanwal Rekhi and KB Chandrasekhar have been working to influence policy. For example, they have worked with the Securities and Exchange Board of India to develop the venture capital industry. I think that creating some kind of exit option like the American NASDAQ for venture capitalists is a very important element of this model.

In each of the places that are trying to imitate Silicon Valley there are particular things that need to be addressed collectively. None of them are insurmountable. India still needs to improve its telecommunications infrastructure. China needs to develop its capital markets and the rule of law. Both need to deal with intellectual property rights.

Each place has its own particular history, institutions, and resources, so no place will be exactly like Silicon Valley. The key is to create an environment that supports entrepreneurship, experimentation, and learning. For these, the main prerequisites are well- trained people, sources of technology and of high risk financing, and open flows of people and information between the universities, industry, and the financial community.

What about Europe and Japan?

There is a general pattern that I have observed, not just in Europe but in parts of Asia as well. The places that were most successful in the old industrial model are having a harder time adapting to this new "bottom-up" entrepreneurial model. I'll term the old model the "National Champion model." Success in this era depended upon an alliance between the state and the large corporations that were designated as national leaders. In this era, every country sought to create its own IBM.

In Europe, the big, established electronics and communications companies typically developed privileged relationships with the state. Those relationships worked when markets were national and technologies were stable, but they also tended to hinder local entrepreneurship. First, the most talented engineers and managers worked for these established corporations, depriving aspiring startups of skill. Moreover, the "national champions" typically dominated the government market for telecommunications and electronics-related products, thus limiting the opportunities for startups. Meanwhile the lack of competition for these "champions" often resulted in a lagging pace of technological advance.

It is interesting to note that the places that are emerging as successful in the new era are those that have traditionally been considered peripheral to Europe. Ireland, Israel, and Finland have all emerged as centers of innovation and entrepreneurship, while France and Germany continue to lag behind.

Or think back to the 1980s, when Japan was the model. When I started writing about the Silicon Valley people said to me, "You're crazy. The big Japanese corporations are going to gobble up all the small companies in the Valley." The large and integrated Keiretsu in Japan provided lifetime employment to the most talented professionals. Like their European counterparts, they were successful in an era of mass manufacturing but failed to keep up with the accelerated pace of market and technological change in the 1980s and 1990s.

How will Japan, for example, break the mold?

I think that it's going to be a long process. It is likely to take generational change to achieve the institutional changes needed to shift from the old model to a more flexible and bottom-up one. It's proven very hard to break up the alliance between the politicians and bureaucrats in the powerful ministries on one hand and the leading corporations on the other. There is a lot at stake. Many people recognize the problem, but the changes are much harder to make.

Will we see a localization of industry segments? For example- innovation will always happen in the Silicon Valley, mass replication will always happen in Japan, software development will always happen in India.

I think you will see localized specialization continue to emerge and I believe that innovation will increasingly occur outside of Silicon Valley as well. Innovation in different segments and sectors will take place in different places as each location builds up its own distinctive technical capabilities. Taiwan, for example, has shifted from a source of low-cost manufacturing labor into a center of state-of-the-art computer and semiconductor manufacturing. India has the potential to develop as a center of innovation in the software and service sectors. Most front-end product definition and design will remain in Silicon Valley as long as the leading customers are here. But as new markets open up, I can imagine new product definition emerging in other places as well. The case of Nokia in Finland is a good example.

If you look at the other side of the coin, what should India, Japan and Germany not learn from Silicon Valley?

First, they should recognize that it takes more to replicate the Silicon Valley phenomenon than a science park. There are many places in the world that are building science parks and these are, as far as I am concerned, just real estate deals, or perhaps an alliance between real estate developers and politicians. A science park is just a building. It alone has little to do with innovation or entrepreneurship aside from providing infrastructure. Second, they should learn that they cannot create venture capital from the top down.

There are many government-funded and government-run venture capital efforts emerging around the world. These efforts ignore the fact that venture capital must be part of the local technical infrastructure and networks in order to succeed.

Planners and policy-makers typically adopt some variant of the "high tech recipe," believing that if they combine a research university, a science park, skilled labor, and supplies of venture capital in a nice environment they can "grow the next Silicon Valley." What they fail to recognize is that the relationships and social networks are as essential to Silicon Valley's continued dynamism as the presence of educational institutions or supplies of skill and capital.

Will the Valley phenomenon be self destructive because of being over crowded and other reasons, like people jumping ship from company to company? Do you see any fundamental changes in the Valley, or will it continue its growth?

People have been predicting Silicon Valley's demise for a very long time. The first thing that I wrote about the Valley in 1980 was that it was going to stop growing. I argued that Silicon Valley would stop growing because the housing prices were too high, transportation was too congested, and that all future growth in high tech would occur in Austin or Seattle. But this did not happen. That's what led me to understand that the Silicon Valley environment offers advantages that outweigh its high costs.

Silicon Valley will continue to attract the best and the brightest talents in the world. And they will continue to benefit from its open and mobile and meritocratic environment. There have been a lot of great companies built in the Valley in the past. This is the environment that spawned Intel, Oracle, Cisco, Chiron, Yahoo, eBay, and many more of the world's leading IT companies. There is no reason to believe that process will stop now.

Of course there are still physical and economic limits to large-scale expansion in the Valley, which is why you will always see Silicon Valley companies expanding to other regions of the U.S. and other parts of the world. This is good for Silicon Valley because you can't do everything here. Nor is this a zero-sum game. Silicon Valley companies benefit from the emergence of new centers of technological excellence. Meanwhile, the region will continue to serve as a crucible for leading-edge entrepreneurship and innovation in the near term. I don't expect that in the next decade either the technology will slow down or the environment here will deteriorate significantly enough to undermine its accumulated regional advantage.

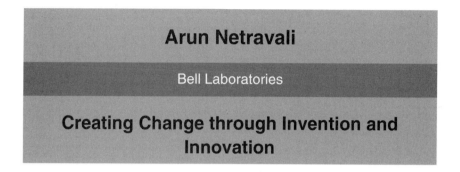

Arun Netravali

Bell Laboratories

Creating Change through Invention and Innovation

Dr. Arun Netravali is President of Bell Laboratories, the research and development arm of Lucent Technologies, where he heads a workforce of 27,000 people. Dr. Netravali has been at the lab for 23 years and has held a variety of leadership positions in the visual communication, computer systems and communications sciences research areas.

Dr. Netravali is regarded as a pioneer in the field of digital technology and led the research and development of Bell Labs' high definition television (HDTV) effort. He holds more than 70 patents in the areas of computer networks, human/machine interface, picture processing and digital television. He has co-authored three books and more than 170 technical papers and received many awards for scientific achievement.

He received his undergraduate degree from the Indian Institute of Technology, Bombay, India, and master's and doctoral degrees from Rice University in Houston Texas - all in electrical engineering. He holds an honorary doctorate from the Ecole Polytechnique Federale in Lausanne, Switzerland.

This interview took place in two sessions. Dr. Martin Levetin, who knew Dr. Netravali in the seventies at Bell labs, Raghu Batta and I conducted the first phone interview. The second interview was conducted at 6:00 am the following day, after I received a call from his executive secretary (CeCe) informing me that Dr. Netravali was scheduled to leave for China very soon.

Dr. Netravali enjoyed sharing his views and thoughts on a wide variety of topics. The primary focus of our interview was how the role of Bell labs has morphed to meet the challenges of the new economy. We compared the Bell labs of today to Silicon Valley. We discussed the role that Bell labs plays as a driver of invention and innovation. Dr. Netravali shares his seven predictions for the future. Towards the end, we explore what it takes to lead the world's largest think tank with a workforce that includes over 12,000 Ph.Ds.

"The most important attribute of leadership is to set aggressive goals and allow people to achieve them with authority and accountability."

Bell Labs is certainly known as a center of innovation. Silicon Valley also has a reputation for being a center of innovation and in some sense one could describe them separately as ecosystems with flows of capital and technology. We were hoping that you could compare the Bell Laboratories environment with the Silicon Valley environment in the context of Bell Labs today as well as Bell Labs pre-divestiture?

Prior to Lucent's spin-off from AT&T in 1996, Bell labs was a center of invention but not necessarily a center of innovation. The philosophy in those days was to get the best possible minds from the academic world and watch where they go. Once in a while they will discover something terrific that might lead to product development. And some of these inventions really helped create entire new industries.

That period at Bell Labs was incredibly prolific. It produced the transistor, the C computer language, the Unix operating system, and cellular telephony, to name just a few. But I don't think we were motivated to do things quickly in those days. The Bell System was a regulated monopoly and received a fixed rate of return on the investments that it made. Our main motivation was to make sure that the quality of our product was fantastic, offering the longest life. The drivers for Bell Labs in those days were very different from what drives us today. So there are several contrasts between then and now. Invention is no longer enough. Now innovation and initiative, and getting the invention to the market quickly, before our competitors, are vital. Meeting the specialized requirements of different customers at the lowest cost is another important driver today.

The second change is in terms of the areas we are focused on. Today we have a clearer focus on the areas that are important for Lucent's success. That doesn't mean that the freedom to look at broad or longer-term issues is gone; what is different is that the areas of focus are very clearly defined. Our recruiting and our research efforts are focused on certain areas, and we are determined that in those areas we absolutely cannot fail. This is a very important change.

Speed has become a dominant theme, and innovation in addition to invention has become essential.

Thirdly, we now recognize that in order to bring a product to market there are many other things that have to happen besides the invention itself. There needs to be a strong partnership between the people involved in the development -- the technologists -- and the people who are in marketing and sales. Most importantly, we value very early participation by customers who are on the leading edge, customers who want this new technology to work to their advantage. So we have transformed ourselves into an innovation factory. We have these small, multi-functional teams organized towards getting us to our goal speedily, much like what a Silicon Valley venture might do. We try not to constrain these teams with elaborate processes or cumbersome bureaucracy. So speed has become a dominant theme, and innovation in addition to invention has become essential.

So the similarities between the present Bell Labs and Silicon Valley have increased because of the small team approach, taking the inventions to the marketplace in the shortest possible time. Given that the universe has a number of different centers of innovations and inventions, what are your strategies for being successful in that environment?

You are right. When you go back thirty or forty years, Bell Labs was the universe; there was no other large laboratory focused on communications and networking technology as we were. Now the universe is much larger than Bell Labs, and we try to learn from the rest of the universe what practices are most effective. In that spirit I have learned a lot from watching the small companies that have been created in Silicon Valley, the Boston Corridor and elsewhere. Studying these companies has helped us organize and manage ourselves differently. We have taken the best of what we have seen and incorporated these ideas into our corporate practices.

In your study of the startups, what is most important thing that you have learned?

Most of these startups have processes that create cutting-edge products for leading customers as quickly as possible, with direct customer involvement from Day One. They bring a product to the customer and improve it using customer feedback.

In the past the process could be described like this: we would sit behind a wall and design a product. After testing it within our own labs we'd declare the product done. There was always the danger that the product would not meet the customer's needs and expectations. Sometimes, we would have to re-engineer the product many times. All this took a long time.

What we do now is very different in that we seek the customer's input very early on. These customers are part of an extended team that is constantly watching, monitoring and working with us to create a product in record time.

Bell Labs already has the infrastructure defined, whereas an incubator or startup has to go through the entire process, and that cuts the cycle time by a good, I would say, 25 to 30 percent for Bell Labs.

You are right. There is a lot of knowledge here gained from experience: Where do we build the products? Should we outsource? How do we conduct the testing? What was the experience before? There are a lot of things we have gone through in the past that we can leverage.

The other thing that is different at Bell Labs from the Silicon Valley situation is that communication networks are usually made up of many different products. Our customers are looking for complete networks and solutions, of which a product is just one part. If you create products that do not inter-work or do not fit together, it becomes very difficult to engineer a solution on top of it. One of the strengths of Bell Labs is that we take a more holistic view; when we have several products being developed simultaneously, we make sure that these products will work together seamlessly. I think this approach is attractive to our customers, but you must be careful, because if you do it to an extreme it could also delay the introduction of individual products. The trick is to figure out how these products will become solutions and inter-work, at the same time not letting their compatibility cause enormous delays.

With a budget of 4.5 billion dollars, how does Bell Labs go about defining some of the focus areas?

We get input from customers. We get a lot of studies and input in terms of our competitors. We look under the covers of our competitors' products. We look at technology roadmaps. We analyze potential products in terms of their value creation and revenue potential. Out of all that come a certain number of products that just stand out in terms of the priorities that we need to have.

Lucent is focused on broadband and mobile Internet technologies. We believe that the Internet of today has all sorts of bottlenecks that represent opportunities for those of us with routers and optical equipment that can increase network speed. So, using this analysis, we will come up with a prioritized list of products that will provide the right solutions for our customers.

What about long-term focus if you look ahead 25 to 50 years?

It is becoming more and more and more difficult to look that far into the future. The rate of change is so dramatic that things that I thought would happen 20 years from now have started to become real in just four or five years.

Let me give you some views of how I believe the future will develop in a broad sense. I'll group them in seven or eight areas.

We are going to have a ubiquitous, high capacity network of networks. Today we just think of connecting communication devices but tomorrow we will be connecting all sorts of objects -- refrigerators, toasters, cameras, cars, and so on. Since integrated circuits are going to become less expensive as time goes on, we will use these inexpensive chips to interface everything that can be networked. Almost anything, when networked, takes on new significance as a remotely controlled device. For example, a camera installed in your house and connected to the Internet would allow you to examine your home at periodic intervals from anywhere.

I also foresee the "infra-chatter" between all these networked devices will use up more network capacity than communications involving human beings. The number of these devices will exceed the number of human beings by several orders of magnitude.

Bandwidth will also become abundant and cheap. Today when you make a telephone call from place A to place B, the charge for the call depends upon the distance from A to B, and on the length of the call. That's because bandwidth is expensive. In the future, thanks mainly to the cost-effectiveness of optical networks, there will be so much capacity available that we will think nothing of squandering it in order to make our lives simpler in some way. We will have such bandwidth-hungry services as 3-D television.

Another big change I predict is this: Today, we are offered a relatively limited number of communication services, and almost all of those come from service providers. In the future, there will be a cottage industry of programmers who will be writing communication services on an open network. Consumers and businesses will have a multitude of individualized, customized communication services. And this will do for communications networking what the Wintel platform has done for the PC industry.

Yet another big change that I see occurring is what I call virtualization. Anything that can become virtual in the future will become virtual. We will replace the physical travel of today -- for example, taking a course, going to a doctor or hospital, or library -- by bringing the information and the people contacts required for that particular task together via communications links. This has already begun. We already shop or read magazines and newspapers online. As time goes on, we will understand how to develop virtual universities, classrooms and hospitals. These virtual experiences will improve productivity beyond comprehension.

The networks of tomorrow will be far more intelligent than today's. They will respond to spoken queries and commands, phrased naturally, not in computer-speak. They will figure out where you are and deliver your messages or connect you accordingly.

Basically the networks of tomorrow will be a transparent tool in our lives?

Right. You said it well. Today, communications networks basically just set up connections between human beings or machines. Tomorrow's networks will be intelligent mediators between people and knowledge.

When we become so highly efficient, what do we do next?

There is no end point, no conclusion to this network evolution. Networks will have to continuously evolve. For example, once we have the intelligent networks I described above, we might want to make them language-transparent, so that a Chinese could talk to an Indian with the network doing the language translation.

How do you see the role of personal leadership in this dramatic transformation?

It is tremendously important. When you go through a dramatic transformation, leadership becomes very important in terms of making sure that there is a common vision. At a company like Lucent, the big challenge for leadership is to create a common vision and articulate that vision both internally and externally. Then we must operationalize that vision by parceling out different activities that lead toward common goals and measure our progress toward that vision.

Culture certainly in Silicon Valley and in the startup arena, is of prime importance. Can you tell us about the culture and environment that exists at Bell Labs and how you develop it?

First of all, we hire the best people from all over the world. In the academic world we look for students from the top schools who are number one or two in their classes. In the past it was enough to let our scientists' hunger for discovery and invention drive their work. The cultural change that has occurred here is that our employees feel a greater sense of competition in a market context. They don't just want to do good science, they want to turn that science into products, and do so before our competitors. So one challenge for the management of Bell Labs is to encourage this new focus on creating products in a speedy fashion. Now I am not saying that technology has become less important, because underneath all of our products is technology, discovery and scientific invention. But technology alone is no longer enough. So the cultural change is to rapidly develop products that exploit our inventions in the fullest possible way.

How were you able to successfully morph the culture?

We have done a number of things to implement this change in culture. First of all, we began to educate our scientists and engineers about our competition, particularly where our competitors were besting us.

Second, we brought customers into the labs so that our scientists and engineers could better understand the customers' requirements and generally feel more connected to them.

We constantly confront our people with real-world problems and encourage them to come up with new solutions.

We work in small, multi-functional teams so the R&D people can better understand the roles of the manufacturing, marketing and sales people. All of these groups have to work together in order to get the product out.

We have changed our reward system to make sure the people who create products are well rewarded.

There have been many different things we've changed over the years in order to get us into our present shape.

We understand there is an incubator at Bell Labs?

We have a business ventures organization that takes technology from Bell Labs and constructs small businesses. We often come up with inventions that may not be aligned with Lucent's main business. In the past we used to patent the invention and not do much more with it. Now we see if we can develop viable businesses from these inventions. We have launched 26 new business ventures using Bell Labs technology since the birth of Lucent just 4 years ago.

Do you see this incubator approach becoming more prevalent and do you see it as potentially beginning to evolve into mainline business?

The incubator approach works fine when there is a small, independent product that a small group of people can develop and bring to market. But there are many products that would be difficult to develop with the incubator model. For example, we make large switches that require an infrastructure of many hundreds of people in R & D. My view is that this kind of product may never be in the domain of the incubators.

Clearly, the heart of Bell Labs is its people. What is your strategy to attract, sustain and develop leading edge people?

First of all we have a good brand name.

Second, we have, over the years, continued to build relationships with university faculties. In the past we were focused on American schools, but in the last 7 or 8 years our recruiting strategy has become far more global and we have developed relationships with faculties all over the world.

Third, I believe in order to attract the best in the world you must start early. We bring in students during their summer vacations who we think we might want to hire full-time upon graduation.

Fourth, once you come into Bell, your education continues. We have professors from all over the world come and give talks and short courses. We offer employees an extensive catalogue of on-site courses, as well as a wide variety of CD-ROMS and videotapes for individual, self-paced study. There are a lot of things we do to help employees remain current with the evolving technologies.

Bell labs obviously has a phenomenal record. You file four patents a day. You've patented over thirty thousand inventions since Bell's founding in 1925. These are macro level measurements. What are your micro level measures, indicators such as return on investment, revenue generated, translation of research into reality?

It depends. People who are doing long-term research probably would measure themselves based on patents, papers, inventions or discoveries.

On the other hand, people engaged in creating new products have a plan with micro level milestones.

Some of the business factors -- how much revenue is generated, length of production time, size of market share and so on -- are also included in measurement of the success of the particular product.

In the last two years we have reduced the time from concept to product deployment by about 40 percent. Speed is a very important factor in today's market.

Looking ahead, do you see dramatic technological changes affecting the agenda in the future? DNA computing comes to mind, or perhaps running into Moore's brick wall of fundamental physics limit. Do you see anything of significance in those areas?

The most dramatic change I see coming is the impact of bandwidth becoming so inexpensive that its cost is essentially zero. When bandwidth was expensive, people created very complicated software systems to optimize its usage. What I think will happen in the future is that, once bandwidth is cheap, we will simplify the software in these systems. So the biggest change that I see in the future is a new equation for creating new products in which one of the resources we used to think as expensive is no longer expensive.

Bell Labs operates in 29 countries. How do you leverage your global presence and what is the global strategy of Bell Labs?

We once held the view that most of the world's smart people would come to New Jersey to work at Bell Labs. Realizing that this is not the case, we are now going to where the smart people are.

Also, our customers are located in all parts of the world, so we are decentralizing Bell Labs and setting up facilities in different areas of the world. We look at what the main business propositions are in each country and this dictates what kind of R&D resources we need to establish. In China, for example, we have a large contingent of people doing optical networking R&D because an enormous deployment of optical infrastructure is occurring there. We have a large contingent of people in India developing wireless software, for two reasons. First, there is a big build-up in wireless in India. Second, there is a large community of very good software developers available in India.

What's your leadership style?

I would say that I am a very hands-on manager. In some cases I can even become a micromanager. It all depends on how much trust I have in the people who are executing a task.

How do you motivate your organization?

In a number of ways. First, I make sure we share a common vision. Second, I try to ensure that everyone on the team knows who our competitors are, what their strategy is and how we can do better than them. Third, whenever there is a success to celebrate I do a number of things to express my gratitude. I also make sure that if a person needs something it is immediately made available. When there are people issues I tend to deal with them very quickly so that they don't fester.

Do you primarily recruit people who are fresh out of the universities?

We have a wide spectrum, but a large part of our recruiting is from universities. Remember, we are a high tech company and we need to make sure that there is a continuous input of fresh, new ideas coming into the company. In times like these, with the technology becoming obsolete rather quickly, we have to make sure that people who come into our work pool are abreast of the latest technologies.

With a global playing field, what do you think will be a leader's most important quality?

I think the most important attribute of leadership is to set aggressive goals and then give people the authority and accountability to achieve them. It is very hard to manage a global organization with a localized mindset. The worst thing you can do is try to apply one set of principles everywhere.

What is a typical day in your life?

I get up at around 5.45 a.m. Three days a week I play indoor tennis before coming to work. For about fifteen minutes before I leave for work I read and respond to email and look for technology stories on the Internet. The rest of my day varies depending on what's on my agenda. There might be meetings, project reviews and walk-throughs, or personnel matters. I also do some personal research. So it is usually a pretty full day, ending at about 8:00 p.m.

Give us an example of your personal research?

It is hard to fit it in, given my other responsibilities. I usually do my research in the evenings or on weekends.

In terms of my research topics, I am working on several things. One is how to make the parts of the Internet faster by using technologies like caching and redirection.

Another thing I'm interested in is our ability to infer multi-dimensional information about the world from a two dimensional image. Understanding depth, for example, from a camera view is one of the projects that I am working on.

Who are your mentors?

You might be surprised but my mentor was Lata Mangeshkar. Sometimes we talk of a mentor as someone who has frequent interaction with you. I think in her case she was a distant mentor or a silent mentor. She has been singing for four or five decades. She was a fantastic singer even when I was five or six years old, and even to this day her voice is just as melodious as ever.

She has sung in different languages; she has improvised over the years, remained at the top, even as waves of different music have come along. Her work and contributions, even though in a different domain from mine, have really inspired me immensely

What skill stands out that you can correlate to your Indian background?

I believe the most important value that I can attribute to my upbringing in India is the value of selfless hard work without self-promotion. To succeed in a large company you have to learn to be a team player, and that means working hard and with dedication, and not continuously promoting yourself. This has been an important value I have learned from India.

What role has your family played in influencing your life?

A very dominant role. My parents have been a great source of inspiration. They really valued education, hard work and dedication.

I was always a curious fellow when I was growing up and they allowed me a lot of freedom, letting me do things like taking apart the radio and sewing machine so I could examine them, find out how they worked. They were very tolerant and allowed me to pursue my curiosity. My mother was a housewife, so she was there for me at all times. She was a guiding light.

Raj Parekh

Silicon Graphics, Sun Microsystems, Comstellar Technologies

Technology Strategies and Roadmaps

Raj Parekh is the chairman and chief technology officer of Comstellar Technologies, a meta company. He has over twenty years of management and executive experience in various high technology companies.

Before joining forces with Raj Singh to create Redwood Venture Partners, Parekh served at Sun Microsystems as vice president of engineering and chief technology officer, as well as general manager of Java Products for Sun Microelectronics. Prior to Sun, Parekh was vice president and general manger with Silicon Graphics.

He serves on the board of directors of several companies, including Tharas Systems, Corona Networks, G-Tran, Nazomi Communications, Niksun, Kromos Technology, Magma and PulseCore. He holds several U.S. patents.

Raj Parekh received a B.S. in electrical engineering from the L.D. College of engineering, India, and a M.S. electrical engineering from the Polytechnic Institute of New York.

Martin Levetin, Chief Operating Officer at CopperCom and I conducted this interview. Since Raj is a pioneer and a well-known technologist in the Silicon Valley, it was appropriate to focus this interview on the technology aspect. During the discussion we targeted three core areas: technology and product road maps, technology models and strategies, and technology trigger points.

Raj explains the world of technology strategy. He defines the difference between the companies, which focus on technology and find a place in the market vs. the company, which develops the technology depending upon the need of the market. Raj explains the concept of disruptive technology as well as the ups and downs associated with it. He shares the technology development strategies utilizing examples of Lucent, Cisco and Comstellar.

The later part of the discussion was on the logic of the new Comstellar business model, and organizational logic behind it and how they studied the leading diversified companies and tried to clone the best DNA and combine it with the attributes of a VC firm.

Raj is extremely soft-spoken, a charmer at times but, at the end of the day a core technologist. He takes complex issues and topics under discussion and expresses them in simple language and very much to the point. Raj uses lots of examples and analogies to communicate the underlying message in a very persuasive manner.

*"One must not get married to technology but
married to the hole in the market place."*

How important are technology and product road maps for a startup's success?

There are two kinds of startups. One focuses on technology and finds the appropriate place in the market. The second type of company does the exact reverse. They first locate the hole in the market, then identify the technology required to fill that hole.

In general we see the second kind of companies succeed a lot more than the first kind. I would say there is a 5:1 ratio. The trick is to find the hole in the market, quickly assemble the team and identify the required technology. One must not get married to technology but married to the hole in the market place.

The technology oriented company also succeeds, but it is much more difficult for them to succeed and the probability of success is lower. For example, artificial intelligence is a great technology from an abstract point of view; however, they are still looking for applications in such a way that they can be a major force.

If you have a fundamentally disruptive technology it is worth developing as it has a chance to create a dislocation in the market place. In the mid-seventies semi-conductor technology fell into this category. Today optical technology is another form of disruptive technology but is in its infancy. It is in some sort of a raw form of technology and is still not wrapped or packaged yet. The technology has tremendous potential. For example, if somebody comes along and modifies the signal, while it is still in the fiber, twists the fiber or coats the fiber with metal, provides electro-magnetic fill to the fiber, or induces some sort of impurity into the fiber and polarizes it in a different way, all of these technologies could have a very profound impact.

Statistically speaking, disruptive technology products in the market are phenomenally successful, with the probability of success being low. I usually look at the fundamental technology, which will cause the dislocation. The success rate may be low, but the success outcome could be so large that it is worth pursuing.

Those who have a tremendous passion for the technology usually start such companies. They are willing to do whatever it takes to develop the technology.

Are there any examples, besides the advances made in the optical space that you believe are good examples of fundamentally disruptive technologies?

The other example is the wireless devices domain. Each one of them works on one set of protocol and one set of frequency. But if you can create a wireless device, which will work with GSM, TDMA, CDMA and also with a Blue-tooth, GPS device and 3G, this kind of wireless connectivity from a singular device, would be extremely important. Although some development is going on in this area, the world has not yet seen success.

What should the deployment strategies be in terms of technological changes to infrastructure and services?

Typically, you never change infrastructure and services at the same time. Whatever you do, the chances of failure are extremely high. Nobody has succeeded in changing both at the same time. So typically the right approach in this kind of scenario is you don't change the infrastructure until you provide the application first. Internet was a very good example of that. Any telephone from anybody's home, using a modem can access the Internet. Once people get hooked on the Internet and say this is great, but it is slow, they will go ahead and spend money for DSL or any solution for high bandwidth connections.

If the approach would have been - install DSL or you won't get Internet, I can promise you that both Internet and DSL would have been a lot less successful than what they are today. So enable the new services and then bring in the infrastructure then people will embrace it.

Let us ask you a question about the different ways different companies employ product maps in their business strategies. Can we take Sun and Silicon Graphics as two examples? What is your view with respect to technology and product roadmaps that these companies have employed and how have they contributed to their success or lack of?

Historically, Silicon Graphics came out with a new paradigm, saying that you can describe any object in 3D by virtue of the motion, although the screen is actually 2D. So by using the motion, corners and dimensional attributes, we can show a third dimension to it. The belief behind it was very simple. The world is 3D, and if we can represent the things in 3D and operate it that way, we will solve somebody's problems slightly better. There was a lot of skepticism with regards to this idea. Even Wall Street Journal wrote an article in 1982 questioning the need for 3D saying that there was no market. In a nutshell, they concluded by saying that the Silicon Graphics model was flawed.

Nevertheless, by the virtue of creating a device that will actually process in 3D and fortunately the way they did it was with the use of the same infrastructure, networking, and by ensuring that the look and feel of the product was very similar to what people were used to. Subsequently, organizations working on large complicated problems such as airflow analysis and dynamic analysis became the first users of Silicon Graphics equipment. Thereafter, it became very clear to engineers that there is a whole new world behind this 3D, which is called visualization. You could create artificial realities, you could create movies, and you could create scripts, which could never be created under normal circumstances by the camera. That particular product concept made Silicon Graphics take-off as a company.

In the case of Sun Microsystems, the PC that came into the market was focusing on the word processing and the spreadsheet applications. Sun Microsystems targeted the engineering markets. The PC was not addressing the engineering problems, and instead focused largely on the enterprise application market. Engineers required the floating-point computation, which the workstations had, and PCs had no external floating points at that time. As a result, Sun Microsystems captured the high-end engineering market. That is how they came into existence.

We take it from your response, that Silicon Graphics situation is reflective of disruptive technology whereas Sun Microsystems' approach was finding the technology to fit a market void?

Absolutely!

As you look at potential companies that you are interested in, what would you regard as most relevant metric in measuring your interest in them?

First, we separate very quickly whether it is a product-based market company or a technology-based company. In both cases, we look at different attributes including the team.

If it is a technology company, then we are looking at the fundamental strength of the key members of the company. Determine what they have accomplished? And under what circumstances have they created innovations? How many innovations have they done? Are they coming up with the innovation by virtue of accident or they are actually planning the innovation on the subject until they actually achieve something? Those are the most important criteria. We have found that a person with five solid patents is more likely to come up with three more than the person who has never done it before.

Then we look at the pragmatic piece of it. How many millions of dollars and how many months will be required to truly prove that the technology is viable, feasible and practical. That is our key gate. We will only fund a company if we get proof of the technology in a clear way. If the company is able to demonstrate that, we will then invest significant time and energy to take the technology into the product space and see where we can address the market. Initially we are not even thinking about the market.

For example, in the areas of fiber optic and wireless technologies we are just looking at the proof of concept.

So the team is always important and crucial in this particular regard?

Exactly. Let me tell you the counter side of it. If it is the product company, we are really focusing on how well they understand the hole in the market. What is the size of their Rolodex? Which company can this person go to, communicate with, and convince to use this new product? If it is a product company, sales and business development functions are just as critical as the ability to innovate.

One of the biggest challenges a lot of hardware companies face is being able to alter or morph their product and technology road maps. Is that something you have seen?

Let me give you some examples. If Apple would have ported their software for the PC, licensed their hardware platform, Microsoft might not have been what it is today.

If Silicon Graphics had started the personal systems division where the goal was to move the hardware, which instead of being tied to the workstation was tied to a PC, and make the PC play into a similar market the workstation was playing, the story would have been quite different. That whole project was canceled by internal anti-bodies because every-time a unit is sold there, potential hardware revenue of the workstation was compromised. The company could not see beyond the fact that if they don't do it, somebody else will do it.

Even Sun Microsystems made a mistake. At one point Andy Bechtolshteim and I went to the executive staff and told them, we need to make our own networking hardware, such as switches and routers. This was in the 1992-93 time frame. They replied: "Why? Everybody is telling us that this workstation is the best "switch" in the world. Why don't we make it cheaper, better and faster?" I explained to the staff that only 27 percent of the cost of what we are putting into the workstation is useful for switches hubs or routers.

Rest of the things such as - the operating system, floating points and graphics, disks, all of those things are really not useful for that market. So when you have a substantial portion of your gizmo that is not being utilized, then you have a problem. Because somebody else will be able to make the targeted gizmo better than we can and take the market. And not long after, Cisco did exactly that.

So...it was fundamental?

It is very fundamental for every company, both from an external and internal point of view. That's where in my mind the true strength of a CEO comes in play. You need a CEO who can look beyond the current P&L and say how we can do that.

Now, let me also tell you that it is not easy to do this since it will be suicidal if they are wrong or if it takes a little bit longer, the market will not forgive. So the strategy in this case is to either invest in or work with a startup company outside, coach them and counsel them and work with them and when the time is right buy them. Yes, you will spend the money but now it is no longer viewed as a risk. Cisco has deployed this strategy very successfully. They basically outsourced their R&D. Sun Microsystems on the other hand, historically speaking has not been able to do it very successfully. Although in the past three years, Sun Microsystems has embraced the acquisition model.

This particular phenomena gives rise to something we call as spin-in and spin-out. Sometimes you want to spin-out the technology that has been developed in-house because within the organization it may choke itself and die. Once it matures to a level it is spun-in. This strategy works as it can be applied without disrupting your current product line.

In the Lucent model you create technology yourself and in the Cisco model you create technology elsewhere and purchase, then it would appear that the Cisco model has been more robust and successful?

Absolutely. It is very easy to say that now as today Lucent has been beaten. But I would say, believe me, a long time from now people will still be making the same mistakes they are making now.

Corporate culture seems to determine the strategy of a company in selecting one model vs. the other?

It is more than the culture. Cisco started implementing this strategy and demonstrating the success, but even today in Cisco it is the same issue.

There is a good deal of debate on what should be developed in-house and what they should leave for other people to develop and then purely acquire.

Cisco is consistent in saying that they will continue to do some development in house but if the market timing is not internally met, and an outside company is doing it then they will acquire them. It is a difficult strategy to embrace because it actually creates de-motivation inside the company that they are not the most favorite people in the world, and they can be replaced through the purchase of any company off the street. So maintaining the morale of internal development, when you are acquiring so many companies is a continuing struggle for companies like Cisco.

Whereas in companies like Lucent, internal development gets a little "too comfortable" and protected. No matter what happens they are not going to buy a company from outside, and even if they buy, antibodies will most likely kill it. If you look at the roots, the telephony came from that angle. Lucent always did their own thing, whether customer wants it or not or when they want it.

You shared your views on the different business and technology models, the Cisco model to acquire, the Lucent model to develop. With Comstellar, would it be correct to say that you are somewhere in the middle?

Well, yes we are somewhere in the middle. We do acquire the business when the opportunity is right and when people come up with good ideas. Thus we will invest and provide operational support and keep on adding value and try to make them successful. Our strategy is to acquire based on Comstellar's technology and product roadmap requirements. This approach allows faster growth.

We start our companies because we could not find the right kind of companies for the right kind of price and right kind of people. We basically lay out our infrastructure needs for two, five, or ten years down the road. From our point of view, the challenge is to stay two steps ahead of the market all the time.

We will do some technology development, which are very big bets and we absolutely do not go for small technology development. We will take calculated, well-specified big technology bets. They may or may not work out. But we are completely prepared to have a 100 percent failure in the technology side. At the end of the day we want to achieve the highest market penetration and highest valuation, collectively as a whole group. Our job is to keep on adding value and filling the hole in the management structure of each individual company.

When you see a complementary company that may fill the technology niche that you are looking for you may go and acquire them?

We do more than that. We scout the world for great sources of innovation-universities, research institutes, research labs and other R & D organizations that are likely to fill our roadmap requirements and we go after them.

Can you give us some examples that have been publicly announced by Comstellar to illustrate the strategy with respect to different models? Anything that has been publicly disclosed?

On the technology side, the one company, which has been publicly disclosed, is Kromos. Kromos is developing a new method for processing the signals. No other company has that level of signal processing capability. It starts with the fundamental mathematics and it solves the signal-processing algorithm in a totally different domain. We are going to spend time and energy on Kromos and we may be able to spin a dozen companies out of it or we may come out with none. The company is still in the proof of concept phase. That is our technology and we have not licensed any piece of it to anybody.

A different example would be one of our portfolio companies, RealChip. We know most of our companies will need their own custom designed semi-conductor chips. Having a company, which can design chips very quickly with all kinds of intellectual property and experience, tools, knowledge and foundry relationship to be in place, was extremely important for us, or else Comstellar's companies would have to depend on other companies. Thus we founded Real Chip.

Why do you think the Comstellar meta company model or strategy will work better than Cisco or Lucent?

It is very simple. It has four major attributes.

First, the people at Lucent or Cisco or any other company have the same kind of stock options and it is spread across all the VPs, directors, managers and engineers like peanut butter. Maybe it is chunkier in some places, but it is still peanut butter. Now by virtue of that, it will limit the extraordinary growth and potential of the people because even though they are doing three times better than their colleagues, they don't get three times more shares. Maybe they will get 10 percent more. So with that disparity in place, the big companies or the conventional companies will keep on bleeding the top-end of their people.

What we have is that each division is organized as a company with its own stock option plan. What it allows us to do is if one division grows three times faster than the other division, people in that high growth division can take advantage of it. That is one fundamental thing, which both Cisco and GE are missing. GE, Cisco and Sun all have common stock. All the divisions of Cisco own Cisco stock. Whether division A works five times more successfully than division B, you can create some artificial difference into the compensation scheme. We are slightly different in that each one of the divisions is tied in such a way where both the Comstellar stock and that particular division's stock come into the play. So most of things under an alignment perspective under Comstellar are seen as an entity. At the end of the day, the reward system is such that, employees at companies that are doing better than the others are better compensated.

Second, when the top end of the people leave the corporate world, they don't want to just go to any startup because of the risk factor. But when they look at Comstellar, they realize that their risk is spread in many ways because they will be working on more than one company. Once they know for sure that they have a tremendous passion for a particular company, they can very easily go from Comstellar into that company and be the CEO or VP of engineering and run the company and be successful that way. And when it is time to come back, they can come back to Comstellar. We believe that this kind of mechanism that we have worked out makes people very comfortable.

Third, we are not creating one startup but we are very focused in the communication and networking infrastructure companies. We are focused all the way from intellectual property (IP) to chips, to sub-systems to systems to deployment, service all the way to aggregation and integration. Since we work on this whole process, the customer feedback comes in very accurately and is very well spread and understood within the Comstellar family of companies.

Fourth, is the technology, which works in exactly the reverse. Technology goes from bottom-up and requirements come from top-down. We work on both of those angles and provide the information to all our companies.

Think of Comstellar as just like another GE where we are a whole bunch of businesses somewhat independent but still aligned. We have a federation of loosely coupled but highly aligned companies. Each company has freedom to do what it wants to do but stays highly aligned. That makes a huge difference to us. Scott McNealy, CEO of Sun Microsystems is a master of this strategy and I respect him a lot. This strategy of strong alignment, in conjunction with a loosely coupled management, is what I learnt from him. That is what Comstellar is practicing.

Jack Welch, CEO of GE also practices this highly aligned, loosely coupled style of management. So the difference between Comstellar and GE is interesting. Like GE we also have all these divisions, however unlike GE where employees are granted only GE stock, at Comstellar, the employees have equity of the parent company and the respective portfolio companies.

Would it be correct to say that Comstellar's scalability and diversification is both customer-centric and technology-centric?

It is customer-centric, technology-centric and people-centric. It is three-dimensional. Clearly our roadmap is both product and technology dependent. We do have a mold for both the technology and product roadmaps and we invent and acquire based on Comstellar's needs.

Each of our portfolio companies has a unified sales and marketing organization. It is very hard to have a singular sales and marketing organization and have each of our portfolio companies dependent on that. That goes back to the Cisco model.

Vinod Khosla boldly predicts that 90 percent of all optical companies will fail, while only 10 percent flourish. Your comments on his prediction?

We have found out that close to 26,000 companies claim that they have something to do with optics. Believe me that is a big optical illusion! We are absolutely sure that there are massive number of companies that will fail. They will fail because most of them will run out of money. This mad rush of investment into anything that starts with "O" has now stopped. Therefore, this creates an enormous opportunity to potentially pick up people as well as half developed technologies that have potential.

And after all that chaos, eventually only three or four eventually survive.

Exactly. The consolidation is already happening as we speak.

How does Comstellar ensure that it will be in the 2 to 3 percent success space?

First, we have the financial clout, a healthy valuation, and thus enough money in reserve to work even in an economic downturn.

Second, our relationships are very strong with both equipment vendors as well as service providers. We spend a lot of time and energy in working with them and make sure we provide them the solutions they are looking for. Therefore, they become our partners. By looking upstream at the service providers who are closest to the customers, we are kept abreast of all of the issues and challenges facing our customers. In contrast the chipmakers and equipment makers are lower on the totem pole; they react to what the service providers are saying. So we plant ourselves right in the middle to see the market and then we look internally to validate the solutions we ought to be creating, in order to fit into the changing market.

What are some of the challenges Comstellar is facing?

It is a combination of the technology, product and the market dynamics. We have to look at all three simultaneously and create a balance very quickly between how we get engaged with a company and how we get out of the company. Both are extremely important for us. We want to make sure we continuously provide value and the day we find out that we cannot provide value we figure out how can we eventually disengage from the company. While engaging with a company is very crucial, disengaging with the company is even more crucial. At Comstellar we have to keep a very delicate balance between the two.

What are the issues that keep you awake in the Comstellar business model that you want to guard against?

In the Comstellar model, the thing I worry most about is very fundamental, which is; are we living within our means or are we biting more than we can chew? Are we overdoing our investments in too short a period of time? That is what we have to guard ourselves against and why we need to take a breather all the time and evaluate current investments and new opportunities with available resources. My concern on the financial side is already getting eliminated since we have access to adequate capital.

The second worry is how quickly can I motivate all the executives and have them devote the time with the most familiar thing they know. How do I bring the employees with the right skills and help them hit the ground running?

Ultimately, both of these worries are really tied to taking on more companies than we can manage. That is why we have to measure ourselves against different models all the time and make sure we are staying ahead of time.

Let us ask you a fundamental question. What makes a good CTO?

A good CTO knows how to stay one step ahead of the market, not half a step or three steps. He is able to come up with the right strategy and product at the right time. Most importantly, he keeps his feet on the ground with his head in the sky.

Vinod Khosla

Kleiner Perkins Caufield & Byers

Starting Up in High Gear

The Internet has opened unparalleled opportunities for entrepreneurs. But the mad rush to cash in is raising hard questions about the way new ventures are funded and brought to the market – as well as about their long-term prospects. Vinod Khosla is in an ideal position to discuss both the opportunities and the challenges facing entrepreneurs and their backers today. He's an accomplished entrepreneur himself, having co-founded Sun Microsystems in the early 1980s. And since joining venture capitalists Kleiner Perkins Caufield and Byers in 1986, he has helped steer companies like Amazon.com, Excite, Juniper Networks and Cerent to success.

Vinod Khosla, general partner in the venture firm of Kleiner Perkins Caufield Byers, has lived in Silicon Valley for over two decades. Even as a youngster growing up in Delhi, Khosla dreamed of starting a company in Silicon Valley.

Vinod is armed with a bachelor's degree in engineering from the Indian Institute of Technology, Delhi, a master's degree in biomedical sciences from Carnegie Mellon and holds an M.B.A. degree from Stanford University.

In a wide ranging interview conducted in February 2000, at the Kleiner Perkins offices in the heart of the Silicon Valley, Khosla shared his thoughts on the Internet's impact on business and the economy, the state of new venture creation and financing, the success of entrepreneurial success and the way Kleiner Perkins capitalizes on new business ideas. He also offered some cautionary words to established companies looking to shift their business onto the Internet.

Note: *This interview was conducted by David Champion and Nicholas G. Carr and was published in Harvard Business Review, July-August 2000 issue. It is reprinted with the permission of Harvard Business Review.*

"I try to get people to think in terms of miles, not inches."

Have the keys to success for entrepreneurs changed much since you started Sun 20 years ago?

Yes and no. It has always taken a certain combination of fearlessness and naiveté to be a successful entrepreneur, and that hasn't changed. A few years back, when I was learning how to hang glide, I watched an instructional movie that ended with a dedication like this: "To those who dare to dream the dreams, and then are foolish enough to try to make those dreams come true." That's a perfect definition of an entrepreneur. You have to have the big idea but you also have to be foolish enough to believe that you can pull it off. When we started Sun, if we had any idea how hard it is to build a computer company, we never would have tried. We were in our twenties, and we had no clue about the challenges that we were facing. We just plowed ahead. Each obstacle became something new to conquer. All entrepreneurs are like that, I think.

What has changed though is the landscape in which entrepreneurs operate. Everything moves much faster now, which means there's a lot less room for error. In the early 1980s, it didn't matter to IBM what we were doing at Sun – we were just a sneaky little start up. Even when our revenues had reached $100 million, we were nothing next to IBM's billions, and they couldn't be bothered to pay attention to us. Back then you had miles of runway before you showed up on the radar screen of large companies. That's not the case today. Amazon may have flown under Barnes and Noble's radar, but even Amazon had a much shorter free ride than we did at Sun. Now you have almost no time before you are under attack. Every corporation in America has its eyes focused squarely on startups.

The notion that entrepreneurs have to spend a lot of time creating business plans has always seemed silly to me, but now in most cases it's completely absurd. In the past you might have been able to write a business plan that could last a year or two before you had to change it. Now you have to change course all the time – you have to adapt, not plan. The best you can do, I think, is to have a sense of direction – an intuition about where the big opportunities are. Sure I want to know that the management team and the entrepreneur are capable of coming up with a strategy – but I now view that process as a discovery process, a way to hone ideas, rather than as a planning process.

The last few years have been a great time to be an entrepreneur. The Internet has created seemingly unlimited opportunities for new businesses. How long can it go on?

We're just a few minutes from the big bang. We've probably got 10 more years of strong economic growth ahead of us, powered in large part by the expansion of communication bandwidth and the economic transformation enabled by the Internet. The first growth wave of the new economy was set off by the dramatic reduction in the cost of computing power. A lot of us at Kleiner Perkins believe we are now going to see the same thing in bandwidth as optics and other new networking technologies roll out, bandwidth will become so plentiful that it will be essentially free. That will accelerate the shift of commerce, particularly business-to-business commerce, onto the Internet, and it will open even greater opportunities for entrepreneurs. Just as oil fueled the old industrial economy, bandwidth will fuel the new knowledge economy.

To put it in perspective, compare the Internet industry to the personal computer industry. In its first 10 years, the PC industry created $100 billion of new wealth in new companies – that's not counting the wealth created by established companies like IBM and Hewlett–Packard. The Internet crossed the $100 billion mark in just 4 years. Ultimately I'd say we'll see four or five trillion dollars of new wealth or reassigned. That's an incredible amount of money, and much of it will end up in the hands of companies that didn't even exist just a couple years ago.

A lot of people look at the traditional measures for the economy and start scratching their heads about this long period of growth that we are enjoying. That's because the traditional measures are industrial measures; they miss what's really going on. The old econometric models take into account the cost of oil, but they totally ignore the cost of bandwidth. The old yardsticks don't make sense anymore because what's going on today is a fundamental change in the structure of our economy. It's a repeat of the last major economic upheaval, when manufacturing displaced agriculture. A hundred years back, agriculture accounted for more than half the all the jobs in the United State. Today, it accounts for only about 3%. Twenty years ago, manufacturing was the biggest employer – accounting for half of all jobs. In thirty years, manufacturing will probably account for less than 10%. The knowledge economy will be the new employer.

To create the kind of new wealth you're talking about, we're going to have to see massive investments in the Information technology. Where's the money going to come from?

It's going to come out of corporate budgets. Companies invest wherever they're going to get the biggest returns, and right now that's IT. Look at the trend in capital expenditures. Twenty years ago, information technology accounted for about 10% of the capital expenditures in the United States. Today, it's 45%, and it's still going up. The payback time on the Internet investments is measured in months, which is far, far shorter than the 2 to 5 years that have been the historic norm. As long as you have such quick paybacks, you're going to see more and more money pour into IT. And remember, much of the rest of the world hasn't even begun to make those investments. There'll be plenty of money.

The rush to capitalize on Internet opportunities has set off a flood of venture financing. According to one study, more than $14 billion in venture capital was invested in the fourth quarter of 1999 – a fourfold increase over the year before. Do you have any concern that there's too much money out there?

A bit. What's positive about this is that every conceivable economic experiment is being tried. All that cash is driving enormous innovation everywhere in business, and that's one of the fundamental strengths of the U.S. economy right now. About 40% of our GDP growth is coming out of the tech sector, and most of that can be traced to the vibrancy of entrepreneurial initiatives. If you take tech growth out of the equation, the U.S. economy looks a lot like the European economy and not much better than the Japanese.

That's the good news. The dark side is that we're very much in the greed cycle. As we make this transition to a new economy, we're going to alternate between greed and fear, and greed holds sway right now. On a macro level, we can see greed in the stock market. Over the long run, people who invest in the tech sector will earn great returns because the winners will be big winners. But at the moment I'd say about 90% of the public companies in the sector are over valued. We'll see a great deal of volatility in stock valuations for some time. The danger is that when the price corrections happen we'll overreact on the fear side. Investment will dry up and the pace of experimentation will severely slow, putting the health of the overall economy at risk.

What concerns me even more, though is the effect of the current greed cycle on entrepreneurs and their infant businesses. Today, if you have a plan for a new business, you circulate it in the venture community and you get funded in a week. What you don't get is an honest, painstaking critique. What are the downsides in your plan? What are the shortcomings? What are the weak links? The strengths of your idea get a lot of attention, but the weaknesses get ignored – and ultimately it's the weaknesses of your plan that kill you. A start up is only as strong as it's weakest link.

> *A startup is only as strong as it's weakest link.*

So I think the venture community is doing a disservice to entrepreneurs by funding them without forcing them to undergo a tough, critical examination. In the long run it cripples new businesses. Take the issue of talent, which is the most critical issue any start up faces. Usually an entrepreneurial team has only one real skill set – they're great technologists or they're great marketers. When the venture process works well, the VCs help the entrepreneurs build the complete team. Without the full team, you can have early success- you can have strong traffic growth on your site, you can get to $50 million in revenue, you can have a hot IPO – but after that, things begin to break down. The lack of managerial skills, for instance starts to foreclose further growth – and you add those skills later because the top talent isn't going to want to join your company once it's gone public. As a result, great ideas never reach their full potential.

Frankly, the velocity of money is so high now, it's getting ugly. Too many people have too mercenary an attitude. When companies like Intel and Oracle and Apple and Sun got started, it wasn't about money. It was about passion, vision, and a desire to create something new that would have a lasting impact on people and the economy. The financial rewards flowed from the bigger vision. There are still entrepreneurs that are driven by passion, but I fear that many of them – and many of their backers – are more focused on the deal, on the big payoff. It's distasteful to see this sort of money grab.

Business to business commerce has been an area of tremendous entrepreneurial activity over the past year. According to Vinod Khosla, remote services may be one of the next hot opportunities. Here are his remarks on the topic.

Pretty much everyone now acknowledges that business is being completely reinvented. Because transaction costs are much lower on the Internet than in traditional channels, companies are rapidly shifting their business functions supplier relationships onto the Web. United Technologies, for example, is saving upto 40% on supplies by purchasing them through Web auctions hosted by Free Markets. Using the Internet saves Cisco more than $700 million annually in customer support – it has 80% fewer customer support employees per billion dollars of revenue than competitors like Lucent and Nortel.

But the Internet doesn't just make traditional transactions more efficient, it changes the very nature of the buy-or-make decision. It lets companies outsource many functions that they once had to handle themselves. I'll give you an example. I was scheduled to make an early morning presentation recently and I didn't have time to think about it until the afternoon before. I patched a bunch of slides together from older presentations, but it was a jumble of different formats and fonts. I needed to have it professionally designed and it had to be done that night. I posted that job at a site run by eLance.com, a company Kleiner Perkins has invested in and in a half hour I had bids from 10 freelancers. I picked one who offered a good price and showed an impressive portfolio, and in a couple of hours I had a first draft. I made some changes and shot it back, and by midnight I had the final copy. I have no idea who did the work – it was probably someone on the other side of the world.

There is no reason to suppose that in the future, customer support, bill processing, accounting, or any of the traditional functions of corporations will need to be done within a particular corporation or geographical area. Even critical functions like engineering design, architectural design and manufacturing are being virtualized. They will be offered as remote services and you will be able to purchase then when needed, just as you would buy a drink or place a phone call. Thanks to the Internet it will be possible to perform all these services in the most efficient place, be it Fargo, North Dakota, or Delhi, India. The remote service marketplace will be worth trillions of dollars and, more important, it will truly be global.

As we get more and cheaper bandwidth, we'll see a proliferation of such remote services, and they will fundamentally change the way we work.

The lure of riches is pulling many new players into the venture arena. We're seeing management consulting firms setting up incubators for startups and big companies launching internal VC efforts. Are those kinds of efforts helping or hurting entrepreneurs?

At their core, a lot of them aren't even about the entrepreneurs. The McKinseys, the Bains, and the BCGs of the world have a big problem right now: they're losing their best people, especially the people who are really action oriented, to start ups. So a lot of these incubator initiatives are employee retention programs more than anything else. They're a way to give employees a taste of – and hopefully some of the economic rewards of – a start up within the safety of an established firm. It's a way to provide equity compensation in an economy that, in technology at least, is more and more an equity economy, not a cash compensation economy.

The problem is, most of the organizations rushing in to help entrepreneurs aren't qualified to do so. Just because you raise venture capital doesn't make you a venture capitalist. Just because you call yourself an incubator doesn't mean that you have the skills to bring a business idea to fruition. Entrepreneurs need to ask themselves: Have these people ever really helped build a small company into something big? Have they dealt with our area of technology at a level detailed enough to provide valuable assistance? It's not enough to have just one piece of expertise – a strategy piece or a systems integration piece or whatever. You need to see the big picture as well as the little pieces, and that kind of ability only comes out of direct experience. Unless you have built a company yourself, you are not qualified to advise entrepreneurs.

As for big companies incubating start ups, that's very hard to do. It has been done – companies like Charles Schwab have done a wonderful job- but by and large it fails. Again, it's a matter of talent. Big established companies neither attract nor nurture the kind of people who know how to create new businesses. These companies have little or no experience with entrepreneurship.

That's not to say that new forms of venture assistance aren't needed. As the amount of investment pouring into the venture arena has increased, many traditional VC firms have had to shift their focus to bigger deals, and that's created a need for newer players to advise early stage start ups. But if I were an entrepreneur looking for such advice, I don't think I would go to an institution that has no experience creating new businesses. I'd probably turn to angel investors who have succeeded as entrepreneurs – people like Jim Barksdale and Tom Jermoluk.

Given the current "velocity of money", it must be tempting to rush through the development process. How do you give ideas the critical attention they need, and how do you get entrepreneurs to focus on building companies that endure?

> *Unless you have built a company yourself, you are not qualified to advise entrepreneurs.*

We're blessed with a pretty good brand, and that encourages people to come work with us, especially second time entrepreneurs who know they need a lot of things besides money. We also do far fewer investments per partner than most other firms, so we can be more selective and spend more time with each of the companies we back. And we try to stay focused on the long term. In evaluating each other, we look back 10 years and say, "How have your investments done?" That's the metric we've always used – you're judged according to how well your companies have performed over the long haul. The assumption is that you can never sell a stock once you have bought it.

We also genuinely challenge the entrepreneurs who come to us. The most common failing in entrepreneurs is that they underestimate the scale that they should aim for. Getting to the $1 million in revenues seems such a big challenge to them that it blinds them to all else. As a result, they may miss out on opportunities that will get them to $1 billion in revenues. I'll give you an example. I'm on the board of a start up called FireDrop, which just launched its product – an e-mail based communication platform called Zaplets. FireDrop started last September with just 2 people. Now it has about 60 employees. The founders had no idea how high to aim – they were talking in terms of 10,000 page views a day. But I told them, "It's not material until you get to a hundred million." I try to get people to think in terms of miles, not inches.

Our other focus is on getting the right mix of people. A company's gene pool gets established early and determines the company's direction and performance for years to come. So we try to make sure from the start that the people in the company have a wide range of skills, operational biases and strategic beliefs. The companies that can manage conflicts between different points of view are the ones that will break new ground.

In the final analysis, though, our single biggest advantage may be the fact that we screwed up in more ways than anybody else on the planet when it comes to bringing new technologies to the market. That's a big institutional asset. Our hope is that we're smart enough not to repeat old mistakes, just make new ones. There's no short cut to good judgment – you can only learn it the hard way.

Kleiner Perkins is known for it's pioneering investments in companies exploiting the biggest new technologies, from the Internet to fiber optic networks? What's your secret?

The first challenge of course is to uncover the new ideas and to do that, you have to do a lot of digging. I spend a lot of time visiting new companies, for example, and in the course of those visits I'll often hear about an interesting new technology. Then I'll start talking to experts in the technology, and I'll go to the right conferences and do some background reading. I'll discuss the opportunity with some of the other partners here, and if the basic economics look attractive enough – if there's a large potential market – the firm will launch a formal initiative.

That's what we did in 1994 with the Internet. We laid the groundwork by following the bulletin boards and early chat rooms, because back then those were the only places to really learn about the Internet. That turned into a formal initiative, which led to a series of investments and ultimately to the launches of Amazon, Netscape and Excite – all at roughly the same time. More recently, we've gone through a similar process with optical networking.

We're also very fortunate in that we have the best and the brightest minds coming to us. Every single day, people walk into our offices and educate us in a new area – the technology, the market, the economics. It's through discussion with these people that we start to develop ideas of our own. Then we go back to the same people and they critique our thinking from many different points of view. It was people like Dave Huber at Corvis, Jim Foster at Cisco and Pradeep Sindhu at Juniper who helped me develop my thinking on optics, for example. Foster originally got me thinking about how much a big leap in bandwidth would change the way we build networks and the components we use to build them, and that led to a lot of ideas about big business opportunities. To be honest, I feel decidedly dumb next to those people – I think of them as my teachers.

When you look back at all the companies you've had a hand in launching, which one would you point to as the best example of a venture building process?

> *I try to get people to think in terms of miles, not inches.*

It's hard to point to just one. The smoothest, best-executed deal was probably Juniper Networks, which we helped develop from day one. Pradeep Sindhu, Juniper's founder, had come up with a technological breakthrough in the way enterprise routers work. But he had never worked in the router business, and he didn't realize the full commercial possibilities of his ideas. He didn't see that enterprise routers could also serve as Internet routers. So the first thing that we did was to help him define the market for Internet routers. Then we gave him a crash course in building a business. I had him take an office for 3 weeks next to Milo Medin, who was then at @home. As Milo's shadow, he absorbed what it meant to run a public Internet – protocol network – what the big issues and problems were. It was a fast way to bring him up the learning curve.

When he got back, we started having weekly staff meetings, just Pradeep and I. The first thing that we focused on was getting the right set of people for the company – the right gene pool. We started out on the technical end. Pradeep had helped architect the Ultrasparc processor at Sun, so he had strong skills in building technical architectures and could apply those skills to routers. But he needed somebody with experience in building and operating an IP network, and he needed somebody who'd done operating systems software for routers and somebody who'd done protocols for routers. So we drew out a map that said, "Here are 10 different areas of expertise we need." Then we made a list of the companies doing the best work in each area, and we listed the five people in each company who would make good targets. We went after those people, and piece-by-piece we assembled a multidisciplinary team that could make Juniper a leader.

On the top of the technical layer, we put together a management layer, recruiting Scott Kriens, who'd founded StrataCom, as the CEO. We needed the technical layer in the first place, because without it we couldn't have attracted the top management talent. At that point, the company was off and running, and I basically just got out of the way. There wasn't much else I needed to do. So from my point of view, it was the most bang for the least buck – the buck being my time. It was the perfect incubation. Our starting investment was $200,000, and now the company is worth many billions.

Juniper is an example of a process where from the start, everything goes right. But the real test in venture capital is what you do when things go wrong. I'm equally proud of my work with a company like the chip maker NexGen, which endured a lot of hardships as it grew. NexGen had a very good technology, but it was competing against the Intel monopoly, and in the early 1990s it just ran out of cash. Even though we were originally a small investor, our firm was the only one to help them when things got tough. We helped shuffle management and recruit a broader engineering team, including a new VP for engineering. We helped redefine the company's strategy and got additional financing in place. Most important, we mentored the management team on dealing with day-to-day issues.

The effort was intense, but it has paid huge dividends. In 1996, AMD bought NexGen for almost $1 billion. More important than the money, though, is the fact that the NexGen chips – the AMD – K6 and, more recently, the Athlon – became the first true challenge to Intel. NexGen broke Intel's monopoly and made an important economic contribution. From a personal standpoint, working with struggling companies like NexGen is rewarding precisely because it entails such a difficult journey.

Let's shift from startups to incumbents. Why has it been so hard for many established companies to adapt to the Internet?

There are a number of reasons. One of the most important is that their top executives still tend to think of technology as a tool. Back when I was in business school, we were taught that first you develop your strategy and then you pick your tools – and technology was just one among many. But now technology is a driver of business strategy. The answers to questions like "What business model makes sense?" and "What strategy makes sense?" are now a function of your assumptions about where technology is headed. And inside your company, your technology architecture determines how you procure supplies, how you provide customer support, how you configure your products, how you manage your sales channel – everything. It's naïve to think of a website as an "Internet Strategy." The Internet is causing a complete overhaul of all aspects of business. It means new business models and new sources of competitive advantage. It demands new assets and different strategies.

An obvious consequence is that the CIO has suddenly become the second most important executive in a company. For a long time, the number two strategic person tended to be the top marketing executive; now it's the technologist. A visionary CIO – not the old model of the CIO – is the key to the company's success. Some big companies understand that – and I'm thinking of Cisco, Schwab, Wells Fargo, Federal Express, Wal-Mart – but most don't.

As the speed of business picks up, we're seeing other basic assumptions about strategy being overturned as well. Think about the concepts of scale, for instance. It used to be that the bigger you got, the lower your costs were and the better you did. Economies of scale were everything. Of course, being big also meant you were less able to adapt to change, but that didn't matter much because the rate of change was fairly low. You could get McKinsey to give you a new strategy every five years. Being big and slow was better than being small and nimble. That's turning around. The rate of change has become so high that the drawbacks of scale are outweighing the benefits. We are seeing the diseconomies of scale.

A similar thing is happening with the business processes. It used to be that the best companies had well documented, state of the art processes that all their employees knew and followed. Everything they did, was carefully planned. But now with decision making time shrinking rapidly, the slowness of highly planned processes is a big disadvantage. I'll give you an example from the late 1980s. IBM had a great product planning process, and they applied it to the first few laptops they developed. Following the process, they methodically researched every element of those machines. The laptops were beautifully designed. Unfortunately, they never got to the market. By the time IBM finished the development process, the products were out of date. We're seeing this problem all over the place today: great processes that are completely unsuited to the new pace of business.

Yesterday, you optimized your cost and performance. Today, you have to optimize for flexibility and adaptability. Change is continuous now; it's not a discrete event anymore.

That's a pretty scary thought if you're a big company that has spent all its time building up scale advantages and optimizing its processes.

It's a very scary thought if you're unwilling or unable to change. Large traditional companies are unsuited to the new environment for a host of reasons. First they tend to be risk averse, which is a big liability. There's so much experimentation going on right now that avoiding risk is the biggest risk you can take. If you're not experimenting, you can be sure you'll be shut out.

Second, they're too hierarchical in the way they communicate. Information moves slowly, and they just don't have the free flow of ideas that you need to succeed. Some hierarchy is necessary in decision-making, but it should not extend to the flow of information.

Third, they don't have the right talent. When you can no longer depend on process and planning, instinct becomes very important. But big companies have never rewarded people for making gut calls, so over time they've bred the instinct out of their organizations. And it's very hard to teach instinct. Process can be taught – anybody can learn to follow a process – but to get good instinct you really have to bring in new people, create a new gene pool. One CEO recently said to me, "I hope 30% of my senior managers are not here at this time next year." That's a harsh thought, but a necessary thought. This isn't "be nice time" time – it's a shake up time. If you don't make the hard decisions now, the best talent will continue to flow to start ups.

In the end, though, it's not the big things that are going to kill you; it's the accumulation of little things. Most companies always do the top 3 or 4 critical things right. They start a website, they do the stuff that Bain and BCG tell them to. The problem is, everybody gets those things right. It's the micro decisions – the thousands of little decisions that a company makes every day – that are hard to get right. What ad agency do you pick? Which engineer do you hire? The little things separate the dot-coms from the incumbents. A new company has no baggage. It can rethink everything from scratch and tune every decision to the new realities of communications and computing. But in a big company, the whole infra structure and culture acts like gravity, pulling you back to where you started from. You can never reach escape velocity.

When I have some young entrepreneurs stepping up to bat against Wal-Mart or Ford or AT&T, I tell them, "Guys, you're going to go up to the plate with 2 strikes against you. There are a lot of things you don't have – like brand, like distribution, like scale, like staying power. So you can't make too many mistakes. But you've got one huge advantage: your competition has minor – league pitchers." It's not that the big guys' assets aren't valuable. They are. If they could apply the instincts of an entrepreneur to those assets, the big guys would be unbeatable. But that almost never happens because big companies, whatever they might say, aren't open to change.

Anil K. Gupta

University of Maryland, Stanford University

Business Strategy

Anil K. Gupta is a world-renowned strategy scholar. He is a visiting faculty member in the Stanford Technology Ventures Program at Stanford University and a Distinguished Scholar-Teacher and professor of strategy and global e-Business at the University of Maryland's Robert H. Smith School of Business. His core research interests focus on "Managing in the Digital Age," "Managing Globalization," and "The Quest for Synergy." He has published over fifty papers, including several in major journals such as *Academy of Management Journal, Academy of Management Review, Strategic Management Journal, Organization Science, Sloan Management Review, and Journal of Business Strategy.* Dr. Gupta's book, **"The Quest for Global Dominance",** coauthored with Vijay Govindarajan, will be published in the summer of 2001.

Dr. Gupta has worked actively as a consultant with several large corporations including IBM, National Semiconductor, Marriott, Rauma Group and UPM-Kymmene Group (Finland), Cemex Group (Mexico), and IRI Group (Italy). He serves on the board of directors of two Silicon Valley technology companies, NeoMagic and Vanigai, and an asset management company, Omega Worldwide.

He has received numerous awards, including the Distinguished Scholar-Teacher Award and the Allen Krowe Award for Excellence in Teaching from The University of Maryland, the Glueck Best Paper Award in Business Policy and Strategy from the Academy of Management, and the Broderick Prize for Excellence in Research from the School of Management at Boston University. In 1994 he was ranked by *Management International Review* as one of the "Top 20 North American Superstars" for his research in strategy and organization.

Dr. Gupta earned a B.Tech. from the Indian Institute of Technology at Kanpur, an M.B.A. from the Indian Institute of Management at Ahmedabad, and a doctorate in business administration from the Harvard Business School.

He lives a bicoastal life, with homes in both the Silicon Valley and Washington D.C. areas.

We spoke with Dr. Gupta at Stanford University in October 2000. We started off the discussion by examining the importance and creation of organizational design and business strategy in the startup world. Dr. Gupta explained the core makeup of an organization and the key components behind an organization's business strategy. We then explored the various avenues that companies have implemented in order to grow, scale, and become leaders through utilization of various globalization and diversification strategies.

> *"The strategist must also be like an artist –*
> *somebody who strives to break the mold, to*
> *change the rules of the game."*

Should a startup look at strategy first or should it focus on the organization?

I think that the two are really dealt with in tandem, because most startups will begin with a good idea. Of course there are situations where three or four smart people working in a roughly similar kind of field have a burning desire to do a startup. So they know that they are going to work together but they don't yet have an idea. Or, it could be that one or two people come up with a brilliant idea and then try to create a team. It could go either way. But if you have a burning idea, the next thing you should think of is putting together a team. Or if you have a team, then before you begin to try to raise money, you have to be clear about exactly what your business idea is. In short, you have to deal with both issues. The central question in strategy is: "What business am I in or do I want to be in?" And one of the key questions on the organizational design side for a startup is: "What is the composition of my team?"

How do you define "organization design"?

Organization design refers to both the formal as well as the informal aspects of what makes the organization more than the sum of the individuals. For new ventures, organization design also includes the top-level leadership question: "Who are my team members and what role will each individual play?" You can't have everybody doing everything because that leads to a waste of resources and sooner or later it will lead to conflict. You have to decide on how the responsibilities will be distributed among the team members.

Once you have differentiated the responsibilities, you have to think about how you will integrate the viewpoints of different people in the process of making key decisions. Let's say somebody is in charge of marketing, somebody else is in charge of human resources and somebody else is in charge of technology; how will their different perspectives become integrated? Another aspect is the distribution of ownership rights in the company. And a closely related issue is reward and compensation.

Next, I would focus on culture. Culture refers to the shared values and beliefs of the people involved. For example, there are some companies that are very techno-centric, where everybody seems to believe that leading edge technology is what counts the most. There are other organizations where people believe that the customer is king and that customer relations are far more important than technology. If you lead the company with a "customer is king" philosophy, you are saying that even if you are behind in technology you can always go and acquire it. So different organizations often have differing sets of beliefs. Usually these beliefs get imprinted very early in the organization's life.

Contrasted with culture, which refers to values and beliefs, the concept of structure focuses on the distribution of authority and responsibility and the nature of reporting relationships. You could take the same company and create functional departments or multi-functional business units. The same number of people can be grouped in different ways. You have to choose which design makes the most sense, because not every structural design would be equally effective or efficient. Also, structure can range from highly formal to highly informal. For example, some companies believe that there should be no formal organizational chart or formalized reporting relationships, whereas others believe that you need to have a clearly defined set of responsibilities.

Finally, the last dimension I would include under organization would be information and control systems. For instance, the total life cycle approach, that's really about business processes, about information and control systems. An example of information and control systems is the "flash report" at Yahoo which gives the company's senior executives a one page summarized report on all key parameters on an ongoing basis. Organization means organized activity and organized activity essentially means activity that is structured rather than random. What is it that makes an activity organized rather than random? It's your culture; it is your reward system; it is your information and control systems; it is your people. These are the elements which, in aggregate, define the organization of a company.

How important is all this for a startup?

For a startup, some of these things are very key. The three that are the most critical at the early stages would be the composition of the founding team, the reward system, and leadership and culture. Obviously a startup should not get tied up in the rigidities of a highly formal structure. I must add, however, that what you need is balance. Have too little organization and the new venture runs the risk of disintegrating into chaos. On the other hand, have too much organization and the venture runs the risk of dying from lack of flexibility and creativity.

Now let's move on to business strategy.

There are three key components to business strategy. First, what financial and non-financial goals are driving the company? By financial goals I mean revenues and profitability, and by non-financial goals I mean things like market share, number of customers, types of customers, customer satisfaction, and the like.

Second, what is the market space that we want to play in? What's the business domain? What customer segments are we after? What products and services are we going to deliver to them? What geographic market will we target? Take the case of Yahoo! From the very beginning they have seen themselves as a "media" company rather than as a "technology" company. Defining themselves as a media company has meant that the Yahoo! portal must be exceptionally customer friendly, must build a strong brand, must have a broad customer base and generate all of its revenues from advertising and commerce rather than subscription fees. As compared with Yahoo!, eBay and Amazon have defined their market domains quite differently. eBay is an enabler of person-to-person commerce whereas Amazon is a retailer.

Third is competitive strategy; that is, how will we play within that market space in order to win? No matter what market space you take, there's always more than one way to play the game. In operating systems for servers, you have Windows versus Solaris versus Linux. Or take the personal computer industry. Throughout its life, Dell has played the PC game one way, with direct selling and build-to-order, whereas companies such as Compaq, IBM, H-P and others have played the same game quite differently, selling through retail stores and resellers and building-to-stock. As the performance of Dell versus its competitors over the last five to ten years illustrates, not every approach to playing the game is equally effective. Every company has to figure out as early as possible what the winning approaches are, pick one of them, and learn to effectively execute that particular approach.

So business strategy involves our goals, our choice of market domain, and our competitive strategy within that market domain. Once you achieve clarity on these three issues you can say, "Yes, this is our business strategy." Obviously, nothing remains the same forever. Over time, your business strategy answers to these three questions can be expected to change.

In developing a business strategy, the new venture team should begin by first achieving clarity regarding the targeted market space: What customers, what products, and what services? You then need to ask "What's different about my company and my products and services?" This is important because the moment you go to talk to your angel investors and VCs, one of the first questions they are going to ask after they understand your market domain, is "What's your unfair advantage? Why should you be the winner?" Once you have achieved clarity regarding the market space and your competitive strategy, you then have to focus on strategy execution. As is obvious, if you can't execute the strategy, it's not worth the piece of paper it's written on. In order to execute your strategy, you get into issues centered around the people and the organization. So you loop back to questions such as: Who are the members of my team? What types of people do I have? What kind of incentives do I put in place? What kind of culture do I need to build? It's through people and organization that the company executes the strategy.

What are the strategy issues pertaining to scaling up the business?

Once a venture is up and running, you immediately start facing the question of scaling up, and when any business is scaling up it can be done in several ways. First, you can scale up by creating and expanding the size of the market. For Yahoo! that would be akin to asking themselves how they can increase the number of Internet users and the amount of time that these users spend on the web.

Second, you can grow by expanding your market share. An example of that would be Dell going from less than 5% of the PC market before 1990 to over 15% now.

A third way that you scale up is by going after the global market rather than just the domestic market. Take a company such as Keynote Systems. Until early this year, they were focused almost exclusively on the U.S. market. However, they are now very active in Europe and are also moving into Asia.

A fourth way to scale up is by diversifying your portfolio of products and services. For example, look at Amazon, which started out with book retailing and since then has diversified into retailing of toys, music, videos, among other things. Or take a company such as Lara Networks, which started out by focusing on silicon chips. At some point they said that instead of just selling silicon chips they should also sell subsystems and systems. Now when you're selling subsystems and systems, you are selling a much bigger bundle of products and services. Why does Lara Networks want to make that switch from just selling silicon to selling subsystems and systems? It's because they want to scale up. Companies don't need to think about diversification early in their lives, but once they have gone beyond the beta test phase into commercialization, then for a whole variety of reasons, like pressure from the VCs and the market cap, you want to scale up the company rapidly. And that leads you to think about how to grow the market, how to grow market share, how to go global, and how to expand the bundle of products and services.

What do you think about the subject of global strategy?

There are companies of all stripes. There are some, such as Sycamore, that are born global. Or take Broadvision; their first customer was not from the U.S. but from Japan. So we could also look at Broadvision as being born global from the first day. In contrast, I would not view Amazon as a born global company. They started with a focus on the U.S. market, with a U.S.-based web site. For Amazon, globalization has been an incremental, step-by-step story – first the U.S., then Europe, and within Europe, the U.K., Germany, France, and so on. Amazon is globalizing country by country, region by region, as a part of scaling up.

How would you define global strategy?

I would define it as the sum of two components: global expansion strategy and global competitive strategy. Global expansion strategy includes issues like how rapidly you should become global, in what sequence you should enter different countries, what your entry strategy should be for different markets, and so on. These are some of the key elements of global expansion strategy.

The second component, global competitive strategy, kicks in as you begin to build market presence across multiple countries. How do you act in a concerted manner in order to convert that multi-country presence into competitive advantage? Look at Nokia versus Ericsson versus Motorola; all three have a global presence. So on the globalization front, the battle really is about who can convert global presence into global competitive advantage. Or take Texas Instruments, one of the most global of the semiconductor companies. TI has quite consistently and explicitly said that they are very conscious of trying to convert their global presence into global competitive advantage. If you are a semiconductor company you need to build massive fabrication plants. The cost of capital is not the same in all parts of the world. Let's say that you are able to find a country where the talent and infrastructure is sound and the government is quite keen to have your presence and able to lower the cost of capital for you; then it makes sense to locate the plant in that particular country.

Should companies in the Internet space go global from day one?

It's true that the Internet is global, or as they say, the Internet is worldwide. But just because the web is worldwide and you can access a site in any part of the world, it does not necessarily mean that it is desirable for a startup to go global from day one. Yes, for some startups it does make sense to be born global or to go global very early on. However, for the vast majority of U.S.-based startups, even in the technology arena, going global from day one or very early in the company's life is neither necessary nor desirable. It depends on how much local adaptation your products and services require for different markets. So let's say that if you're selling a router or a switch, then there is minimal localization. Language is not an issue; content is not an issue. Also, you are selling to technical people, senior people in large companies, who speak the same global language. On the other hand, if you are Amazon and you are selling books, you have to deal with the fact that more than 80% of the books that Germans read are in the German language rather than in English. Your whole library of English language books targeted to Americans is, by and large, irrelevant for the German market.

So Amazon has to go global in an incremental, sequential fashion?

Yes. Of course, this approach creates its own challenge. By the time you enter the new market, whether it is Germany or France, somebody out there, a local player, has already been busy cloning your business model. People around the world have been studying what Amazon has been doing, which means that when you go to foreign markets there will be incumbent players.

Then how and what should a global strategy be in order to address such bottlenecks?

I don't think that there is a simple answer. When you are a young company, you are very short on people, you're very short on formal organization, and basically you're very short on organizational bandwidth. You are just learning to be a company; you're still trying to figure out what your strategy should be even in the domestic market, and you're engaging in a lot of experimentation. On top of that, in a market place like the U.S., you are likely to have a massive number of competitors trying to imitate your business model. If you start to globalize pretty early, you may get distracted and your management and organizational attention may get diffused. You may end up, in fact, losing your U.S. position to a competitor who says, "To hell with globalization, all I'm going to focus on is the U.S." If the need for localization is strong, rapid globalization is very risky and you may die everywhere. In such a case, you have to pursue slower globalization. Slower doesn't mean forty years; slower might mean five years. Of course, that itself also implies a price, because during the time that you are focusing on the home market, on the U.S. market, let's say, somebody else in Germany or Japan or France is busy studying you and cloning what you are doing or maybe cloning with a difference, with a localization difference. So when you enter that foreign market, the marketplace already has an incumbent. Of course you can acquire them, but then you pay a price for acquisition. Or you can say that you will fight and displace them, but that is not going to be inexpensive either. So if the need for localization is very high, there is no way that you can avoid paying the price that the quest for globalization will impose on your company.

Can you elaborate on the topic of localization?

I would say that we could break localization down into several important components. One is local adaptation of products and services. Another would be distribution channels and access to local customers. A third would the issue of whether or not you need local operations. With some businesses you may need to localize your products and services but you can deliver them remotely. The hardest is when you need high localization on all three dimensions.

Would it be correct to say that local adaptation is one component of globalization and technology the other?

I would say that in the technology arena, simplifying a bit, we could break down companies into two types: those that create platform technologies and those that create applications that ride on the platform technologies. For example, Google is a platform technology whereas Yahoo! is an application that rides on Google. So the companies that are in the platform business generally need limited localization, and for them rapid globalization from the beginning is feasible, is relatively low risk, and is extremely important. Whereas, if you are in the application business, then most applications tend to require localization and therefore being born global is often not a wise strategy; you need incremental or sequential globalization.

Let's now look at diversification strategy.

When a company starts to think about diversification, it must typically choose one of two paradigms. One paradigm is to stay focused on the targeted customers and diversify the portfolio of products and services that you offer to these customers. In this type of diversification, the company is choosing to leverage its knowledge of targeted customers and its relationships with these customers. In many ways, we can look at Cisco's diversification as being driven by this paradigm.

Second is techno-centric diversification, where you say: "I have this core competence; what are the different types of products and services that I can create from this core competence?" Those different products and services may actually have nothing to do with each other and may go to very different target customers. Through much of its history, Corning has been such a company. Corning's core technology has been specialty glass. From those technology roots you end up with the light bulb, which was their first business, but you also end up with cookware, television picture tubes, flat panel displays for laptops, and -- lo and behold -- fiber optics. Obviously, the customers for fiber optics, light bulbs, and cookware are very different. But what ties all of these together is that they share the same technological roots. So what Corning is really doing is saying, "We have this technology so let's unleash the power of this technology in a thousand different ways." In contrast, under the first paradigm you say, "I have this customer. I know this customer, I have a relationship with this customer, and I want to leverage this relationship through a thousand different products and services."

When do you use these two different strategies?

For a young company, to do both at the same time adds too much complexity. Early in the company's life, you should pick one of the two. But if you become a larger company, like Cisco by the mid-1990s, then you can pursue both. Or, as in the case of Corning, you create divisions - a fiber optics division, a TV division, and so on. Then, each division can take a customer-centric approach, whereas the overall company takes a techno-centric approach.

Diversification is always challenging because no matter which of the two approaches you pick you have to learn to do something very different. If you are pursuing customer-centric diversification, you constantly have to figure out how to internalize new technologies. On the other hand, if you are pursuing techno-centric diversification, you constantly have to figure out how to access new types of customers. For a young company, it's often too challenging to pursue both types of learning simultaneously.

Should a startup develop a diversification roadmap at the time of its founding?

I would say that in the early stages it would often not be very easy to predict what type of diversification you'd be pursuing two years down the line – whether it would be customer-centric or techno-centric. During those two years, the market space you are in, what customer segments you are going after, or what the product or service is that you're going to bring to those customers may evolve. My inclination would be that in the first couple of years a startup should pretty much ignore the question of diversification and really focus on the basics of business strategy and organization design in order to create a viable business. Once you have created a viable business and have a set of customer relationships and you have a certain technology competence and need to scale up, you should look at what kind of diversification makes more sense and pick either the customer-centric or the techno-centric route. When you make that choice you may find that the capabilities of the company are not optimal for that particular type of diversification and you may then need to make changes in the management team. However, all of this evolution might be hard to anticipate early on.

Is strategy the art of making good predictions?

No, strategy is only partly about prediction. Strategy is the art and science of defining and constantly redefining what game you want to play and how you will play it. "What game you want to play" is the definition of market space. "How you play that game" is the definition of competitive strategy. This process of constant definition and redefinition requires a combination of "smart prediction" and "smart experimentation."

Being very good at predicting the future of a market space or the future of a technology is not the same thing as being able to predict the strategy of a specific company two years from now. In any market space there are several competitors and the strategy of a company depends not just on the size of the total market, the movement of the total market, and the emergence of new technologies, but also on who the competitors are and what their strategies are. You simply can't predict all of the key parameters accurately. Obviously, every entrepreneur, every leader, has to try and do the best job possible in terms of anticipating the future. However, in a dynamic and highly competitive market it is very dangerous to become a prisoner of your predictions. You must also cultivate the ability to engage in smart experimentation and adapt to the unexpected.

Any final thoughts?

I like to think of the business strategist as analogous to an architect, some-one who is part engineer and part artist. Like an engineer, a strategist strives to create something functional, something that will serve as a means to an end. Also like an engineer, a strategist must work under various constraints and obey certain laws, such as the laws of economics. Yet the strategist must also be like an artist – somebody who strives to break the mold, to change the rules of the game. This is how CNN rose from nowhere to become a leader in network broadcasting, how Southwest became the best performing U.S. airline, and how Cisco became one of the world's most valued compa-nies in just fifteen years.

Romesh Wadhwani

Aspect Development, i2 Corporation

Great Companies are Built on Vision

Dr. Romesh Wadhwani, founder and former chairman and CEO of Aspect Development, Inc., is now vice-chairman of i2 Technologies and a member of the i2 board of directors. Over the past nine years Dr. Wadhwani has spearheaded the emergence of Aspect as a leader in the fast-growing B2B e-commerce arena. This dominance led to Aspect's merger with i2--the largest merger in software history.

Dr. Wadhwani was previously chairman and CEO of Cimflex Teknowledge Corporation, a company specializing in products and systems for computer-integrated manufacturing. Prior to that, he was chairman and CEO of a company specializing in information systems for energy management. In addition, he has been a director on the boards of several companies and organizations.

Dr. Wadhwani received his B.S. degree from IIT Bombay and his M.S. and Ph.D degrees in electrical engineering from Carnegie-Mellon University.

Raghu Batta and I met Dr. Wadhwani on a sunny California day at his house in Los Altos. We sat around his dining table and spent several hours immersed in stimulating conversation. Dr. Wadhwani has a very arresting personality. He answered every question in a systematic manner, always bringing our attention to the three most important rocks. Dr. Wadhwani's presence is solid. Not only does his voice communicate his belief and conviction, but his eyes express sheer passion and will. He constantly looked us straight in the eye and his every act and every sentence reflected his belief and conviction.

Dr. Wadhwani shared with us his vision about building great companies. He described in detail the conception, rationale, integration, and challenges behind the largest software merger in the world.

"Great companies are built on vision."

Sanjiv Sidhu, Dr. Deshpande and you are a handful of Indus entrepreneurs who have actually conceived the idea of a company, taken it through the IPO and have continued in leadership positions in the post IPO phase. To what do you attribute this?

Post IPO phase is a phase which, surprisingly I don't hear too many entrepreneurs talking about, yet I believe it is the most important thing; it drives the whole culture of a company, which is to build a great and lasting company. It's not just "life after IPO", in the sense of the immediate after-life; it's what you are planning for the next five years after IPO. Great companies are built because they were conceived of as lasting companies from Day One, as compared to companies that were only thought of as IPOs – with an exit strategy from Day One. The whole company is then geared around a culture of "We'll get to an IPO. Our job is to create short-term market cap; after that who cares what happens to the company". Entrepreneurs need to take a holistic view of building a company. The IPO is nothing more than one simple milestone in the life of a business. The focus is to build a great company, and in the process of doing that you can do an IPO, or you might get acquired by Cisco or you might have a great private company - all are perfectly legitimate alternatives. And by the way, if you do an IPO, it's largely a capital-raising event; it's in a slightly different way a liquidity event, but other than that life goes on. It's really about building a great company and that needs to be the focus of entrepreneurship.

Before I moved to Silicon Valley about 10 years ago, I had built two companies in Pittsburgh, Pennsylvania. When I first moved here, for the first several years my sense was that everyone I met was focused on building a rock-solid company and people viewed IPOs pretty much as capital-raising events along the way.

Over the last three years there has been a pretty dramatic shift in thinking in the Silicon Valley. While this perception may not be true anywhere else in the country, certainly in Silicon Valley the standards of success have changed. People believe that the IPO is the end event, not just a milestone along the way. People believe that stock options are a God-given entitlement. People also believe that stock options are a one-way program that only goes up; if they start coming down, there is no loyalty to the company or even to the idea.

Great companies are built on passion. Particularly in the early days of a company, the passion can't be about stock options and IPOs; the passion has to be about the business, about the product, about the market, about the customers. That needs to be a life-long passion. It can't be a passion only up to the point of an IPO and then all of a sudden: "Who cares about the passion? By the way, I quit because I have the next startup that's in my future. So good luck Mr. CEO and Mr. Customer!"

Can we attribute this mindset, this lack of vision, lack of long-term growth strategy to a lot of failures?

Yes. Things are going to go back to the old ways, because if you look at long market cycles, people always somehow go back to fundamentals. Some of these cycles may be three year blips, where people forget the fundamentals. They may be ten year blips, they may be twenty year blips. I think here it's a five year blip. But ultimately people will go back to fundamentals.

There are some strong fundamentals on which companies must be based. Anyone who forgets those fundamentals, whether they've gone public or not, is doomed to failure. Great companies will get great valuations, but it's a sustainable valuation. With mediocre companies, these great valuations are only temporary. Then, when things change and the valuation goes down, employees leave, customers leave and the company goes into a down spin.

Let me give you an example of what Sanjiv Sidhu, the chairman of i2, and I both did independently. When I started Aspect, the statement of value of the company and the mission of the company was focused on one key principle: delivering enormous measurable value to our customers. I had a particular way in which I defined that; Sanjiv had a slightly different way in which he defined that, but right from the get-go both of us have built companies focused on delivering value to the customer. It's not about a notional, parallel, blind statement along the lines of: "We shall strive for customer excellence, we shall deliver customer satisfaction, we shall delight our customers." Everyone's got that statement.

Are you stating that the vision should be quantifiable and measurable?

It should be value-based. What does delighting our customers actually mean? Kodak sells that and look at their stock. Do you know any company that doesn't say it? Take the top 50,000 companies in the world and they all say it. Who doesn't have a value statement that says: "We shall do great stuff for our customers"? What does that mean? Sanjiv did it by saying he was going to deliver 50 billion dollars in value to his customers in the next 5 years. Aspect did it not by giving a hard number but by saying: "We will deliver a tangible, enormous value proposition to our customers." And just see how it's affected both companies. It was a value statement that was made on Day One. On Day One the value statement was not: "We shall have an

IPO, we shall have a market cap of 43 billion dollars, we shall make the employees rich, our stock options shall go up 100% or 10,000%." It was about how we actually deliver value to our customers, because there was a notion that if you did that, everything else would fall into place. If we didn't do that we wouldn't have a sustainable company in any sense of the word - sustainable customers, sustainable stock option value, sustainable market value, IPO value, all that good stuff.

It's interesting to look at the actual numbers through the end of last year, because they were at the heart of why we were able to merge the two companies so easily. i2 had delivered 7 billion dollars in hard, measurable, tangible value through December of 1999. Aspect had delivered 3.5 billion dollars through measurable tangible, hard benefits delivered to our customers. That's a combined total of 10.5 billion. So when Sanjiv and I met for the first time with the idea of a merger, in early March this year (2000), we went in six hours from "Does this make sense?" to shaking hands on the deal. This is a 9.3 billion dollar deal, non-trivial, the largest software deal in history. What made it possible? It wasn't about who's going to run what in the joint company. It wasn't about how this will affect your stock value and my stock value. It wasn't about what this is going to mean for the shareholders. The notion was we had an identical business philosophy. It's about building a great company; it's about giving value to customers and everything else is purely supportive. That meant we didn't have to worry about vision, didn't have to worry about culture, didn't have to worry about whether we'd be compatible partners. We already knew from our original mission statements, going back ten years, that we thought the same way. Six hours later we shook hands on a deal and that led to a definitive agreement in ten days after the handshake, something that has never been done before in the history of the software industry.

So has that actually translated into less of a challenge in terms of integration, because the value systems of both i2 and Aspect were so similar?

Yes, absolutely, and I'm not trying to diminish the people issues in the integration because they are important. I'm not trying to oversimplify either, but it has absolutely, definitely made it a lot easier. The impact of that kind of thinking goes all the way to the first day of the company, and defines the kind of people you hire, the kind of teamwork you create. It goes to the heart of how you incent people. It

> *The long-term view is to build a great company; the short-term view is to build a great IPO.*

shapes the kind of IPO you do and when you do it. It sets the expectations correctly with your employees before an IPO, during an IPO and after an

IPO. All these are affected by whether you have a long-term view or a short-term view. To me, the long-term view is to build a great company; the short-term view is to build a great IPO.

I gave you one example of how it affects the mission statement of a company on Day One. I'll give you another example. What types of employees do you want in a company? Broadly speaking, potential employees fall into three categories.

There is one group of executives and employees who are passionate about the market that the company is going to be in, passionate about the product, about the technology, about serving the customers and about delivering value. Their passion is a long-term passion. It's not driven primarily by option price or the date of an IPO.

There is a second group of employees that I would say are largely financially driven. Their focus is on what the option plan is. When is the IPO going to happen? What price can you guarantee or confirm as to what might be the IPO? Clearly these are not people who don't care about the products, but to them the passion for the market and the product and the people is secondary. The passion for the IPO and the stock options is primary.

Then you have a third group of people who are somewhere in the middle. They have some sense of passion, but in the end their decision will still be guided more by comparing their stock option plan to someone else's. This is more important to them than whether they will enjoy the work they're going to do.

My philosophy in starting Aspect was to try to bring on board executives and managers who were passionate about the business we were in, who I felt would be committed to the business through the up cycles and the down cycles and who would enjoy their work. The reward from an IPO and a stock option program would be a byproduct of their passion rather than principal reason for being with the company.

How successful were you in doing that?

You can measure it in a couple of different ways.

One way to measure it is the number of years the employees stay with the company after the initial four-year vesting is up, and we have had a very high percentage of people staying with the company. I would say our turnover has been less than 12 or 13% on average, which is less than half of the geographic average. In particular, that turnover is lower with employees who have already vested their first 4 years of stock options than it is among employees who have just started with the company. To me, that is the ulti-mate test; the people who have been vested are still here at the company.

Another way to measure it is to see what happens when the stock takes a downturn. As you know, we had a major slip in Q1 last year (2000), with the stock going from 30 or 40 bucks down to about 6 bucks. The company was nine years old so many of the employees had already vested their options. It would have been very easy for every employee to say good-bye at that point. There was a pretty high percentage of employees who felt that the best the stock would do, coming out of that slip over the next 2 years would be to get back to around 25 or 30. I think if I had polled the employees then and asked how many of them believed the stock would be at $100 in less than a year, there would have been only one employee and that would have been me! And the reason I say it would have been me is that when I spoke to the employees on the 1st of April 2000, telling them that we had just missed the quarter, I said that it would be easy to get caught up in the fact that the stock was down to $6, but that we'd always shared a long-term view of the market and taking that into account I personally believed that the stock would be back at $100 in less than 2 years, possibly as early as a year. And even though the employees may not have believed that, the fact that I did was very important to them. I did actually believe it; otherwise why pick $100? It seemed like an impossible goal. Why not pick $30, $50 or $60 or a much more achievable goal? But that's just the way I felt - passionate about the business in my tenth year of running it. So this wasn't just a starry eyed first year view.

The net result of all this was that we were actually able to keep all of our employees. We didn't have any turnover. Compare that with the experience of companies that have focused more on the IPO - the Silicon Valley is full of them- and you will see that when they have a slip or the market changes on them and there is a downtrend in the B to C companies, the stock values come down by 30% to 95%. The turnover in those companies is phenome-nal. It's 50, 60 or 70 percent. We didn't have that at Aspect.

When the stocks fell off on Wall Street, it must have been a huge challenge for you.

Big challenge! But that, in my opinion, separates good CEOs from flashy ones. I consider myself to be a passionate, intense, driven, focused CEO who keeps his eye on the fundamentals. I don't consider myself to be a flashy CEO or a celebrity CEO. So what is the difference? I could've chosen to spend my time over the last 10 years promoting myself rather than building the company. Everything takes time. I think publicity-driven CEOs move the focus away from where it belongs, which is on the executive team and the employee team that makes a great company. They move the entire focus away from the organization on to one individual, and in the process of doing that they lose sight of what is fundamentally important in building a great company.

What is fundamental?

What is fundamental is having clearly articulated values. Fundamental is great products and great people who are passionate about the product and market. Fundamental is delivering actual measurable value. Fundamental is giving as much priority to customer satisfaction as to sales. Fundamental is building the right kind of infrastructure and process at the right inflection points in the growth of a company. Fundamental is sharing the credit and the rewards with all the employees in the company. These are all fundamentals in the building of a company.

When the stock price of Aspect was near the bottom, what was the root cause and how did you attack the situation in order to turn it around?

I'm a very strong believer in the 80/20 rule and usually focus on the top three things.

The number one thing, the immediate root cause, was that we had not grown, commensurate with our bookings. The end result was that we were increasingly dependent on a small number of large deals to make every quarter. Also the sales force did not grow in 1998 like it was supposed to. I hadn't focused enough on it. At that time we were also going through a change of COO in the company; ours had left earlier that year. I was bringing in a new COO who didn't join till April of 1999, which was almost 14 months after the first one left. During that time I had a lot of responsibility on my shoulders and unfortunately I did not focus on these issues. That was the first root cause problem.

The first thing that I wanted to do was to change the sales organization, to double it over a nine month period from April 1 through December 31, 1999. So we did that.

Second was the repositioning of the company. We had begun to develop a lot of technology that would reposition us from being a client server software company to being a web-architecture based software company. But that wasn't obvious to the market or to Wall Street, so the second decision was to completely change the positioning of Aspect towards being a web-centric company. We actually had to do that in three steps. We first announced our Internet strategy in August, 1999. The market responded more or less with a yawn. The stock had gone back up to the 10-15 dollar range, so in one sense it had doubled. But in another sense, the market said: "Interesting story, a little complicated, we don't get it, we'll wait for the proof of the pudding." In October of 1999, I began another road show because we had made even more progress in terms of our technology and our whole approach to the market. From October through December 1999 our stock began to climb pretty successfully - based on reality, not on hype. It was based simply on getting our messages out, because when you slip a quarter no one wants to listen to you. This was actually a very tenacious, persistent process of getting people to continue to listen, continue to see the upside. Another step was taken in February 2000 when we actually had a major analyst meeting. We showed them some of our latest technology and there was a lot of excitement about it. We announced our marketing partnership with i2, so the buzz began to climb, with the end result being that the stock began to take-off. If it hadn't, a successful merger with i2 would not have been possible, because we would have had too much of a valuation imbalance. I felt intrinsically that our company had a lot of value that wasn't being reflected by Wall Street metrics. Had the value not gone up to where it did, I would not have merged the company with i2. That's also part of what made the merger easier.

The third piece was strengthening the management team of the company. I felt that the company had run out of management capacity.

In what way? Scalability?

One was scalability and the other was having a head for fresh thinking, that is, new ideas from the outside. The same management team, more or less, had been in place for about four or five years and much of it is still there. It wasn't that I had a problem with the management team; I think the team-members we had in early 1999 were all-star performers. But at every key inflection point in the company you need to keep bringing in fresh ideas. Fresh ideas can sometimes come from the existing management team, but sometimes they come from the outside. The key is to keep bringing in new blood, keep bringing in new ideas and of course to listen to them and integrate the good ones, because a lot of the new ideas that come from the outside can also be useless. I brought in the new president and COO; I brought several new people into the content business.

You made a decision, a controversial decision, to spin out a major portion of the content business. What were the reasons?

One was to provide a focus on the content business. This was because inside Aspect the content business was surprisingly being lost as it was only generating a small percentage of our total revenue. So most managers tended to ignore it and forget it. I felt it actually represented one of the crown jewels in the company; I believe in the next 5 years, in the B-to-B space and the E business space, content is going to be one of the biggest drivers of success. In fact it was one of the reasons why i2 wanted to merge with Aspect. And yet inside of Aspect, content wasn't being given the level of respect and funding it deserved.

The second reason I had for spinning out a portion of it was to fund it at the right level. I actually went to Wall Street and told them I was going to spin it out. I said, "I'm going to invest another twenty million bucks in it that I can't take through Aspect because you guys will shoot me, since I won't be able to make my quarterly plan. Therefore we are going to make it transparent; we're going to break it out in a separate Profit Center." It was a very innovative approach to Wall Street, one which analysts actually bought into. As a result I was able to start dramatically increasing my investment.

Third was focus. I felt that this would provide a very strong focus to the content part of the business.

What effect did the spin-off have on Aspect?

A dramatic increase in the stock price, because the feeling was that we were thinking of new business models for the Internet, for the "new" economy. We were being innovative at the same time that we were being transparent. We weren't trying to hide this or fudge it. It was all being shown completely and openly. In fact, in Q4 1999 and Q1 2000 I believe we actually had two sets of P & Ls announced. We had the core Aspect and we had what we call the Infinite Supply Business. Analysts were perfectly OK with it. It's very rarely been done successfully, but in our case it was successful because I was able to fund the business; I was able to attract a very good talent pool into the business. That was an example of the new thinking that came about after the April slip of 1999.

The idea was to completely transform the company, focus it on the new economy, focus it on our big strengths. Content was one of our strengths, so we invested in the content business wisely. But since we couldn't do that through the Aspect P & L, we split out a piece of it, making it transparent to Wall Street. These were examples of all that we did. All through this we had to do a lot of customer hand-holding, a lot of employee hand-holding and lot of shareholder hand holding, because obviously words are cheap, and people are looking for performance. The good news is that we reset expectations in April 1999 and then against those reset expectations we delivered scrupulously in Q2, Q3, Q4, 1999 and Q1, Q2 2000.

Switching gears to global strategy, did Aspect think global right from the get-go?

In the first 12 months we set up our operations in Bangalore, India and started our European business. We were in Japan in the second year of the company. In hindsight, I think I could have done things better and differently in Europe and Japan. For example, when we started in Japan we did a partnership with Digital Equipment Corporation. I think they were the wrong partners. They were driven mainly by hardware rather than by solutions selling, even though they told us that solution selling was very important to them. They did produce some good sales for us in the early days, but they also mispositioned us as a low-end part search engine. Instead of doing large enterprise-like deals in the millions-of-dollars each, we did small deals in the hundreds-of-thousands of dollars range and this mispositioned the product. It's taken many years to get that position changed to where it is now and where we wanted it to be.

Did Aspect morph over the years? If so, in what way?

Yes! The customers wanted larger value propositions. Our whole sales process changed from selling technology to selling value. All this happened beginning about 3 years ago. Our technology itself changed, at my strategic direction, from being a toolkit that customers could use to create solutions for part management to being off-the-shelf configurable solutions for strategic sourcing, design collaboration and content management. I changed the sales strategy to a value selling approach, changed the technology strategy to a solutions-driven approach, changed the sales force to support. I also changed the messaging, branding and positioning with customers in order to reposition us. We began this process in early 1998, and by early 2000 the transformation of Aspect was pretty much completed. To some degree that probably made us more interesting to i2 and other potential acquirers.

What industry did Aspect go after first and why?

Our core expertise was helping companies make better decisions about what they buy, from whom they buy, what price they should pay, what quantities they should buy it in, with the view being that we wanted to reduce their product cost by 15%, reduce their design cycles by about 50 to 75% and increase their asset utilization by some 25 to 30%.

We started with electronics because of several factors - fastest rate of change and the fact that our technology provides decision support for rapid and better decision making. Ten years ago the rate of change in electronics was far greater than it was in most of the verticals, so it's not surprising that almost all of the 200 largest electronics companies in the world are customers of ours. Today you can arguably say that the rate of change is high in all industries.

Next, as we began to move more and more towards asset management, we targeted the chemical and gas space. Chemical plants are basically a collection of a million products, just like a PC is a collection of 700 parts. So we applied the same basic decision support technology and content technology to help oil and gas companies increase the efficiency of utilization, keep their plants' uptime higher and reduce their spending on strategic MRO purchases by 15%. As a result, BP Amco became a customer, Shell became a customer, Occidental became a customer, and most of the large oil and gas companies became our customers.

From there we went into automotive, industrial, aerospace and defense, consumer packaged goods and utility.

Now let's go into the micro level of the merger between Aspect and i2. You had mentioned that Sanjiv Sidhu had given you a call. What happened next?

Well, it was an interesting scenario. i2 and Aspect had already been marketing partners for about 6 months. We were both, unknowingly bidding to buy the same company, SupplyBase. I felt that this was becoming adversarial. I sent Sanjiv an e-mail basically saying: "Why don't we buy the company together?" And a couple of days later he called up and said, "I have an even better idea ... how about if we buy both Aspect and SupplyBase? Then we can make this a 3 way partnership." I told him that I would like to think about it for a few days and a few days later I called him back and said the idea made perfect sense.

Why did it make sense?

First, it was based on our business values and our business culture. We were very compatible companies.

Second, Sanjiv had a company on a much larger scale in terms of size of sales force, size of delivery capability and number of customers. I felt it would take a long time to catch up to that scale and in the meantime I saw, in this B-to-B space, a 12 to 24 month window of opportunity which I could access on my own and keep adding to. But I could only keep adding within a level of the profit plan that I had committed to Wall Street. That meant I couldn't go out and add 300 sales people, because it takes a year for the sales guys to ramp up. That means during that year you miss your Wall Street expectations. The problem was that I didn't have the ability to invest as much in the business as I needed to in order to achieve or to take advantage of the market opportunity. i2 offered an alternative way to take advantage of that same market opportunity faster, better and cheaper, without having to make the same investment, because they had a very healthy infrastructure in place.

The third reason was that the product suites complemented one another, if you look at the complete e-business set of processes that makes up a complete solution. Aspect provides inbound supply chain solutions -design & source; i2 brought supply chain management, product lifecycle management and customer management -content planning and fulfillment- to the table, and Supply Base provided a piece of the content and solution.

The vision was very simple. When Sanjiv and I met I told him, "Look, these three companies (i2, Aspect, & Supply Base) together are my idea of a full e-business process, the full e-business solutions field. What's your view?" He showed me a diagram that he had done which was absolutely identical to the one I had shown him. Then we asked ourselves: Does every customer need all the pieces together? The answer was yes.

What's the best way to get there? Obviously, one alternative was for i2 to simply develop the various components. The other alternative was for them to buy a small competitor and then try and create a larger competitor to Aspect. But my philosophy and Sanjiv's philosophy were the same. He didn't want to go with a second or third tier partner. I didn't want to go with a second or third tier partner. We agreed that our companies were the absolute world leaders in our respective markets. We concluded that a merger of two world leaders covering different parts of the e-business process was the best way to go. This discussion lasted for three hours and the next two hours were about the value, the price i2 would pay to acquire Aspect. The last hour was spent on the logistics of pulling the deal together.

Was it just you and him one-on-one?

One-on-one. There were no investment bankers at all. That's the only reason it happened so fast. The previous night I had had dinner with Greg Bailey, the president of i2. He and I hit it off quite well and he was very positive and eager to do this deal. When Sanjiv and I were meeting one-on-one, the next thing we talked about was value. We figured there were two ways we had to look at the value equation.

We looked at the relative revenue contributions and revenue ratio of the two companies, going backwards and forward. Depending on various assumptions, Aspect was somewhere between 16 and 18% of the total combined revenue. I also felt I needed some premium on the deal, so we ended up with a ratio of about 19% of the combined company. That was what we shook hands on. It was not a very complicated set of arguments. It was based on the assumption that they had a high market multiple because they were the leaders in their space and we had a high market multiple because we were the leaders in our space.

It took ten days from the day we shook hands to the day we signed a definitive agreement, which is a record, in addition to the value of the deal. Then I would say most of March and April of 2000 was spent basically explaining to the employees and customers of both companies why this merger was going to be good for them.

How did you go about the integration?

That was done by about half a dozen key guys. Bill Beecher, the CFO of i2, and I both went out to the key investors of both companies and spent two weeks on the road explaining to them why this was a good thing. That caused the stock to stay very stable, which is a very critical thing, because in many other large mergers like this, the stock declines. Every Wall Street analyst could immediately grasp this picture and say, "This makes absolute sense, two great companies coming together." In fact, most of the investors were investors in both companies for that same reason. So they had to do nothing except combine their shareholdings together.

We could have integrated the company in a variety of different ways. i2 had a functional organization and Aspect had a functional organization. I actually proposed to Sanjiv that we treat this integration not purely with a narrowly focused view of how to merge Aspect inside i2, but make this a really extraordinary opportunity. We should take a far-reaching view of i2's organizational structure, think ahead and say what i2 wants to be three years from now and support that vision of that future i2. Why not design that future organization and do it now?

We concluded that we wanted i2 to be a 5 billion dollar revenue company in three to four years, and that kind of growth would be facilitated by having a business unit-oriented structure rather than a functional structure. This was the perfect opportunity to reorganize the company and that is what we did. We actually organized i2 by the end of June as a company with 5 major business units - a design unit, a source unit, a content unit and a planning and fulfillment unit, which includes all of these functions. Then we had the platform unit, which does the B-to-B platforms. There is a unit called global business solutions, which basically takes all of these solutions and packages them together into standard market place solutions for horizontal markets, vertical markets, covering all the different verticals we have.

What was the strategy behind this organizational model?

We thought this would be a much more efficient structure; we would be able to empower the heads of the business units and hold them accountable, both in terms of their performance and their budgets.

Second, this would allow us to attract top-notch executives who would want to run the businesses; they would then become part of the expanding executive team of i2.

Third, this would allow us as well to target our competitors and our markets in a much more precise, laser-like way. Because i2, as a functional organization, would have 30 competitors with design having a bunch of competitors, source with a bunch of competitors and plan with a bunch of competitors. However, if you're inside the business unit you can pick your top 3 competitors and nail them, really go after them. So this was very much a market-driven view of the organization rather than an internal view.

Would it be accurate to say that it took a good 9 months to complete the integration?

Yes. The good news is the executive support for it and the employee support for it. The executive team of i2 has a very problem-solving attitude. And certainly at the highest executive level of i2, Sanjiv, Greg and I are working very well together. The next level of management is also working extremely well.

After the integration of i2 and Aspect, how did the executive team align and organize in terms of customer and employees?

What we try to do in the top-level team is share responsibility for executive sponsorship across different customers. For example, I was the executive sponsor on the Seimens deal. For about 4 or 5 months, from the time I got involved to the time we actually closed that deal, I ran that entire sales process. I managed the relationship with Siemens' CEO, their board members and the president of the e-business group inside Siemens. Similarly, Greg, was the executive sponsor for Caterpillar and Sanjiv was the executive sponsor for K-Mart. These were our three largest deals, and each of them was done by a different executive sponsor. That's how we work in terms of the customer side.

On the employee side, we again divide it up in terms of influence. Greg, for example, has the global sales organization and the supply chain planning business unit. I've just turned over the design and source business unit, which was part of Aspect. The reason we did that was that we felt we needed to have one top executive look at the complete supply chain holistically, from beginning to end. We basically do logical things that are not driven by ego or by who has more people reporting to him or her. It's driven by what's the right thing for the customer, what's the right thing for the employees. Many of the strategic decisions are made collaboratively anyway, but in terms of operational decisions of a day-to-day nature, they are made by the executive sponsor who owns that business.

Switching to your personal side, after having started so many companies, what keeps you going?

I have to feel an incredible passion about what I do, because when I go, I go non-stop. I cannot work half-heartedly for anything or anybody, whether it is for me or for anyone else. So I either feel deeply passionate about the business I am in or I become a very dangerous guy to have in the business because I'm not probably going to make the best decisions possible. I usually know when I'm not passionately engaged; when I'm not, I would rather disengage than be halfhearted about it. What has made me passionate about Aspect for 10 years and keeps me passionate today on behalf of i2 is the fact that I think we are in the middle of an incredible revolution, one which is transforming the whole business-to-business space.

My feeling is that the real big win, the big value proposition, the trillions in value that are yet to be delivered, come from collaborations between businesses, much tighter partnerships between businesses. It comes from the exchange and sharing between businesses, from shared decision-making between businesses. Two years ago Dell made all of its decisions on its own. It got information from suppliers but then said, "OK we are going to make the decision, and you, the supplier will do as you are told." That was two years ago. Today Dell makes its decision collaboratively with its top 50 customers and top 50 suppliers. Making those kinds of decisions requires a whole new approach to process and to the technology that enables that process. I believe that i2 is uniquely positioned, with the domain expertise to provide help to companies for their processes and with the technologies that the companies need to automate these processes. I believe that this revolution is just taking off and will continue to accelerate over the next several years. Through all that I find myself in a very good place. I am with a good company. I have a great deal of knowledge that the CEOs of our customers value and the boards of our customers value. I have the ability to synthesize business strategy, technology strategy and marketing strategy, both on behalf of i2 and on behalf of our customers. That is a pretty powerful combination of contributions that I can make. As long as I feel that I can continue to make those contributions and generate value and success for our customers and shareholders, it's a very good reason to wake up early and start making calls at six in the morning. It's a very good reason to keep working till eight at night and a very good reason to continue to work on weekends.

Looking at a typical month, how do you allocate your time?

When it was just Aspect, an average workweek was probably around 70 to 80 hours. Following our merger with i2 it's upped from that. Typically, 10% of that workweek is spent on strategy, about 30% with customers and 30% on operational issues, specific business, technology or market place challenges. The remaining 30% is spent in a broad sweep of i2's operations. It could be meetings related to marketing programs, recruiting, employee-related matters, reviewing financials, or meetings in Dallas to ensure that we continue the communication and dialogue between the business units.

How do you stay ahead of the curve in terms of what's out there in the future?

It is hard. I get a lot of information at the investor conferences at the time of making presentations. I take the time to talk to analysts and learn their perspective on i2 and their perspective on market trends. I tend to read a lot on weekends -- everything from industry analysts' reports to Wall Street analysts' reports to semi-trade publications like Fast Company and Business 2.0 to business pubs like Forbes, Fortune and Business Week. Occasionally, I read technical magazines as well. Reading does consume a lot of my time.

What role has your family played in your success?

My family has provided extraordinary support in terms of putting up with the fact that I spend most of my waking hours on my business rather than with them. I spend most of my weekend hours on my business, not with the family, and I travel a lot. On average, I travel about three days a week or more. It requires a great deal of family support to do that, without any complaints or pressure. You can either do it with peace and calm at home or in the face of stress at home as well as at work. I have to say that I have virtually no stress at home.

My wife Kathy's values and honesty, her kindness and focus on the family in terms of communications and relationships, have been very instrumental in my success.

Is there anything such as a balance to such a life?

There is a balance, but I haven't found it yet. I would think the perfect balance would be more in the favor of the family and less in the favor of business, but it is really hard in the midst of the changes we are going through and because of the opportunity that i2 has. I'm sure there are people who are able to make giant contributions on the basis of having one great idea a year and for the rest of the time they can coast. I can't do that. I have to be engaged intellectually and physically all the time. So I would say that it has been harder for me to find a balance.

What are your comments on Sanjiv Sidhu?

I would say that Sanjiv has turned out to be everything I expected him to be. He's a good visionary; he's very good with customers. He's able to communicate the vision and the passion of i2 to them. He's very good at providing an up-front articulation of the vision of i2 and the benefits that i2 can deliver to the customer. His passion for the business is phenomenal.

What, in your opinion, makes an entrepreneur?

I would say an entrepreneur is someone who wants to add value to the economy by creating a business through leveraging his knowledge, his passion, his dreams and his desires. The definition of an entrepreneur covers the full spectrum of individuals who want to be catalysts for enormous change and can do so in a variety of different ways.

You know, entrepreneurs fall into many categories. There are entrepreneurs who know how to start things but don't know how to run them. There are entrepreneurs who are great idea generators but are not business leaders. There are entrepreneurs who are good evangelists and missionaries but are not good managers. They don't all have to be business leaders; they don't all have to be great managers. However, they need to recognize what they are good at and what they are not good at. Then they should focus on leveraging what they are good at and bringing in help in the areas where they need it in order to realize their vision. If they can do this, they can achieve great success.

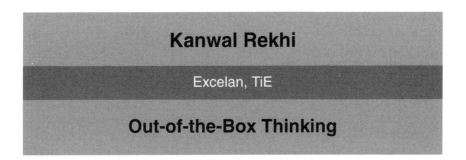

Kanwal Rekhi

Excelan, TiE

Out-of-the-Box Thinking

Kanwal Rekhi is chairman of TiE (The Indus Entrepreneurs). He is a leading entrepreneur and angel investor, and is on a mission to build bridges with India.

Rekhi founded Excelan in 1982. When Excelan merged with Novell in 1989 he joined Novell's board of directors and was later named executive vice president and CTO. In 1986 he was named as "Entrepreneur of the Year" by the Arthur-Young Venture magazine. Now retired, Rekhi serves on several public and private company boards.

He earned a B.Tech from IIT-Mumbai and a master's degree in electrical engineering from Michigan Tech.

Rekhi is a person of clear views who knows where he stands. He is a man with the heart of a lion and will go out of his way to offer help. He is known to be very fair and passionately devoted to cultivating entrepreneurs and helping them succeed. With Rekhi, what you see is what you get. He speaks his mind without mincing words.

This interview was conducted over three sessions. The first, at the TiE head-quarters in Silicon Valley, the second, while I dropped Rekhi at the San Francisco airport (He was on his way to meet the Indian Prime Minister) and the third over lunch at Togo's (a popular sandwich shop in Silicon Valley). We cover a lot of ground in these three interviews. Rekhi shares with us the story of Excelan, one of the first Indus companies to receive VC funding and make it big in America. He explains in detail the turnaround effort he orchestrated at Excelan, highlighting the drastic steps that were required to save it from going under. We then discuss his involvement with The Indus Group and his passion for mentoring. We end with a closer look at the personal side of this passionate individual.

"The sense of fair play is at the heart of everything you do."

Today, you are one of the most successful Indians not only in Silicon Valley but in the world as well. You went from being a successful entrepreneur to an even more successful investor and an icon in the Indian community. How did it all begin?

I like to believe this all began during my undergraduate years at IIT, Mumbai. IIT was for me the window to the world of science and technology. All of us had a hunger, a desire to do something, to become someone great. I was, like many others, swept up by a passion to come to the United States. I arrived in 1967 and received my master's degree in electrical engineering in 1969. To pay for my education I had to wash dishes at a restaurant. To many this may seem like menial labor, but I drew hope from it. If I could earn that little and still live on it, I was already making a profit, even back then.

At the time you graduated, the Vietnam war had just ended, leading to a recession. Engineers were not the most sought after professionals. Was that a difficult time?

Yes, it was not a great time to be an engineer. I was laid off three times but I knew I was going to succeed. I kept bouncing back and traveled all over the country before finally getting a job with Singer-Link in Sunnyvale, CA.

If you look at the history of Indians, those who came early on to the United States were very focused on succeeding. Becoming part of the society, being accepted and competing in order to move up was very important to us. The density of Indians was very low and we did not have much of a support structure. The early immigrants were very focused on success, but eventually most of us started to hit the glass ceiling. The immigrants from the Indus region were seen as techies, engineers, programmers and doctors. The technical track only took you so far. We discovered that we needed to inculcate a certain skill set, and change in order to grow. Several of us felt that we could not do it, that entrepreneurship was the only way available. Only a handful of people were able to make it up all the way up the ladder - Rajat Gupta of Mckinsey, Dr. Netravali at Bell Labs, Krish Prabhu at Alcatel and a few others - but these were only a few.

You obviously broke through this glass ceiling. How did you go about it?

I attacked the issue head-on. You have to make sure that you become absolutely focused on performance and take action. You can't ask for a break from anybody. You have to let your actions speak for you. You have to think "out-of the box" and take unconventional steps. I was one of the first to go to the VCs for money; I needed to do it like everyone else here. I felt that the society was fair and open and that we should not have an issue getting the funds. It was to be the first milestone.

John Barsh, a VC, once gave me sound advice. He said, "Just show me the revenue numbers." When you start to execute you cannot make excuses; every step of the way you have to show the numbers. At the end of the day, performance translates into numbers.

How did you identify the market opportunity? Where did the idea come from?

Everyone thinks of the Internet age as a once-in-a-lifetime opportunity that is changing the world. Any time when there is a rapid change or discontinuous change it usually presents an opportunity. What that typically means is that something fundamental has happened and the previously established order, where average people had an advantage, ceases to exist. The technology has moved on, the present technology has become obsolete, the cost structure has changed and that's when opportunities emerge very quickly.

At the end of the day, performance translates into numbers.

We had a similar change when the PCs came about in the late 70's. The fundamental change that the PC made was that it brought the power of the computer to the masses very cheaply. The early PC, even though underpowered, was still very good. For a couple of thousand dollars you could get the CPU, memory and HD. This allowed the notion of personal productivity. Most of us who grew up with mainframe super-computers saw this as a transition, a revolution. The whole world was turned upside down. The mainframes were designed to be cheaper when they were bigger. When you needed more compute power you bought a bigger and bigger machine. There used to be a well-established IBM formula "twice the power at 40% more money". So, instead of buying two computers you bought twice the CPU. The PC turned this whole way of thinking upside down. If you needed twice the power, you bought two computers. You started small and very flexibly increased the compute power by adding more PCs. This was a fundamental change and we saw the opportunity: These things would have to be tied together into a network. The industry was going through a transition. The PC was being positioned as a stand-alone desktop personal productivity tool. We saw this as a starting point rather than an end point - that the productivity tools would have to tie together and that they would have to tie back into the mini computers and mainframes, and networking would be a very big deal.

Excelan's idea was to network these computers together and to the other machines. In fact, when the PC was announced, Inder Mohan Singh, Navin Jain, and I were already playing around with the idea of designing networks for these PCs.

How did the three of you meet? What did each of you bring to the table? How did you function as a team?

All three of us were equal partners. After working for Singer-Link for nine years, from'71 to' 80, I ended up going to work for Zilog, where I met up with Inder and Navin. I was the logic design/system design expert; Inder was a mainframe computer expert and Navin was in charge of the software world.

So now you had a good team, a great idea; what was next?

When Ethernet was announced as a standard, the idea of networking computers together became an opportunity. Ethernet was straightforward, a standard backed by Intel, Xerox, and Digital; this ensured that the standard was well thought through and was designed to be very broad and open. Intel said that they would design the network chips and targeted an introduction time of two to three years.

I had grown up with the transistors, SSI chips, MSI * LSI chips, and was able to design quickly without having the chips available – a very complex function. For the new engineers, if the µP wasn't available, if serial I/O was not available - they could not design it. I realized that I could design very complex systems without the chip.

With this expertise in design the team felt that we could design the network chips to go with Ethernet in weeks rather than years and that it would be simple. One day I just sat down and started to sketch the Ethernet design on paper and in a couple of weeks came up with a design that would fit on the board easily. Intel had done some board-level design, but their solution consisted of two large boards and was awkward. We came up with a single board design that was half the size and at the same time a lot more original and powerful. The issue was now whether or not the paper design would work.

I was confident that it would work and this became the basis of Excelan. We could design the board level adapters for all types of buses- multibus, geo bus, Unibus, IBM PC bus- and before the chips were available. We became more of a board company and were able to do intelligent boards very rapidly, so we were almost instant hits. If chips became available then others would be able to do it too. We had to get out there and establish ourselves early. So Excelan got ahead of their competition and became leaders in high performance networking boards for various machines. Excelan had a solution that could connect the Minicomputers, Vaxes, Micro Vaxes, PDPs, to the PCs and to all sorts of Unix machines. So the boards solution was considered to be the early magic.

Your betting on the TCP/IP as a protocol appears to be a key component of Excelan's success. Again, this was contrary to conventional wisdom. Why did you take this bet?

Yes, backing the TCP/IP as a protocol was another win. Intel and Xerox performed the hardware standardization with the Ethernet but they all adopted different software standards. Digital adopted DECnet, Xerox came up with Xeroxnet, Intel adopted OSI protocols. All three solutions were different and incompatible with each other. None of these solutions made sense, as the machines could not talk to each other. Most people bet on the Xeroxnet, but we bet on TCP/IP as it had already been proved, on the slow networks, to work with all the machines. The department of defense (DoD) and most universities had adopted TCP/IP as part of the Defense Advanced Research Project Administration net (DARPA). DARPA net was the original Internet and had used TCP/IP.

You knew you could transfer files between various machines using TCP/IP and I sensed that if you took the TCP /IP protocols which are proven on the DARPA net and Ethernet, which is a very solid standard, and put them together you would have an instant solution. People could do things instantly rather than wait for chips and standards.

This turned out to be a good insight, because people were beginning to buy PCs and they wanted to run their CAD programs on VAXES. Excelan was able to let PCs do virtual terminal sessions, file transfers back and forth, and were able to offer their customers rapid solutions.

You were one of the first Indians to go to VCs for funding. What made you take this step?

Yes, I was one of the first Indian entrepreneurs to go the VC route. My thinking was: If we are going to succeed here then we have to be like the other people here. We have to be ready to compete. If we have to compete for the customers down the road we have to compete for the money now. If we are not able to compete for the money now, what makes us think we will succeed later? You have to sell yourselves to the VC, then to the employees, and then to the customers.

Excelan had opened its doors in April 1982. We had put up our own cash and no one received salaries for six to seven months. The first hardware design was already in the hands of customers and we already had our first purchase order. The board was beginning to work well and customers were beginning to show interest. The dream of networking was also a believable dream by that time. We had already differentiated ourselves with the board, so we felt confident to approach the VCs for the money. John Barsh, who funded us, looked at us and told us bluntly, "You guys don't have much bargaining power, do you?" When we said no, he said, "I'll make you one offer and that's it" He gave us two million dollars for half the company. This was a very fair and generous offer at the time.

1983 was a disastrous year for Excelan. What happened?

Excelan was in trouble. We were not making our numbers and the VCs were not happy. We committed the common mistake of "over promise and under deliver". When the numbers were falling we were hiding rather than addressing the issues with a correction plan. We began to blame others. We were actually doing well in absolute numbers but you are compared against the numbers you project and promise. The strategy should be "under promise and over deliver", not the other way around. We were projecting way beyond reality.

For example, we received VC funding in 1982 and promised 5 million in annual revenues. In 1983, neither the product nor the team was ready. It was not possible to bring in 5 million dollars for the year. It would take Excelan six months to develop the product and at least six or more months to deliver. Excelan earned only half a million dollars in revenue that year.

Excelan was obviously in serious trouble. You were asked to take the leadership on an interim basis to steer the company in the right direction. How did you go about the turnaround?

Drastic times required drastic measures. The company was not focused. They wanted to adopt all standards. The team was split in many directions. The same thing was happening with the protocol side. I stepped in and immediately dropped every project that was not related to the boards and TCP/IP protocol, the prime revenue generators. One must establish realistic goals and be on top of the game plan every step of the way. I cut the work force by one third. With fewer resources but a very focused approach you can actually do more. From a hardware perspective, the focus was on boards and all the software people worked on the TCP/IP solution. We had good boards but software was an issue. It's very hard to sell boards without software, so I attacked the issue by hiring outside expertise to develop TCP/IP software for the boards. Within two to three months we came up with a working solution.

I took the risk and bet the company. I shifted the focus to serving the customers who needed the solution right away. I knew this opportunity existed for the next couple of years. The solution worked and the customer need was immediate. If the customer has a headache he doesn't want to wait for aspirin. He wants it immediately. Excelan was able to provide the painkiller immediately.

As time progressed it became clear that eventually the Excelan solution was going to win. We had maintained the lead by keeping focused. Excelan was the only game in town that could connect the PCs to the Unix machines, minicomputers and mainframes. It was a high performance solution. By late 1985, purchase orders were pouring in. Customers were buying; growth was exponential. In 1984 revenues were 5 million dollars with losses totaling 3 million. By the end of 1985, revenues went up to 10.1 million and Excelan saw profitability of $100,000 for the first time. By 1986, we had 22 million in revenue and 2.5 million in profit.

Yet another first was the sale of software over the phone. What was the marketing strategy behind such an approach?

We placed advertisements in all the trade publications. Excelan could not afford a sales force; we relied heavily on trade magazine advertisements and sold over the phone with a money-back guarantee. With a limited sales force of 3 to 4 employees, where a typical organization had over 15, this was the only way to reach the customer. No corporation had sold high-end expensive solutions over the phone before. With limited money resources this was the only way to market. We were the first ones to sell a complex piece of software and hardware over the phone. The quality of the products had to be good to support such a policy.

Earlier, the strategy had been to market through the OEM. Excelan had hoped that the OEMs would sell for them but this strategy failed. All OEMs were themselves startups and were focusing on their own issues. The OEMs themselves did not have any significant presence in the market. So I switched gears from OEM to direct sale to the customers.

You now had the company moving in the right direction. What was next?

The next thing we did was come up with a three month plan to box everything into an end-user product including the board, transceivers, the software and cables. When the customer called he would be sent a complete solution. We focused on integrating customer needs. We made sure that the box would contain everything the customer would need, right down to the screws needed to mount the cables. I pulled Duane from the technical group and made him the marketing guy. Duane and I wrote the trouble shooting flowcharts for the customer service group. When the phone rang, the customer service agent knew exactly what needed to be done. I put smart engineers on the technical marketing group, again utilizing an unconventional approach. This ability to tackle the problem from a system perspective and the hands-on approach to convert customer needs into reality was what got us the customers and their long-term confidence.

Your product pricing strategy to increase the price of software was soon to become an industry norm. What was the reasoning behind this?

It was common sense! Earlier, the software had been priced very low at $70 per copy, while the boards were way up near the $1,000 figure. Naturally, software was not very reliable and not very good. Customers were always complaining, service and support phones were busy. I simply did the math. The revenue generated by the sale of the software was not enough to maintain the design, testing and support of the software. There was something drastically wrong; something did not make sense here. It was quite obvious that to do the right job profitably, we would have to price the software at ten times the price, at $700 a copy. Everybody in the company thought I was crazy. The sales and marketing folks threw their hands in the air in disbelief. It did not make business sense, but I took the bet. There was nothing to lose, as it was clear that the VC would not provide additional funds at that time. Drastic action had to be taken quickly.

The customers initially questioned the tenfold increase. As luck would have it, most of the customers were new. The software quality, along with customer service, improved tremendously with the additional revenue. This ultimately led to customer satisfaction and turned the lose-lose situation into a win-win situation. The entire industry then adopted this model, pricing the software products at higher levels because it made good business sense.

What's your advice to the entrepreneur regarding the turnaround effort?

An entrepreneur has to be able to think financially. He has to be able do the math of his business. I was making calculations on what the pricing had to be and how many calls and refunds the system could tolerate... this is all financial thinking. One has to know the underlying cost structure right down to the bones. The product needs to be priced right. Anybody who prices products based on the pricing of the competition is in trouble. You have to know your cost structure. I do not like anybody utilizing the low cost strategy. Low cost strategy is a sure way to end up out of business. You have to do value pricing. You must deliver value to the customer– "the best bang for the buck."

I recall my father saying, *"Mehnga roye eak bar - Sasta roye bar baar"*. That has stuck in my head. That means if you raise the price, the customer will be upset with you initially but if the stuff works and the service is good he will be happy with you. On the other hand, if you sell your product cheap and it doesn't work, your service is poor, and you don't have the margin to give him the quality he needs, everybody loses.

Business is math, financial thinking and marketing.

By 1986, you had taken all these bold, "out-of-the-box" steps and the company had made a fantastic comeback. Yet when it came time for the IPO, another CEO was brought in. Why not you? Was this an example of the "glass ceiling"?

The VCs wanted to bring in an external CEO as they felt I might not be able to sell the show on the road. It was explained to me that by hiring an external CEO they were preserving my investment. I had gained a lot of confidence in leading but was still learning the ropes, so I agreed with them. Interestingly, in the same year I was named "Entrepreneur of the year" by the Arthur-Young/Venture magazine.

When was the IPO?

It was in 1987. The IPO was at $12, and it went up to $18. It then went down to $7 during the stock market crash in the'87/'88 timeframe.

When were you brought back in to take the lead?

In 1988 the CEO exited, due to personal issues. I think by then I had proven my mettle repeatedly and was totally ready to take on the CEO position officially. We finished the year with $66 million in revenue. Profits were at $5 to $6 million. The things we had done in the years 1985 and 1986 were finally paying off in 1988 and 1989."

Excelan merged with Novell in 1989. What made you consider Novell over companies like Microsoft?

Excelan had by now become a key networking player and Microsoft and Novell had both shown interest in a merger/acquisition. We were the TCP/IP experts and with us it had emerged as the leading networking technology. The Novell offer was better; there was better chemistry between us. They were very easy to work with. The dream and common vision that Ray Noorda (Chairman & CEO of Novell) and I had of becoming a networking giant was very clear. With Microsoft you would just be one of the players. Networking would have been incidental. With Novell, networking was mainstream. It turned out to be a nice merger. Merger is all attitude. It is how you transmit the attitude. Of course you should do it because it will be beneficial and there should be no doubts. Honesty and openness, of course, are a given.

You were with Novell until 1994 and became president of TiE in 1995. How did you get interested in TiE and why?

When I left Novell in 1994 I was very tired emotionally and physically; I was burned out. I went through surgery for sleep apnea and it changed my whole life! I felt like a new person; I had so much extra energy. Once I recovered I had no fixed agenda and just started to come to the TiE office; I had no other place to go. I realized that I had not got my hands dirty for a while and I needed to get back. TiE offered this to me and thus I started my affair with the TiE group.

How did your decision to become an angel investor come about?

While I was at TiE people began to drop in and ask for help. I started looking at peoples' business plans and provided guidance to the budding entrepreneurs. I think the word spread very rapidly that you could bounce ideas off this guy who had already done it. I had become a business guy with experience in hardware, software, and networking.

I would ask the basic key questions: Who is your customer? Why would they buy from you? How would you make money? Who is the competition? How does it fit into the scheme of things? I started to focus on the heart of the business. Mentorship at TiE became my new life. I never focused on the investment; investments just happened. It was not an intentional or planned activity.

It is said that you have a "good nose". If you are in on the deal, people take a look at it. How do you recognize great ideas and convert them into home runs?

I am not enamored with the idea of investing. I look at the person and ask myself, "Is he able to think robustly and intellectually engage me?" I have trouble with people who are very sure of themselves to the point that they are not able to see beyond the lines. I like people who are smart enough to know what they don't know. At the same time I don't like the people whose ideas are so weak that you have to spoon-feed them. You don't want a person who is overconfident and makes up answers as he goes along. You can see through all this very quickly. You want people who have high levels of energy and intellect, people who are very, very focused. I have trouble with anyone who undersells the competition. I look for the entrepreneur who is able to think out-of-the box, someone who is able to learn very quickly and adopt new ideas and thoughts, take challenges head-on and does not get offended easily. I have invested in a variety of businesses ranging from EDA to software to service. All the companies I fund are mainly dependent on the team and the people. That is the underlying thread.

Forbes magazine recently called you "The sage to Silicon Valley's affluent Indian community". Why did you decide to become a mentor?

I began to redefine myself as a person. I did not need the money anymore. The mentorship felt good and was satisfying. It was a win-win activity. You don't only do it for others; you do it for yourself as well. You begin to believe that you can mentor smart people. If you are able to produce results, this mentoring process turns into a relationship very quickly. I become part of the team. The teams always felt that I was extremely tough on them. I never gave them a chance to become lazy thinkers; I challenged them. I never was an easy investor. Once you start getting engaged, you always want to protect your name and reputation. You get involved enough to provide guidance intelligently. I am a hard taskmaster and am constantly keeping them on track by asking tough questions. I focus on 3 to 4 companies at a time. My involvement ranges from a daily basis, especially at the beginning stages, to monthly meetings.

Take Exodus for example. Chandrasekhar, the founder, is a very very sharp, intellectually honest and adaptable person. In the initial stages, Exodus had been defined as an ISP/VSP. He could not differentiate himself. I challenged his business ideas and he was not able to defend them. After a few sessions of brainstorming we honed in on another opportunity with no one else on the horizon. We weren't sure how big the opportunity was, so we sat down and did some analysis and realized that the market was potentially huge. Chandrasekhar was quickly able to adopt this change in direction. One thing I like about him is that once he understood the change he was able to execute it with great precision and pace. Once he was convinced, he would execute flawlessly. We filled up the data center in six weeks. We had thought initially that it would take up to six months. Instantly we knew we had something that everybody wanted.

You have said that your personal goal has shifted from making investments to TiE. Is this your payback to society? Tell us about the concept of TiE. What are its goals and focus?

Nowadays, I feel investments tie me down. You have to invest both money and time, and to spend time you must understand the market, the customers, their positioning. These days I find that extremely cumbersome; as a result I am now investing to a lesser extent.

TiE was started with the express desire to bring together entrepreneurs from the subcontinent. We don't distinguish between people from Sri Lanka, Bangladesh, Pakistan or India; there is no reason to. We do not allow any issue, other than economics, to enter into our domain. Here you have to co-prosper. There is no religion in TiE. The focus is on how to create success for the individual, the family, the environment and the country. In fact one of TiE's first leaders, Safi Quereshey, is from Pakistan.

One of TiE's main goals is to be a mentor to startup companies. TiE is not about venture capital funding; it is about angel investing. The focus here is to identify a good idea that has not attracted any money and then fund it, with money coming from the members. The environment is traditional in the sense that it follows a Gurukul of sorts, where the gurus transfer knowledge on business plans, management strategies and survival kits to new TiE members. It's about transmitting, top-down, the accumulated wisdom of doing business and succeeding at it; it is to help the new entrepreneurs reach their goals faster and better.

Part of the thinking at TiE is that you first create the wealth for yourself through entrepreneurship. Having done that, you then focus on becoming a social entrepreneur. You start creating an impact around you which is beyond your home or community, drawing a larger and larger circle. The U.S. has been built by entrepreneurs. When JP Morgan retired, he built 3000 libraries in the country. Why did he do that? He did that because he wanted to plough back into the system and have an impact and influence. TiE's goal is to get high achievers engaged in this process not only in the Bay Area but nationwide, worldwide. The idea is for these people to give back to the system. This is not charity; it is something people should do as responsible members of the community. It, of course, is also an investment opportunity which is both mentally and intellectually satisfying. It is a win-win situation that produces results.

How does TiE function? What, in your mind, are its biggest achievements?

> *There is no religion in TiE. Everyone is equal and participates equally.*

They way each chapter starts is by gathering information about the people who may become involved in that chapter. We form a charter group that meets several times to discuss the logistics involved. We then set up a launch meeting and invite well-known entrepreneurs to participate. Through these meetings we attract membership.

We hold a forum once a month where people gather. A speaker is invited. That itself has an enormous value. The other value is, of course, the opportunity to network. We foster social values as well; successful entrepreneurs can also be successful social entrepreneurs. The ability to take ideas and convert them into home runs is all done by individuals. The investments happen at these forums. Investment is not a TiE activity. It is one of the results of networking, which is a TiE activity. At the end of the day, the entrepreneurs are encouraged and inspired; they seek out mentors and investors. This becomes a focal point.

Several chapters are being launched not only in the U.S. but in Europe and in India as well. We want to build an organization of successful, like-minded people and use it to showcase our method of working together. Indians, by and large, are focused on individual family rather than the community

The notion of Indian technology firms being featured on NASDAQ arose out of TiE. We are having a major impact and have been able to break several mindsets. For example, we have proven that Indians are as just as good business people as they are technologists. It has changed the question from whether Indians can succeed to how many Indians have done so. A majority of business plans submitted to VCs in the Silicon Valley are now by Indians. What's more, a significant number of projects funded today are headed by Indians. TiE can take the lion's share of credit for this.

You have achieved a lot in this lifetime and you continue to give so much back to the society. Have you had any mentors along the way?

The one person I look up to is Mahatma Gandhi. He was an innovator, a thinker. He was a man who did his thinking out-of-the box. He was able to bring everybody together for the cause. He was sharply focused on one great single cause: the freedom of India.

What do you think is the key to the success of Silicon Valley? What do you think is coming next?

My personal sense is that somehow the sun, the moon and the stars have lined up in the Silicon Valley and it has become a fountain of wisdom, a source of inspiration. I think the electronic renaissance will last another half century. It is the Grandfather Theory. The grandfather comes up with a new idea and works hard to develop it. He is the innovator, the doer. The son, though used to a good life, remains aware of how it came about and works hard to sustain it. But the grandson simply assumes this to be his birthright. He has no idea how it happened or what is necessary to sustain it. As a result he unthinkingly destroys it. Now the process must begin all over again. In the Valley, we are going through this cycle and I think we are currently in the "son" phase.

Can you compare and contrast the differences in the macroeconomic environment between India and the U.S. and its impact on entrepreneurship?

The environment is very progressive in the U.S.; there is a constant desire to improve. In India this is not the case. The civil society movement basically says that the society's strengths come from its citizens and not from the government. We need to strengthen those institutions in India that are civil in nature and not political; churches, for example, and universities, private organizations, charitable institutions. These are the institutions that focus on day-to-day life. Societies that don't have a strong civil infrastructure have been unable to build strong foundations. A civil society movement is at the heart of America's infrastructure.

But with liberalization, power in India is being disseminated very rapidly. People are now beginning to take charge and we are seeing a change in the right direction. We need to ride this change and put people, rather than the government, in the driver's seat.

U.S. democracy is based on the simple saying: "You can fool all of the people some of the time, some of the people all of the time, but you can't fool all of the people all of the time". Indians are now beginning to follow this philosophy. Democracy is functioning and power is moving away from the government and back to the people.

> *It is only when you are out of your comfort zone that you grow.*

My general sense is that India, with the right amount of help and a slight push in the right direction, can become a superpower. We need to challenge the people. We have the faith, we have the velocity, we are on the right path. We have the talent, the training, the democracy. We have the legal system and the civil system. The only issue now is to focus on the economic reformation. Economics should be at the top of the agenda. To compete in the Global Economy, to become a member of the United Nations, all depends on a strong economy. The only way to get there is through a free market and entrepreneurship.

Looking back, what would you say is the primary reason for your success?

I became an entrepreneur by totally thinking out-of-the box, not focusing on design alone. I focused on how to deliver value, how to price it right and how to make sure the customers come in. I had to become a true general manger overnight. One thing that was key was the realization that you stagnate when you get into your comfort zone or niche. It is only when you are out of your comfort zone that you grow. I have seen this over and over again. Every time I am outside my comfort zone I begin to think more effectively, really use my brain.

What are your hobbies?

I play tennis fairly frequently. I read a lot. I am very much of a history and economics buff. I am a semi-expert on British-Indian history and the history of the U.S. civil war. I also very much enjoy traveling to various places.

On a personal front, how are you bringing up the kids?

My kids know that the number one thing in their life is education; number two is health, which keeps you strong, and number three is family. And that's it.

What's next? What are your goals for the future?

Hopefully, I will amount to something some day. At this stage, I have accomplished more than I ever thought possible. It has been an unbelievable journey so far.

Saiyed Atiq Raza

NexGen, AMD, Raza Foundries

Operational Excellence

Saiyed Atiq Raza is the founder, chairman and chief executive officer of Raza Foundries, Inc. Prior to establishing Raza Foundries (RFI), Atiq was president and chief operating officer of Advanced Micro Devices (AMD). At AMD, he oversaw the development of AMD's processor roadmap, brought the AMD-K6 family of processor products to the market and laid the foundation for the development and manufacturing ramp of the new Athlon processor. Atiq became part of AMD's executive management team after the merger with NexGen, Inc. in January 1996, where he was chairman and CEO. Prior to joining NexGen, he spent fifteen years in various engineering and management positions, including vice president of Technology Centers at VLSI Technology Incorporated.

Atiq obtained his bachelor's degree with honors from the University of London, and a master's degree from Stanford University.

We met Atiq at his office. He is friendly, passionate, full of charm and energy. Atiq exemplifies the force that builds great technology companies. Very rarely do you find a brilliant technologist and a master executive business manager cast in the same mold. Atiq captures the essence of both.

During our discussion he shared with us his presentation, "Creating Great Companies" that he had prepared for the alumni at MIT. The overall focus was on the importance of "building critical mass" at warp speed in a startup company. During the course of his presentation we asked Atiq to share his insights on team building, leadership, operational excellence, corporate culture, scalability, valuations, high growth markets and setting expectations. Toward the end we explored the personal side of the man.

> **"Knowledge in technology, products, and markets - these are the three dimensions that are extremely important in order to create great companies."**

You have been involved with several startups. What do you think is more important - the founding team or the idea?

The founding team is more important than either the idea itself or the innovation. I have sometimes taken members of a founding team who had an idea that I knew to be flawed but with the potential of being transformed into an idea that would become a compelling product. You can always morph an idea into something I call compelling, something a customer desires very badly. It does not have to be something that the customer knows that he desires. Say a customer has a bicycle and you go to him and ask, "What do you need?" and he says he needs a faster bicycle. In reality, he needs a car but does not know that there is such a thing as a car. You interpret the customer's need and combine it in the form of an idea- an engine- and provide him with a car. That is the kind of non-linearity that comes from people. So that it is why the fundamental ingredient of a startup is people. The founding team that I try to get involved with is one with experience and a track record. There have been cases where I have worked with pure creators - people from the university who have not had prior experience, but I have then combined them with an experienced team. A close-knit team is another important factor.

What do you mean by close- knit?

In a close-knit team there should not be any friction amongst the team members, which sometimes becomes very apparent early on when you are presenting a business case. What is important is not simply the absence of friction, but the ability of team members to communicate among themselves on an on-going basis. That is not because I like it or it is more pleasant; it is because the most important thing in a team is its ability to coordinate its capabilities in order to create a single product or single service in record time, because they will be intercepting a dynamic market. This is only possible if they are in complete harmony. Their interaction should be free of any noise and noise is created by all the things that distract from the smooth functioning of the team. I do, however, consider a healthy disagreement to be an important part of a closely-knit team. A close-knit team is one where the disagreements are all based on evaluating the various aspects of what it takes to create the final product. And next is their sense of *mission and drive*. These provide the energy that propels the team towards its objective.

Once you have the founding team and the compelling product defined, what is the next critical step?

Once the product concept has been validated the next step is to form a critical mass of capabilities as quickly as possible. Two things represent critical mass around which the rest of the corporation can be built.

The first is to form the engineering core team, other than staff in other functional areas, to provide a full set of operating capabilities. At RFI we attract world-class talent and we do not compromise on what that is. It is one of the most important things we do. A definition of world-class talent is that these people have amazing intellectual capability and are good team players. All members of Raza foundries get involved in attracting this talent and we have a near 100% hit rate when we go after a person. Building the team has two parts. One is the core and then there is the rest. If the core is not A-plus then you will have to contend with second grade talent for the rest. So the quality of the core is extremely important. The second element of critical mass is to create any needed corporate alliances or key service agreements. We must create critical corporate alliances between the partner companies and strategic technology, product, sales and marketing companies who would not otherwise enter into a relationship with a startup. With the core in place the founding team immediately executes on the strategic activities of product definition and development.

Once you have the critical mass in place, how do build upon it?

The third phase is the execution of product ramp. Execution of product ramp involves establishing processes and setting up tools and an environment for product development. You have to be very systematic about it.

The startup must build disciplined and detailed operating processes in all functional areas to ensure effective and efficient execution. Detailed schedules for product development, prototyping, manufacturing ramp, and entry into the marketplace are fundamental parts of this stage. The methods also result in consistency of approach between development, marketing and manufacturing on a fastest-time-to-market schedule.

The fourth phase is that of building the company. The focus at this point should be to achieve excellence in corporate operations and structure. This includes hiring the final members of the senior management team, ensuring that the succeeding rounds of funding bring the smartest and most influential investors into the company, and mentoring the management team on creating a great, long-lasting corporate culture.

A high-quality management team is fundamental to the steep trajectory of a company as it transitions out of the startup phase. Each company is different, but the first priority in most cases should be to find a top quality experienced CEO. Additionally, the final senior management team members such as COO, the vice president of sales, and the chief financial officer (CFO) should be recruited as appropriate.

The follow-on rounds of financing bring in additional investors who add more than just money. Potential business or technology partners for the company, potential customers, top tier venture capital firms, and investment banks all can provide value beyond money to the company.

What product development strategy do you execute to shrink time- to- market?

We combine the core engineering team with highly productive design tools, whether it is software or systems or optics or silicon. Also important is schedule management - both front-to-back and back-to-front. Front-to-back is normal schedule management and we have templates for managing the schedule of a product as it is being developed. The back-to-front is methodology unique to RFI, where you actually put yourself in the mode of ramping into production and imagine that you are shipping to the customers. We ask all developers to imagine what they are shipping to the customers and understand what the customer is expecting. This is when there is a shock because people have forgotten what the customer wants, the path for upgrade-ability, the documentation, the ability to debug if something is going wrong. We force the documentation of customer requirements up front when the product is being developed.

Back-to-front scheduling, in a nutshell, means that once you have a definition of what is required in the market place, you have to put all the features in a product that would support this product being in volume ramp. So RFI designs both forward and backwards.

So you have the new product development cycle down to a science?

We have a very systematic and well-defined new product development process. We start with the marketing requirement document (MRD), which is the definition of a compelling product. Then comes the product design document (PRD), which is far more detailed than an MRD. What we are talking about here is low-level design, precisely what is going to go into the design in nuts and bolts. We remain involved in low level design description, down to the design rules on a piece of paper, down to the silicon, all the way through to exactly what the software is going to do as it is interacting in a customer environment. Through experience, we realize that when details of a product are not specified until development is well underway, it results in reworking of designs and schedule delays. We review all this periodically. A typical VC firm will not do this. Even big companies do it late in the game and I have been in big companies. At RFI, we tend to do it early in the game. This is 3 to 4 months into the development of the product. While the product is being designed we start thrashing it to make sure that it can survive a ramp. At this time we start holding design reviews every other week. These are cross-functional review meetings in which all the key players from manufacturing, marketing and product development get involved. This is all invaluable stuff. The result is that not only is the product developed very rapidly but when it actually ships, the quality of the product is dramatic. Most startups have a terrible initial product that goes into the customer's hands. That does not happen at RFI.

What about management methodologies for startups?

Management methodologies have several components.

First is organization structure. A lot of companies don't understand that the organization has to change over time. This is not just at the high level but throughout the whole organization.

Second is the review process. The progress of developing a product should be reviewed and measured. The key is how it gets reviewed. Who participates? What is reviewed? What is the closed feedback loop? How do you keep the company under control? For example, we form a cross-functional team consisting of the person running the company and the heads of engineering and we have a process by which those guys, along with one person from RFI, will put together a product outline. The product outline is intended to be a product which will be out on the market three years from now. We keep at it until we have defined the product thoroughly. Once they show us what they plan to do in three years, we say we don't have three years and instead we shrink product development time to one year and help jump-start it by using the fast track process.

Third is the tool requirements; this involves defining all the tools required to scale the company.

Fourth is product development flow. Front to back and back to front.

Fifth is scalability: Will you be able to scale? How will you keep on top? What things are likely to go out of control?

Sixth is risk management. Everything we do has a degree of risk associated with it. When we get together we never talk about what you have done or how successful you are, what are your highlights and lowlights. All I want to know is what the risks are in these 6 areas: product definition, product development, market acceptance, financing, management hiring, and engineering recruitment. Once you know the risks, you appropriately manage them.

What role does corporate culture play?

One of the most important things to understand is the building of corporate culture. The first foundation of great corporate culture is leadership, because leadership represents the vision of the company and that vision should be articulated and represented by word and by body language to the rest of the company until it becomes the vision of the rest of the company. Corporate culture is leadership and has to come from within a company, not from outside. If you bring in leadership from outside the company by having an acting CEO, I think it basically hurts the company culture in the long run. It is an understanding of the fundamental concept of what corporate culture is all about.

> *One of the most important things to understand is the building of corporate culture.*

Another key component of company culture is to operate decisively and with integrity.

What fundamental metric do you use to judge the success of RAZA companies? What is your scorecard?

Escalation of their value! How rapidly the company's value increases. It is the only real metric. Our goal is to make them successful in record time. How do they get the highest third party valuation faster than any competitive entity? In these days of global competition, I judge myself against every single company on the planet. I think we have outperformed every single one of them.

For example, Maple Networks, a Raza Foundries company, recently received for their Series B round a $360 million valuation. We funded them in September 1999 when the company consisted of three people. There are a hundred people today (October, 2000) and the team is headed by Bill Jones, a former president at Nortel. When I take a look at how far along they are, it boggles my mind. We have caught up with companies that started one year before Maple.

How do you put value to a company?

I don't do it; third parties provide a valuation. There are competitive metrics utilized in the process. Everyone has a systematic way of valuing companies; however, there are a few basic metrics that are used to do this. How far along is product development? What is the valuation of comparative companies in that stage of development? Is the company's product in beta testing with its customers? Is the company shipping product and if so, what is the market paying for competitive companies that are shipping? These are the metrics used to establish the value of a company. We maintain these charts for the entire industry.

For Series A (first major round) funding, the key criteria are the quality and size of the team, market segment and potential, and the first mover advantage. For series B (second round) funding, in addition to series A metrics, we look at the following; What is the product's elapsed time? Where are they in terms of beta testing? Are they major players in the market? Will they continue to dominate the market? We also look at competitive metrics.

Series B funding (second round) occurs in most cases after 8 months. If we meet all the other requirements of product development and team development and management development along the lines that I described, then a third party VC should come in and see a higher value. If they don't see a high value then we have failed. If they see a high value then we have passed. We keep a scorecard on our series B valuations, comparing them to companies funded by well-established VC firms such as Kleiner Perkins, Sequoia and Mayfield. Our goal is to have a market valuation two to five times higher than the industry average.

Is the method of valuations quantifiable or purely subjective? Can you elaborate?

A good question. Here, judgment is the governing factor. There is no right way to value a company. However, let me list a few important criteria that we use.

Quality of the team. I look for two things in a team; extremely high IQ and good teamwork. Good chemistry in the team results in what I call a high signal-to-noise ratio communication.

The team size typically ranges from 3 to 20 people in the core team. That is a solid numerical way of judging it.

Third is the market segment which is being targeted.

There is one other factor that governs the valuation and that is competitive metrics. For example, we were presented with an opportunity to invest in a company where the competing valuation was $60 million. At RFI we concluded that the valuation should be $15 million. Despite the disparity, the company selected RFI. They thought that we were a better fit for the company and they were looking ahead to the next round of funding.

With your name and recognition you could go to investors (such as mutual funds or pension funds) and get the money. Why did you go to VCs instead to seek out money?

I could have funded it myself but there is an important factor in accelerating growth. We worked with Benchmark Capital (VC Firm) because we knew we would be able to get their total attention. Bruce Dunlevie (general partner at Benchmark Capital) had a strong sense of commitment towards what we were doing. That has really paid off. Finally, it is more difficult to praise yourself than to have somebody who is an objective investor say that you are his most successful investment. When Benchmark was written about in Business Week they said that RFI was their number one investment.

As far as TCV and Bowman (VC firms) are concerned, there was another reason we got them. The dilution was very limited. The reason we got their investment is because we wanted the other investors to step forward and pay market valuations. Once again we needed a third party to validate us. Benchmark wrote a letter to TCV and Bowman and I think we closed the round in 6 hours from the time the letter went out.

I could have received higher valuations from other investors; however, I believe very strongly that everything requires a foundation. Thus, I was willing to give equity away in order to get total commitment of another investor. I tell an entrepreneur, "You are most welcome to get money from elsewhere, or you can get money from us. Share the equity with us and see what we will do. If you don't believe us, talk to all the companies we are involved with. If they say it was worth it, then come with us." Similarly, we were willing to give the equity away to get the total attention from Benchmark. If I have an issue requiring input from Benchmark, I get their response within two to three hours. These are complex issues that we struggle with and we benefit immensely by leveraging the knowledge of people who have been investing for 19 years. No matter how good we are in building companies, we cannot learn in 6 months what these VCs have learned over decades, so that is an incredible amount of value.

How do you select the right investors?

Always pick investors that have domain knowledge; initial valuation is important but not critical. Pick investors that can add tangible value and impact. Pick a board that is willing to spend quality time and have a balance of skills such as market knowledge, marketing, and relationships with customers.

What do you look for when evaluating the quality of investors?

Fundamentally, I look for two major qualities: judgment and leadership. That's how I judge investor quality and that's the report card I hold myself to as well. For example, everyone knows Vinod Khosla of Kleiner Perkins has a tremendous track record, but there are certain qualities that we have determined to be the distinction between a good investor and a bad investor. Judgment is the most important and its manifestation starts when you are actually listening to a deal coming in through the door. Your judgment is being tested at that time. For example, there is a company that wants to raise funds and they describe their technology, product and what the value proposition is. A good investor's judgment is tested when he is listening to the pitch and interacting with the entrepreneur. The first step is whether he is going to say yes or no, and judgment does come into play in analyzing whether it is the right company or the right team.

Once you invest in a company, one's judgment is again tested when creating a compelling product, a roadmap, the right team and extending the business reach of that company.

Don't you expect the entrepreneur to show up with the compelling product, the road map and so forth, when he comes knocking at your door for money?

Oh no, you'd be surprised. If such a guy shows up with all these capabilities I would love to invest in him.

How much control do you have in your companies' choosing their investors?

It varies from company to company. We offer guidance; however, we do not exercise any direct control over their actions. We try to make sure that we have influence but control resides in the internal management of the company. We do, however, help our companies procure funding from other investors. We spend a lot of time educating our core team in the pros and cons and in the process. We are continually educating ourselves.

What is your strategy regarding angel investors?

I try to include angel investors in every one of our investments. My preference is for those investors who have the relevant domain knowledge, or someone who has lots of contacts and will extend the market reach of the companies.

In these challenging times, credibility is equal to achievement. How does one set external expectations?

When you set expectations in the market you better be sure that your achievements will exceed them or you will end up with negative credibility. Do not set expectations in areas that are not predictable. Achievements can be broken down into business achievements, product achievements, technology achievements, hiring achievements, investment achievements and, later on when you are a public company, it is P & L achievements. All of us know only too well the consequences of missing earnings estimates.

The balance between expectations and achievements must be difficult to reach.

Absolutely! You manage it by having very good business processes, managing every one of these events.

You have to have a play-it-safe approach. When a company is young, always play it safe in external image creation until the credibility is so high that you can draw on that bank balance. Then start getting aggressive.

Is this where you as the CEO get most involved? Letting out the information strategically?

Absolutely. That is the review that has to happen. All the CEO's have to carefully manage the image in the marketplace. It has to be down to a science.

What is the significance in using the word "Foundries" in naming your firm?

What do you do if you want to provide these processes over and over again? You create tools that are re-usable. That is what a foundry means. The concept of a foundry goes back to the early days of the industrial revolution, with the idea that a tool was something that was used to make things again and again. It's like the concept of a guild, which was the predecessor of the union; it was an association of toolmakers who were the experts in their field. These tools captured the entire intellect of what was going to be implemented again and again and these toolmakers knew how to build the tool that was used in a press, that would pump out products again and again. That's why I called it a foundry, because in a foundry you build tools. This is no different from a Silicon foundry, wherein the tool is the mask. And now it is three-dimensional replication that is occurring.

What's a typical working day for Atiq Raza?

I get up at 6.00 am and I go to sleep around 11.00 pm. Before I go to sleep I know what my schedule is for the following day. If I look at Monday, which was today, the entire morning was spent preparing for my first meeting, which is a meeting with my extended staff. There are two or three things that the staff meeting focuses on. It focuses on the strategy, the strategic imperatives that we have. It focuses on the cultural imperatives that we have and it focuses on the tactics. All of the above attributes are evaluated using key metrics.

For instance, there was a discussion on what a company has to have when it goes for a series B funding. What are the requirements? We take a look at companies we have already invested in and we look at the next two milestones for each one of those companies. The next discussion was on the eight or ten companies we are currently reviewing as investment opportunities. Where are they and what are the criteria that will convince us that a) We would like to make an investment, b) We would like to pass, c) we should form an alliance with some of them? What is our value proposition to them and what is their value proposition to us? Everyone knows that we have a report card that is going to be generated every time we work with our portfolio companies. Then we take a look at financial goals and objectives. Who owns them and what has to be done and how are we going to get these things accomplished? Finally, we summarize for ourselves. What do we stand for? What is important in order for us to be successful? And then we go around the table. This, properly done, can take a good two or three hours. At the end of this time everyone feels synchronized; there is a complete intellectual and emotional synchronization. You have to do it; there is no other way. In the afternoon, I meet with company entrepreneurs. Normally, we meet with the folks from about four companies and review their status. At the end of the day there are a few more meetings, typically followed by a dinner meeting.

How do you spend your free time? What are your hobbies?

I spend as much time as I can with my wife and children. Time with the family is very important to me. My only hobby is reading.

What skill can you correlate to your background and upbringing?

Something I learned from my family and my parents is to stick to your values no matter how great the adversity. I don't compromise my values because to me nothing else matters as much.

Any mistakes you have made that stand out?

I've made a lot of mistakes during the course of my professional career. I think the one that bothers me most is tolerating incompetence for longer than I should have. Whenever I have made that mistake I have always regretted it.

Who is your mentor?

Over the course of my professional life I have had many mentors. I have learned a lot from various people. For example, I have learned a lot from Vinod Khosla, a general partner at the VC firm Kleiner, Perkins, Caufield and Byers. From Vinod Khosla I learned important aspects of strategic thinking, perseverance, and how to stick to your business model. Essentially you need to keep a relentless focus on your domain. Irrespective of tactical results, once you are convinced that the model that you are using is the right one, learn to stick with it.

I have also learned a lot from Andy Grove, even though I have not worked directly with him. Most of all I have leaned how to manage a large corporation. An example is the development of scalable processes. Scalable and flexible processes are extremely important in achieving your objectives. Scalability and flexibility go hand in hand. A process that is not related to the underlying business and technology factors is bureaucracy, which is counter-productive. The second thing I learned from Andy Grove is how to understand and interpret the future. How do you look for mega trends? How do you identify strategic inflection points?

What role did your mother and father play in shaping your life?

Open-mindedness is an important quality that I learned from my father. He was not fixated on any religious or political beliefs and he always encouraged us to question everything.

> *My mother inculcated in us a sense of fairness and equality and to this day I cherish such values.*

My mother is probably the person who has inspired me the most. She was an entrepreneur even in her time, when women were expected to take a back seat. Her father died when she was in 12th grade, and soon after that she started a girls' school because there was no way for them to make ends meet. In a few years, that girls' school turned out to be the most successful one in the inner city of Lahore, Pakistan. I learned from her invaluable qualities such as perseverance, never being afraid of doing what you believe in and kind-heartedness. Above all, she inculcated in us a sense of fairness and equality and to this day I cherish such values.

What makes you tick?

I like to do things that excite and challenge me, where I have the opportunity, along with a team, to have an impact on the future. To me, success is all about making an impact.

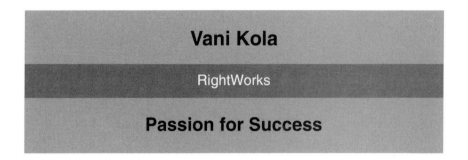

Vani Kola

RightWorks

Passion for Success

Vani Kola, RightWorks Corporation's chief executive officer and founder, started the company in 1996 with a vision of providing business-to-business solutions that enable customers to derive maximum value from the Internet. In early 2000, Kola secured significant financing for RightWorks from the Internet Capital Group (ICG), which acquired a majority interest in the company in a transaction valued at $657 million.

Before founding RightWorks, Kola held senior engineering and technical management positions at Consilium, Inc. and Empros, a division of Control Data Corporation. She earned her undergraduate degree in engineering from Osmania University in Hyderabad, India and holds a master's degree in engineering from Arizona State University.

We met at Hobbies, a health food eatery in the Bay Area popular amongst the Silicon Valley folks. The discussion took place over a cup of coffee.

Vani comes across as a principled, energetic and gutsy woman. In this interview Vani discusses her journey with RightWorks. We touch on a wide variety of topics, including the first few steps, funding strategy, strategic alliances, morphing, organizational culture, the ever-changing role of a CEO, and her approach towards managing RightWorks.

"The problem lies not in the idea but in its execution. That is the key."

You are known in Silicon Valley circles for your vibrance and high energy. To what can we attribute this?

It was probably my upbringing. I belong to a conservative Brahmin family in Hyderabad, India. My father was an accountant and my mother was a home-maker. I have one sister. During the time I was growing up in India, girls were not encouraged to go to college. However, our parents encouraged both their daughters to go to school and college. I was also motivated to excel at a number of different things apart from academics. I always had a lot of energy and from an early age I never considered there was anything I couldn't do.

When I was very young, my parents opened a bank account for me. My father used to put in a sufficient amount for the year and I had to manage my own bus pass, school clothes and books, and I had to work around a budget. It is amazing when you are given that kind of responsibility how much money you can save. I had the choice; I could either buy a book or use the money to party. If I blew it, it was my funeral. Every year I had to figure out when to pay my fees, bus pass and so on. It was good in a way. I had a lot of freedom. My parent didn't put up any roadblocks.

Why did you decide to pursue an engineering education?

Interestingly enough, my parents did not encourage me to pursue engineering. I was very good in math in high school and I wanted pursue engineering. In addition, very few girls were studying engineering during that time, so it was a challenge.

I would get up at 4 a.m. and go for coaching classes and not come home until 10.30 p.m. My dad would get angry and tried to stop me from going to the coaching classes. I starved myself for three days and he finally caved in! I went to engineering college when I was 16 and finished at 20. I was younger than most of the students.

What was the most valuable thing you learned in engineering college?

Well, my parents wouldn't allow me to go to a residential college so I went to Osmania University in Hyderabad, India. Although the engineering university was co-educational, there were only six girls.

In those 4 years I learnt how to be a minority and still succeed. There was a great deal of pressure on us girls to compete with the boys in college.

When did you come to U.S. and why?

I graduated from engineering college in 1984 and came to the U.S. in 1985 with my husband, Sri. We got married right after I graduated.

We came to the U.S. on a Friday and I wanted to enroll in a M.S. program right away. The college, Arizona State University, began classes on the following Monday and I remember going to meet the Dean. I was told that I could not see him without an appointment, so I waited until he walked out of the door and went up and talked to him. He gave me provisional admission, as I had not taken the TOEFL or GRE examinations, on the condition that they could revoke the admission if I didn't do well in the first semester.

I took four of the toughest classes. All my fellow students as well as my husband advised me against it. It was very tough because I did not have a background in computer science and I was up until 2 a.m. every night. However, I got all A's in my first semester. Looking back, I think I excelled because people were willing to help. It is important not be too afraid to ask. If I could not do something on my own, I asked for help.

A company called Control Data (Minneapolis, Minnesota) funded my engineering thesis. On completing my thesis, I was asked by them to develop a product based on it. My husband had received admission to the University of Minnesota for his Ph.D, so off we went to Minnesota. I was happy that I would be building a product, which was a simulation package used by electric utilities to model their grid. I worked at Control Data for 3 ½ years.

After your stint at Control Data you moved to California. How did this transpire?

During my tenure at Control Data my husband decided to ditch his Ph.D after a year and accepted an offer from a company based in Los Angeles. I decided to stay in Minneapolis and complete my project at Control Data. We lived apart for a year and a half and commuted between L.A. and Minneapolis. Once I finished the project at Control Data we both decided to move to the Silicon Valley.

What did you find unique about Silicon Valley?

A number of things: the network, the pace of innovation, the VC presence, access to a wide variety of talent, and the knowledge that we were among the right crowd. If you live among a bunch of Sadhus (religious monks), you have a better chance of becoming one.

How did you get involved with the India Literacy Project?

Three weeks after moving to the Silicon Valley I was working again, at Concilium. Around that time I had decided to become actively involved in giving something back to India, something of lasting value and not just money. In Dharma, there are four kinds of giving. Giving to a known person is of least value; giving to an unknown person is of considerable value. Giving anonymously to an unknown person is of enormous value. Anonymous but self-sustaining giving of a part of yourself is of most value. This is the most unselfish. That is what the Hindu Dharma says.

So, with the assistance of Dr. Parameshwar Rao, I started the India Literacy Project here in the Bay Area. I came up with some innovative ideas, including raising funds by selling grocery coupons. The organization grew and gained a lot of recognition in the Bay Area. People felt good about it. I made the rule that it would be fully voluntary. The fund raising came from the public. We didn't take any money for administrative purposes and the volunteers and I wrote checks from our own pocketbooks. People saw that I worked 30-40 hours a week for the India Literacy Project. I was very actively involved with the project for two years and worked hard to grow the organization. By 1993, the organization had grown and was well recognized. It was then that I decided to pass the mantle of leadership on to another volunteer and prepare for motherhood. My first child was born in 1993.

I feel that once you have created an organization you should eventually pass it along to others. When an organization becomes big, the founder becomes just a shadow. It should not become overly dependent on just one person. Part of my caring for the Literacy Project was to step aside and allow others to become leaders. By starting the Literacy Project I developed leadership, marketing and interpersonal skills. Non-profit organizations provide an excellent source for developing such skills.

What led you to start your own company?

For two years I spent time with my daughter and continued to work at Consillium. I wanted to go back to business school. I was doing two courses every quarter in order to keep abreast of new technology developments. I completed several multimedia courses because I was fascinated with graphics. So between raising my daughter, work, and taking classes, I was quite occupied. I had also taken GMAT and applied to Stanford. During that time, I pondered whether I should go to business school or start a company. Ultimately, I decided to start a company.

How did the idea for your business germinate?

The idea for the business arose out of the rapid growth of the Internet. I had experience with software and I understood by then the potential of business–to-business interactions. The challenging part was not coming up with ideas - I probably had ten different ideas and I could have picked any one. For example, a few of the ideas I was thinking about were market automation, procurement software and security web - a VeriSign type of thing. The problem lies not in the idea but in its execution. That is the key.

How did this particular idea of eProcurement software come about?

My background was in the manufacturing process. I wondered what the key problems in a company were that had not yet been addressed. Where was the core value proposition which I could sell to the customer? I didn't want it to be a productivity tool. The idea didn't just pop out of nowhere, saying procurement is great. I had to pose a lot of questions involving specific problems and find a net closure to all of them. I used to talk to chief information officers (CIOs) about their core problems. I called a lot of companies and said, "I am not selling you anything now, but I have a product idea. Your input would be valuable, as you may be a potential customer. Will you talk to me?" It is amazing how many people are willing to talk to you. For instance, at Juniper Networks (Santa Clara, CA), which is a now a customer of RightWorks, I asked the CIO how he saw the problems fitting in and he provided me with valuable input. After discussions with several CIOs and members of the IT staff, I came up with the preliminary idea of eProcurement, which would help address some of the problems confronted by IT.

How did you build the team?

The first person I recruited was someone recommended by a friend. He was just graduating from college and I convinced him to take the job. I met the second employee at a party. She was thinking about quitting her job and going to law school. I talked her into joining us and she in now one of our top-notch engineers. Then I recruited a neighbor and a engineer from Boston who were also referred to me by a friends. That's how we formed the core team

How did you raise the seed capital to get the company off the ground?

I was smart enough to know that the VCs would not fund me; I had no track record, no product, no customers and no team. These are the four things they look for when deciding to fund a company. So I chose to seek funding from angel investors. Dr. Prabhu Goel and Dr. Suhas Patil, two of the most renowned Silicon Valley entrepreneurs, funded the company.

We had invited Prabhu Goel to speak at an event for the India Literacy Project. After the event, I told him that I would like to talk to him about a business idea. He said he wasn't funding anymore, but I persisted and said, "Listen to me even if you don't want to fund the project". I met him several times and convinced him of my idea and he finally gave me some initial funding.

As for Dr. Patil, it took me six months to convince him that our business model was viable. At that time I felt that I had to get someone not only to fund me with some serious money but to also be a coach, someone who would be emotionally tied to the company and the project. Suhas Patil was all of the above and much more. Dr. Patil stepped in, funded the company and took it to the next level. We immediately hired several engineers and completed the product.

What was the value addition from Dr. Patil? How did he add value to the company?

Dr. Patil is a great coach and a company builder. He has always been a sounding board. For instance, after his investment in 1997, I was pregnant with my second daughter. Apart from my family he was the only person to know about it. I went to his office at Cirrus Logic and spoke to him for about 15 minutes. I was going through an emotional trauma and was wondering how to break the news to him and the other board members who had invested with me. I wondered how they would react to my being pregnant and how it would affect the company. I didn't know many personal details about him at that time. When I told him I was pregnant he cancelled his next appointment and talked to me for an hour. I asked him how the board would react and he said that it would not matter. He gave me a lot of strength. He told me to take care of myself first. It wasn't what I expected from a board member. He has such a humane side to him and that's why I respect him so much. He has a heart of gold.

Now you had a solid idea, a team that believed in it, and angel investors willing to fund you with seed capital. What came next?

The one thing I wanted to do upfront was to retain topnotch lawyers and accountants. I wanted a clean company. Even before I started the company I had reputable professionals lined up to advise us on the correct way to set up a corporation, the capitalization structure and so on. Arthur Anderson and

Fenwick and West, both very reputable firms, advised us in accounting and legal matters respectively.

I called up Arthur Anderson and talked to one of their partners, Gary Methusjack. I asked him if Arthur Anderson would work for us. I told him that it was a startup and I couldn't pay him upfront. I said, "You can invest your time, and when the company goes public, Arthur Anderson will be rewarded". To my surprise they agreed to audit our books for $3,000 per year. Similarly, David Healy from Fenwick and West agreed to draw up corporate bylaws, board laws, articles and stock option plans. A lot of people feel they can't afford these resources, but one must try.

We understand that your first major marketing promotion was extraordinarily successful.

Yes, that is true. We did a lot of research. We made a big foam board cutout with my picture in the center. The banner would say, for example, "Hey! Michael Dell, do you want to save $300 million for your company? Call me direct". We created these things that could be produced for 10 dollars each and we shipped them out to CEOs and CFOs of large enterprises.

To our surprise, we had a phenomenal response rate of 30 percent. Even Michael Dell responded. He sent a reply saying that he loved the ad and gave us contact information on the person to whom we should talk. That was enough. Our strategy was to always start from the top. They would respond or point us towards the right contact person. We got our first customers, including Applied Materials and Fujitsu, before having a single sales person on board.

When did you decide to seek money from the venture capital community?

We survived for about 18 months with funding from our angel investors. After we signed our first customers I decided to seek VC funding. Our first round with the VCs closed in early 1998. We raised $7 million and soon thereafter, in October 1998, we raised another $21 million. In 1999 we raised $21 million in mezzanine money from Lehman Brothers. We also raised corporate funds from i2, and in 2000 we sold 50% of the company to Internet capital group (ICG). We were valued at $1.2 billion.

How did you orchestrate the deals?

That was the difficult part. I did the i2 deal personally. It took me 8 months to put it together. First I had to cultivate relationships and then close the deal. I studied the backgrounds of i2 executives and i2's strategy in depth. I worked hard to find the value proposition which would benefit both parties. In addition, I recognized that sharing thoughts and developing a healthy respect for each other was right not only for RightWorks but for the market as well. Finally, I had to convince i2 that we were a good fit.

What was the necessity of selling 51% of the company to ICG?

I felt that we needed another big deal to accelerate the business because of the pace at which the market was moving. We needed to either sell or go public. I evaluated these various options and began to think about the value of ICG.

They had a lot of credibility, good channels. They could provide us with financial muscle and market expertise. I did some research on ICG and found out that they were on the lookout for someone like us to partner with. Through an analyst friend, I was referred to Paul Slatson at ICG. It took only 6 weeks from the time I first met him to the time the deal was closed. That was because, unlike the deal with i2, there was no need for any kind of relationship. With ICG, it was not about relationship; it was about putting together a win-win business proposal.

What stands out in this deal?

Taking the time to understand their business. Before I did those deals I talked to analysts and tried to understand what worked for them and what didn't. I was prepared on what I was trying to sell them, my knowledge of their business and the industry, what the value proposition was and how my product could help them. If you can't come up with the answers to these questions it is hard to put the deal together.

Looking at the two extremes of expansion, one approach is to try to become successful in the U.S. market first and then expand globally. The other extreme is to invest globally from the get-go. Which path did RightWorks pursue?

We had scarce resources so we decided to focus and win in the U.S. before investing in global operations. RightWorks has now opened offices overseas, but we took our time in doing so. However, we knew right from the start that we could not ignore the overseas markets. One of the reasons we did the ICG deal was to accelerate our globalization process.

There have been a lot of alliances in the past few months. Can you highlight the various alliances that RightWorks is associated with?

Let me address this by first grouping alliances into several categories. The simplest is the technology alliance; that is, build vs. buy. Then there are business alliances, such as channel alliances and mega -strategic market alliances, that result in shaping the overall market. RightWorks has in place channel alliances with Agilera and Breakaway, and a mega strategic alliance with i2.

If I had to do this over again with the network, knowledge, and skills I have now, I would put together deals immediately. It may not always be a win-win proposition; business deals are put together not only for business value but for the strategic benefits gained through sustained business relationships. It is more a "You scratch my back, I'll scratch yours" sort of thing. Those market types of relationships are important.

In the current dynamic environment, opportunity and improvisation have to be there. Is there any rule for strategy and planning?

> *Strategy is a conviction, which is developing a belief system and acting upon it.*

Our method is both long term planning and acting on certain convictions and hunches. I will give a macro and micro example. At a macro level, we said that the world is going to move towards a lot of out-sourcing of procurement. Then we said that if that is the case, trading exchanges will be set up. It was set up in 1998, when trading exchanges were not believed to be a big thing. We went out to get early partners and it could have been a wrong bet that could have hurt the company significantly. That's my point. Sometimes you have to act on your convictions and it's possible it may not always turn out right. That's what strategy is; you should be able to make minor changes and adapt as you go along. We called it multi-organization and trading exchanges and that's what morphed. Strategy is a conviction, which is developing a belief system and acting upon it. Part of it is being able to question your beliefs periodically and that's when improvisation or opportunities arise. As opportunities occur, you question your strategy, test it and realign it.

Did RightWorks morph at any particular time?

RightWorks has morphed from its inception through its evolution. In today's world, the market moves fast. Companies need to be reinvented and people within the company need to reinvent their own roles and, when necessary, new people need to be brought in rapidly. Once a quarter, our core management team discusses where the market is going and what the changes are that drive it. I believe every company goes through this exercise, but earlier on people would do this just once a year or even every five years. We have a strategy meeting every ninety days. We examine what changes are going on in the market and how they will impact us. But I do not believe we have done anything that is sacred or holy. Morphing then doesn't become a radical revolution but an evolutionary one. It becomes part of the process. This is not to be feared or avoided, but should be viewed as a part of surviving. Darwin's theory of evolution says that nature is constantly changing in order to survive. If you don't evolve, you won't survive.

A CEO of the old economy said that if you break your chains you will be free; if you cut your roots you will die. In the evolution of RightWorks, what has remained constant and what has changed?

This can be answered in many ways, but the main thing that has changed is the culture of the company. Core environment within the company is the one that embodies the innovation, the one that motivates risk-taking. For instance, I was talking about the micro example of evolution. Years ago, we thought we should not adopt Java for a client or client interface. It was our belief that the direction would not be toward Java but instead would move toward HTML. All conventional wisdom pointed towards Java and most of our competitors were adopting it. In the beginning we got a lot of flack about this, but it was our conviction and we took a chance on it. It turned out to be a feather in our cap. Java is a server-side thing, not a client-side thing, and what we did three years ago proved to be right. That is why we are rewarded, not for being a 'me too' company, but for acting on our convictions. But remember, if you are wrong you won't get rewarded either. No true leapfrog success can happen by being a 'me too'. The things that have stayed constant are fundamental core value systems. This is a kind of safe haven when everything else around us is whirling like a tornado. The things that haven't stayed constant are, necessarily, the business strategy, the technology platform and the architecture. Those have been up for grabs. The culture of the company is the core. To my mind, it is the absolute center.

> *No true leapfrog success can happen by being a 'me too'.*

What has been the core value system that has remained the center of stability?

First and foremost we have always been a customer-centric company. We changed the core architecture of the product, making sure that we provide an upgrade for the customer for free. Additionally, we made sure we carried the customers with us and made them an integral part of the whole process of change. We are truly committed to customer success. Treating people fairly has also been a big part of RightWorks' culture from the beginning. It is gratifying to me that people who left the company voluntarily often come back to work for RightWorks later on. People are comfortable with the change and know they will be taken care of. They know they will not be compromised.

What is the work culture at RightWorks?

Most importantantly I believe in leading by example. You motivate others by following the philosophy of not asking others to do what you are not willing to do yourself. Be fair, give credit and understand why people work here. It is both for financial and professional success. You have to provide a path for your employees to grow professionally. You also have to let them go when they reach a plateau, and be helpful in the process. Though we work 80-100 hour weeks, we are not burnt out yet. This is due to commitment, loyalty and good communication.

As you look at the strategy of RightWorks and its evolution over the last 3-year, do you see certain elements which have remained fundamentally the same?

The key element which hasn't changed is that we are still an application software company. The core focus of the application was all about efficient trading; that was what e-procurement was all about. So the core focus and the vision have remained the same. During the first phase of the market evolution, the efficiency procurement automated the process cost; we did that The second phase was the supply chain efficiency. The core vision was always giving value and saving cost as the bottom line, but better procurement always stayed the same. The 'how' of it has changed as the market has offered many more opportunities. First, it was process cost and then it became cost of sourcing, where it was possible to do auctioning and bidding, supply chain and vendor management; then it became aggregated buying. So the value drivers have changed along the way. Looking at the accounts payable system, there isn't much of strategy, because it is the backbone of the system and can impact it on the multiple levels of complex things. Strategy and focus can deepen, become richer, or shift.

So the belief system of a company drives corporate strategy?

Most definitely. For example, we believe in the market system and are marketplace enablers, not owners. Where Commerce One made a choice to actually own market places, we said we would be enablers because we didn't want to compete with our customers. These are the belief systems that create a plan of action. To illustrate, I don't believe that with Cisco's first acquisition they said, "We will grow or gain knowledge by acquiring companies." It worked for them and a belief system evolved as a result. This applies to strategy as well.

Are there any other marketplace belief systems? Can you give us an example?

We also said that we would enable open commerce interchange, as opposed to private commerce interchange. That's why we don't have a market site like Commerce One has, but one with which we've partnered; we don't have our own. We envisioned an open infrastructure for the marketplace rather than a mega-marketplace. Look at Commerce One. They have a brand name for the marketplace, operate under the market site and have their own ecosystem. I don't say it is right or wrong, it is just their strategy. We said we would not create a mega-ecosystem like that. We believe that the marketplace will demand free interchange, which is what the Internet is all about. We said we should have multiple marketplaces which will be more of a nodal system than a hub and spoke system.

Switching gears to leadership, how did your role evolve with respect to the changing business climate and organizational growth?

In 1996-97 it was about forming the company, being the visionary, raising money and being involved with sales and marketing. By 1998 I had a good team and my role evolved into that of a choreographer of the team. But I was still actively involved in product strategy, even though I spent a lot of time raising money.

By 2000, it was more about mega-deal making and keeping the vision alive and less about being a conductor, since I now had such a strong team. In 2000, we hired a new CEO, Mary Coleman, formerly of Baan Software.

What led to your decision to bring in a new CEO?

Running a company that is growing exponentially is a lot of work. Moreover, it is difficult for a company to recruit a CEO immediately after it goes public. Either you do it just before you go public or two years after it goes public. I felt that at this stage of my life I had to make certain commitments to my family as well. In the early days of RightWorks I used to be on the road for 20 days a month. Once the company is public, this might go up to 25 days a month. I felt that I was not prepared to take on this commitment for the next two years or more. Also, knowing that someone could do the job better than I could made me more willing to hand it over.

What was your selection process for the CEO?

I had a few people on my wish list and would have been happy with any of them. We were not actively looking, but it just evolved opportunely. It worked for me personally and for the company as well. We looked for credibility, a sense of 'been there - done that'; we wanted a committed person who could take the company to the next level in terms of operations, infrastructure and scalability of the company.

What is your leadership style?

I believe that leaders have to dive deep and I am not afraid of diving deep. There are times when I sit down and Q&A the product; it is important to me. I have learned when to delegate and when to pay attention to detail in business. I don't believe you can run a company without knowing the details. You also have to bring in very competent senior executives from whom you can learn. I always try to hire senior staff-members who are better than I am.

Any mistakes you've made along the way?

One mistake I made was not going for venture capital funding much earlier than I did. Angel money is fine but it is not enough to survive on for too long. I had not approached VCs earlier, on the advice of my board members-advice that I shouldn't have listened to, although it was well intended. Also, angels think the company can be grown on their money, but they forget that it soon gets diluted. Angel investment is not enough to grow a company on. What we need is great people and tons of money quick in order to make the company grow exponentially and succeed.

What is the one skill or value that has been instrumental in your success?

One important quality I have is a strong sense of Dharma; of doing the right thing. For example, when doing the ICG deal, it was never about what was best for me personally, but what was best for the company. A lot of people asked me why I was doing it. It was because of my sense of responsibility towards the company and the community I live in.

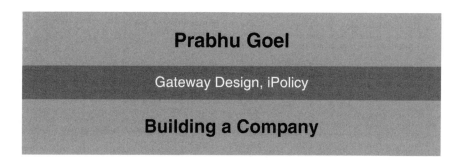

Prabhu Goel

Gateway Design, iPolicy

Building a Company

Dr. Goel is currently chairman of the board of iPolicy Networks, Inc. He is also an active private venture investor and is on the board of directors of several startup companies in the Bay Area.

In 1992 Dr. Goel founded Duet Technologies, which recently merged with Tunnelnet to form iPolicy Networks, Inc. Prior to founding Duet Dr. Goel was division president and director of Cadence Design Systems, Inc., the world's largest EDA software company. Nine years prior to joining Cadence Dr. Goel was CEO and chairman of Gateway Design Automation Corporation, which was later acquired by Cadence Design Systems.

Prior to founding Gateway, Dr. Goel held management and technical positions at IBM and Wang Labs. While at IBM, he received several Invention Achievements Awards and the IBM Corporate Award for Outstanding Innovation.

Dr. Goel graduated from IIT Kanpur and received a Ph.D in electrical engineering from Carnegie Mellon University in 1974.

We met Dr. Goel at the iPolicy Networks corporate office. He comes across as a man of few words, very action oriented, with a razor sharp personality. His responses were crisp and clear-cut. He has the look of a very seasoned entrepreneur, a result of having "been there-done that". He gives the impression that nothing can ruffle him.

Dr. Goel shares his wealth of knowledge on a variety of topics ranging from starting companies back in the eighties (in the pre-gold rush days), to re-inventing a company to angel investing.

"An important reason for my success is the presence of a very secure and supportive family."

Dr. Goel, Where did you start your career?

My first job after graduation was with the CAD group at IBM. I did a fair amount of development there in the areas of test generation and EDA and in the process filed four patents. I've got a couple of invention awards and outstanding contribution awards as well as a corporate award. At the time it seemed pretty big but what it basically did was accelerate my exodus because I was thinking: "What next?" It became apparent that the growth opportunities in IBM were not very significant. I got a call from a former boss of mine at IBM who had joined Wang Labs and I made the transition to Wang Labs in Massachusetts. Wang was a high flyer in those days and I thought it to be a great company, fast growing and thus with great opportunities for growth, whereas at IBM everything was saturated.

When did you move to Wang labs?

This was in 1981. Wang was setting up a new chip facility to make ASIC and testing tools internally. Previously they'd been doing everything off the shelf. So I went in and became part of the operation to support this strategy. Within a year it became apparent that Wang was not going where it was believed to be by outsiders. Management at Wang was too conservative. Dr. Wang was the only aggressive guy but he didn't have the support of the other people there.

So you quit Wang and ventured out on your own. How big a risk was it?

There is always a certain risk involved in venturing out on your own, especially when one has a family. I quit Wang and started on my own around July of'82. I think I had enough money to survive 12 months on my own, so I quit and started consulting as well as writing some software in an area for which I was quite well known in the industry- it was test generation related stuff- and also consulting in the area of testing of chips.

I also had a lucrative contract with Digital Equipment that helped sustain the company at a break-even level for the first year while I went about developing the software. There wasn't enough commercial software developed.

My stint at Wang really helped me see the world outside IBM. When you live inside of IBM you think the world is IBM. When I went to Wang I realized how different the world was outside; realized also that there was no good software available in the test automation space. There was a significant need because other companies outside of IBM, AT&T and Honeywell were starting to develop complex chips and the technology was not available anywhere else.

You were one of the first few to capitalize on the niche in this space. Can you elaborate?

In simple words, you really want to make sure that all modeled failures on a chip are being detected with a test that you generate automatically. And the software available was not able to do that as the circuits had started to grow bigger. The coverage of failures was down to, in some cases, 50% or 60% whereas they needed a 95% pass rate. So when I developed this particular software it had a huge impact.

And I saw this niche clearly as no one else was offering anything in this space. Since I knew how to do this at a technical level, I decided to give it a try. So that's how the window opened and that's when Gateway started.

How did you get your first few accounts?

For the first one year I was solo and basically did consulting. I began to engage with customers like Texas Instruments. They gave me the time of day because of my technical reputation and that's how the business jump-started.

Since I was an engineer and not a sales guy, I didn't understand the sales process. I basically made product demonstrations to the technical teams showcasing the results. They in turn had to do the selling internally themselves. So that is how I landed my first two contracts in the same month for $150,000 each, one from TI and the other from Raytheon. That basically laid the foundation for the company, in terms of now being able to attract more people.

It was persistence that opened a lot of doors. Typically, I would look through articles that people had published in the test area. I would identify all the people who published papers in that area. I went to various conferences and looked up their affiliations, got their business cards and then called them up and said, "Hey this is a product that I have. I know you need this because you're getting into this area, so why don't we work together?" And many times they would say, "Well, we cannot really work with a small company, we've got Company X, Y and Z," or something like that.

But there were always people inside these companies who were risk takers as well. They would actually open the door and say, "C'mon in and let's talk". What happened is that I used to do a lot of telesales, which obviously had to be followed by face to face meetings; you don't just buy products in that price range based on a telesales conversation; they do benchmarks and so on. That helped me immensely. I was in close, direct contact with the customers. I knew what objections they were making, what they were asking for and why they would or would not buy. I had no clue what the VP of engineering was going to say from a budget standpoint or a whole bunch of other factors, but at least on the technical level I knew what they wanted. These technical people inside who could see the value of the product did the first level of selling. Then I would get invited to talk to the management chain.

What were your next steps?

I started to add more people to the company. I hired somebody that I knew from my days back at IBM. Around the same time I hired a person I met in the U.K. who was one of the principal developers of a similar product. I had benchmarked his particular product as part of my Wang Laboratories mission and I quickly realized that the software he had developed was very much state-of-the-art.

In 1983 he contacted me and said that he wanted to come to the U.S. and asked if I would consider him joining my company. I said sure. He came over and lived with us for three months while he was still getting settled in. I gave him a clean slate and said, "You develop the next generation product based on your experience on your simulation side." And that's what gave birth to the Verilog-XL product at Gateway; it really became a hit.

How was your first year?

They were pretty long days; I mean, it wasn't uncommon to have 16-hour days and very little social life. And we were working seven days a week. We were able to recruit more people, increase the staff to about four people. It stayed at four for about another three years. The first two years we were literally running the company out of my house. I had a fairly large house so it was possible to keep the office part separate from the other areas. Eventually we did go out and get ourselves an office space, and for the first four years I was wearing all the executive hats in the company.

What was the growth like in the first four years?

In the first year the revenue was around $60,000; the next year it was $300,000; during the third year we were up to $1.1 million and in the fourth we hit $1.6 million. We became quite profitable. I made sure that I had at least 9 months of working capital before I would spend more.

At what point did you go to a VC?

Actually I didn't go to a VC, they approached me. I had tried going to the VCs after the first year and a half, but in those times on the East Coast, and with my kind of background, the VCs wouldn't even talk to me. What happened was that news began to spread that we were doing something exciting. We were contacted by three venture capital firms and all three made us offers. I knew that we needed more money if we wanted to grow. We raised 2 million dollars then and gave a good portion of the company for it, but I still maintained the majority control. They had the majority of the board members even though we could have named the majority, but it didn't matter. What was more important was getting their advice. So Fidelity Ventures and Greylock Management joined the team and put their money into the company.

We wanted to bring external oversight into the company. If I own most of the equity in the company, I can't have somebody else provide me with guidance unless they have a stake in the company, because that guidance doesn't have the same value, or isn't given with the same degree of intensity. I wanted oversight where the board could sit across the table and say, "You are wrong and we are not going to let you do this" If I had a board that did not have a stake in the company it would be, "Well this is what we think but if that's what you want to do then go ahead and do whatever you want". That is very different in a situation where other people own a piece of it because if they strongly believe in their position they will put their foot down, whereas without the stake they won't put their foot down.

We were looking for some external mentoring, feedback, support, a sounding board. Remember that my background was strictly engineering. I had insufficient knowledge of the many sides of management.

Why did you select Greylock?

We actually took a lower bid. Greylock, first of all, had a better reputation. Also the chemistry with them was incredible. We strongly believed that they added much more value as individuals and we got the chairman of Greylock to be on our board. So that's why it's more important to get quality into the company than being worried about equity percentage. That is why we went with Greylock.

In 1986 I hired a VP of sales and marketing who was one of the best sales executives that I have ever known. Then we hired a CFO, which is what Greylock wanted us to do. They recommended a person for this.

He was a very, very good CFO and he was extremely valuable because he basically took over the entire finance and administration function. I had zero involvement in that area. It was the same with the sales guy; he was handling the complete recruiting and the sales process and used me as an asset to basically sell whenever necessary and to help close deals. I was now confident about sales. They usually had a problem of not having enough feet on the street as opposed to whether we were meeting our numbers or not.

How come you brought these people on board after several years and not right away?

I didn't feel that I could attract these sorts of people at the outset. How could I convince them to come work for me when I didn't have enough credibility established in the market place? It was only after my creditability was established in the market place, and these guys could actually talk to customers like Motorola and others who said, "Hey, this is a great product", that we started to attract attention.

What was the change in strategy after you received funding?

Well, before funding we were operating on an extremely tight budget, keeping our head count down even though we knew that we could use a few more heads. After the funding, since we had an additional two million in the bank which we never did use but we knew was there, we were able to invest more aggressively. We were able to open offices in multiple sites, set up a Japan office. The first was in California as California was the biggest market.

What key inputs did the VCs actually provide? How often did you meet him?

We used to meet with the VCs practically every month. We had a board meeting every month, and I think the key factors the VCs provided us was that they made sure we focused on building a strong organization. We had the finance functions in place and other functions were being put in place to prepare for growth. On my own, these would not have been at the same level of sophistication as it was with the guidance of the VCs.

The second thing that was even more valuable was that when we hired any key people at the senior technical or management level we always ran them by the VC in the interview cycle. Part of our deal with the VCs was that, as we were taking their money, we were going to require them to spend a fair amount of time with us as well. So they gave us a lot of time. The place where we used them most effectively was actually in the recruiting process, because VCs are good judges of people and ultimately it's all about betting on people. So by being able to use them to evaluate people we were able to filter and attract the key people. Also, when we were recruiting somebody and gave them the opportunity to interview with some of the guys on the board, that was a big plus. We'd say, "Hey, we'd like you to meet the members of the board," and this became an attraction as opposed to a distraction.

You obviously hired topnotch people. What were their qualifications?

The Sales VP had an MBA degree and was considered one of the super star sales executives. The CFO had an MBA in finance from a topnotch university and had also been a controller at his previous company before he joined us.

I think the most important job a CEO has is to hire a team. That's his number one job. If he cannot attract the best people into his company then it makes his job very, very hard.

How were you able to become the market leaders in this space?

The microprocessor industry was saying, "Hey this solution is working so well. This is what we need." As a result we signed on several customers like Sun Microsystems and Motorola that were very credible and referenceable.

We used their success story to get into National Semiconductor. We became the golden simulator at three semiconductor companies and finally we leveraged our success to get into just about every semiconductor company out there.

> *I think the most important job a CEO has is to hire a team. That's his number one job.*

We were able to sign a corporate deal at Compaq. Compaq was a user of a lot of ASICs in those days. So they were the ones that started to pressurize the semiconductor companies by saying, "If you want our business you've got to accept the results that we generate out of this product." It was then that Verilog started to become what's called the "reference simulator". Progressively we were able to parlay that into making it the "golden simulator" in just about every semiconductor company that there was. And if the semiconductor company would use our product, their customers would naturally come to us. That was our strategy. That's what ultimately led us to practically own that space.

Seems like you had solid customers and predictable revenue. Were you thinking of an IPO?

Yes. In 1989 we were running bookings of nearly $24 million and were very profitable. That's when we decided to go for an IPO.

In an IPO you basically have to work with the investment bankers and the lawyers to articulate your vision for your company going forward. How are you going to sell it to the public and to the analyst, in terms of what the future of the company is? That's a very significant aspect of what they buy. They don't buy history, they buy the future. So you have to have a very good vision of where you're going to take the company, how you are going to make it bigger, how you are going to make it a compelling proposition for the future. History makes it easier for them to believe in your future.

In our case we were starting as almost a niche company, playing against the likes of Mentor Graphics, Cadence, and Daisy, which had integrated products. There was a lot of value perceived to integration because what you've got is a broader offering; you can sell a whole package to the customer instead of a selling an isolated product. And then integration into those environments is always a barrier to entry that the competitors would use against us. So we had to come up with a very compelling story in terms of how we would evolve.

Why did you decide to go with the Cadence acquisition offer instead of the IPO? It must have been a big dilemma for you, weighing the 2 options of IPO versus being acquired.

It was at the end of 1989. We were actually half way through an IPO. We were preparing for the road show when Cadence made a preemptive offer. I decided I didn't want to run a public company. I preferred to take the rather attractive offer from Cadence.

It actually wasn't that big a dilemma, because I think managing a public company is a very difficult task; you have to manage towards external expectations that are driven on a quarterly basis. By comparison, when running a private company you don't have to worry about the sales performance quarter to quarter to that large an extent. That was one factor that was certainly important. In addition, I recognized that we were still a niche company. We had one product that was the flagship product, and while we had developed other products in timing and other areas, it was still a single product company. If you look at the history of technology companies, most of them have disappeared after 10 years. Exceptions are Intel, HP and those kinds of companies. I didn't want to play those odds, so it made a lot of sense to me, given the valuation we were able to get, to secure liquidity for our shareholders and employees.

Tell us about the merger with Cadence.

We had interaction with Cadence because they obviously needed our product in their environment. I knew Joe Costello (CEO of Cadence during that period) pretty well and it was clear that he had this hole in his product offering. He could either try to build it himself or buy it.

I think there was some personal chemistry working between Costello and me that helped move it along, so the negotiations weren't really all that protracted. Costello just called and said he'd like to talk to me about buying Gateway. It was as simple as that. We came to a handshake and in a few weeks we finalized the deal. I think if they had bought it after the IPO it would have been a lot more expensive.

What was your integration like?

It was basically a transition for me into doing something very different. The agreement was that I would spend some time to help, since I was the largest single shareholder; so I had to make sure that the merger occurred successfully. I did leave two years later. The reason I left was that my style did not work well with a lot of other people at Cadence. I don't spend a lot of time analyzing stuff before making decisions and that probably did not fit well in the Cadence environment. There were too many legacy products that Cadence was saddled with that influenced their decisions in a direction that I might not have taken. So that was another significant factor in my decision to get out of there. I also wanted to do different things. I had already done this for practically 10 years and needed a change, so I chose to leave Cadence.

Did you start Duet Technologies after leaving Cadence?

Duet was started by a few other people. I was mainly the venture capitalist.

A couple of people who used to work with me set up the operation in India. A number of people who left Cadence came over to Duet and that's how it kind of started. The initial idea was to create a software foundry. It was an India-based operation with sales and marketing in the U.S.

What was the trigger point that led you to believe that the Duet business model would not work?

What happened is that one of the big competitors in this space had already gone public just after Duet got involved in the same domain. As a result of the IPO the competition now had 40 million dollars sitting in their coffers and, as a strategy to kill their competition, they slashed the price; they tanked the price of the product (libraries) by literally giving it away for free and making their money through the royalty model.

As a result the revenue growth that we had expected wasn't there. The numbers that we were showing were substantially lower that what we had projected to the investors. It became evident fairly quickly that we were too big in size. The number of people that we had was out of proportion to the revenues that we were generating. Obviously we had hired ahead based on the rosy projections.

Another thing that became apparent was that while we had good people in the area of business, our core competencies were not properly focused. The company was all over the map. We were doing networking, software related consulting, libraries for customers, memory compilers, as well as body shopping and EDA building blocks. So it was a hodgepodge of things. It was becoming impossible to manage, and one cannot be expected to be good at any one thing if there isn't enough focus.

And then to add to the confusion, we acquired Cascade Design.

What did you do to rectify the situation?

The playing field changed dramatically. It forced us to kill the old business model. As a result we morphed considerably into the telecom networking space. We literally transformed the company from one space to another; it was not just changing the business model. We jettisoned one side of our business and were able to raise cash out of that jettisoning process and then redeployed that to a new business area.

What were your key lessons learned from Duet?

Always ask very hard questions. Don't get carried away with someone else's enthusiasm. Do not let hiring get ahead of revenue. It's a very risky thing to do, especially in a services business. In a product business you don't have a choice, but in a services business it's very significant. Always ask, "What is our core competency?" I think at every board meeting one needs to step back and ask, "Are we doing the right thing? Is there something we should be doing differently? Let's go back and test our base assumptions." Because in the first few quarters the revenue growth was exponential. I said, "Wow, things are looking good!" But that's the wrong thing to do. Instead we should have said, "OK, so here we are, are we sure we are doing the right thing?"

Switching gears here, what triggered you to become a VC?

Two things. One, I did not want to become operationally involved, because I think that operations management is a 24-hour-a day job and I didn't want to be a part of that anymore.

The second factor was that I wanted to remain involved with the high tech area and one great way to do that is as an investor, an active investor. So that was the motivation behind the switch.

In today's market, the VC you select is very important to the success of the business. In other words, "founder and funding" have to match beautifully. On the flip side, what do you look for in a company you may invest in?

The most important thing you want to look for in a company you want to invest in is the PEOPLE, and the person who matters the most is the CEO, because if he's right then everyone is right by definition. But really you're looking at the top management team that exists in the company, whether it exists at that point or not. If it doesn't exist, then at least you know that it will be built to a high quality, based on the CEO. That's the number one thing you look for.

Secondly, you ask: What is the problem that they are trying to solve? Is there a real need for that in the market place? And is the need big enough that there is enough money to be made? Is somebody going to pay if there is a solution to that need?

The third question is: Does this company have what it takes to deliver a solution that fits the need, and at a price point, including delivery to the guy that needs it, that still allows him to make a profit?

The fourth thing you would look at are the barriers to entry in terms of someone else jumping into this and what this company has going for it, that will keep them ahead of the competition?

And then you want to make sure that there is a liquidity strategy, that after all this effort is put in there is a way to make money.

What should a startup's funding strategy be?

The thing that you have to ask yourself before you decide to raise five or ten million dollars is whether it is the right amount or should you be raising more? Your next milestone determines that. What is it that is going to take you to your next milestone? You've got to be able to demonstrate that the reason for waiting to take money is because you think that the company is going to be much more valuable, so you'll have less dilution. Now to get there, if it's going to take you longer by not raising more money, then it's not a smart idea. So you want to take as much money as you need to get there. What you don't want is money to become the limiting factor in your time-to-market.

We understand that you were the seed investor in Vani Kola's company, RightWorks.

I was the seed investor in RightWorks (once known as Media Kola). Vani struck me as a person who is incredibly determined, smart, and aggressive. She has the ability to open doors; she can call up people, all kinds of people. I don't know whether it's street savvy or what, but it's something that she has that allows her to connect with people. She also has a strange following; for some reason people gravitated towards her in terms of the people she recruited. We invest in people and that's why we invested in her.

What are your views on the current IT boom in India? What do we need to do in India to get it to the next stage and replicate the environment present in the Silicon Valley?

I think we need to make sure there are enough sources of funds available, that there are competent partners managing those funds who can evaluate the business risk. We need to create a climate where venture capitalists become accepted financial instruments, both in the view of people who are investing as well as well as for the entrepreneurs leveraging it. By and large companies in India get loans from banks who are willing to give money for a company that has a building worth a million dollars, but who would not give any money to a company that has an IP worth 10 million. Those kinds of barriers have to break down.

What will it take to break down those barriers?

I think it's getting there. Look at the success of companies like Infosys and Wipro. I think that there will be people like that who will become the role models for the local environment. I don't think that the role models can be transplanted from here. I think that the role models have to form over there because they have to reflect the local environment. People like Murthy and Premji, these people are role models. People can look up to them and say, "Look at where these guys started from and where they went." Plus, the access to the Internet gives them a lot of access to information elsewhere. So to a certain extent the Internet access is doing for businesses in India what television did for the villagers in India, showing them what can be.

Has success changed you?

I'm sure success changes everybody and I'm sure I've changed in many ways myself. It can't change my values. We have the same set of friends that we had before; we value that much more than the financial aspect. My living style has definitely changed; I live more luxuriously than I lived before. I think it changes your confidence level.

I now do what I think is fun in life as opposed to stuff that is necessary and may not be fun. I think that's what retirement means. When you think of what other people do when they retire, they usually travel, do things that are fun to them. In a similar sense a businessperson or a professional then starts to do stuff that is fun to him as well. For Bill Gates, its still fun to do Microsoft, and he's the richest man in the world. That's his retirement.

What are your strengths and skills?

I would say that I have faith in myself, a quality similar to confidence in my abilities. And I'm reasonably astute in terms of understanding things. Probably my judgment skills are very well developed and I think people find it easy to relate to me. These are my personal strengths. An important reason for my success is the presence of a very secure and supportive family.

How do you motivate people?

I think there are a number of ways that you can motivate people. First, they have to feel good about what they are doing. If the work they are doing does not satisfy them it's very difficult to motivate people, no matter what you do. Second, they have to feel good about the work environment that they are in. Once those two basic needs in a professional environment are met, people need to feel that they are well compensated for what they are doing. Finally, they need to feel that they are making an impact.

What are your goals at this stage of your life?

My first goal is that my children become self-sufficient, have adequate self-esteem and feel good about what they are doing. That's my number one goal now. Number two is that my family life is of a high quality. Number three is to have both calm and excitement in whatever I am doing professionally.

K.B. Chandrasekhar

Exodus, Jamcracker

Market Penetration

K.B. Chandrasekhar ("Chandra") is the chairman and CEO of Jamcracker. Prior to founding Jamcracker he was the co-founder and chairman of Exodus Communications. In 1994, Chandra identified the potential of the Internet and founded Exodus Communications. The company went public in March of 1998 and was one of the most successful IPOs that year. In 1999 Chandra was honored as the Ernst & Young Northern California Entrepreneur of the Year.

In 1992 Chandrasekhar set out on his own and founded Fouress, Inc. Fouress was a network software design and development firm, with clients including Sun Microsystems, Adaptec, Toshiba, and Lockheed. In 1990 he moved to the U.S. as country manager for Rolta, India, Ltd., responsible for business development, marketing and software consultant services to software developers and end users. At Rolta he generated major new accounts including Ford, DEC, ScanOptics and Borland. He began his career in 1983 at Wipro, an Indian information technology company, as a customer support engineer. Over his seven years with the company, he advanced through various sales, marketing and support functions including building highly available networks for satellite applications and managing marketing for Europe.

Chandrasekhar was born and raised in Chennai, India and educated at Madras University.

Even though Raghu and I conducted this interview over the telephone, Chandra's enthusiasm and excitement made us feel we had conducted the interview in person. His responses illustrate his excitement and enthusiasm. Chandra began a number of his sentences with the word "simple", putting us immediately at ease. His friends describe him as an executor. He gets things done while others are talking about it.

During the interview Chandra describes the market penetration strategies utilized by startups to become market leaders, using Jamcracker and Exodus examples. He explains the logic behind the globalization strategies as they apply to various geographic regions. He offers his point of view on scalability and mindset.

"The smart entrepreneur knows which revenue he wants and is willing to give revenue to other people so that he can gain three times more."

How did Jamcracker come about?

If you look at the evolution of computing in the past twenty years, there was first the PC revolution that focused on personal productivity. Once a majority of companies and consumers had their personal computers, they began wondering what came next. "What do we do beyond personal productivity applications like word processors and spreadsheets?" They wanted to communicate, which led to the proliferation of local area networks and ISPs. Now that everything was connected, the next logical step was to deliver reliable content for consumer use over the Internet. This led to the rise of the Internet Data Centers, a market that Exodus pioneered, which made content available 24 hours a day, seven days a week. Once a reliable infrastructure was in place, the consumer began to expect utility computing. For instance, when you go to Yahoo you expect the stock quotes to be there. But at the same time this revolution in utility computing had not touched the corporate market. Usually the corporate sector is 24-30 months behind in adopting trends of the consumer market. When I looked at this I thought that there were two or three phenomena occurring in the corporate sector from which one could profit immensely by embracing utility computing.

First, the existing business models of enterprises were changing dramatically. Second, information needs were becoming real-time and decisions were being made on real-time needs. Third, corporations were stuck with information systems that had been installed several years before and belonged to a previous era, where you felt that 99% of your enterprise was within your enterprise and not outside of it.

So I looked at these phenomena and thought to myself: This is almost like a half-time show at the Super Bowl. In the first five minutes you assemble the entire platform for a great show; the next eight minutes you perform one of the best shows of the year and the following five minutes you dismantle the platform in order to perform another great show, which is the second half of the super bowl show.

In a similar fashion an enterprise must be able to assemble and dismantle the information system based on business needs and not the other way around. That was the motivation behind Jamcracker.

What is Jamcracker's value proposition?

Our value position is very simple. We take the headaches out of a company's information technology requirements. You get it just like you get Yahoo on a simple poster. First, your organization needs information systems that give you a competitive edge. Second, you don't have to pay ahead; you pay as you go. This means an application provider is going to be proving himself every day, not having sold the system and taken the money. Third, you are obsolescence-proof. Once you find your business needs have changed you can discard a particular application and subscribe a more relevant one. We have a platform that allows the aggregation and integration of ASPs.

Which market segment was initially receptive to this idea?

You always want to focus your solutions on the market that most needs them. From that point, we chose high growth companies from the high-tech sector, companies that had a high mobility of workers. We always started with the mid-size companies and moved to the larger ones.

How did you penetrate the market?

Any new concept needs a little bit of evangelism. We started evangelizing from that perspective, emphasizing ease of use, and rallied industry analysts like IDC and Data quest. We felt we were on the right track. We conducted breakfast seminars called 'Living on the fault Line,' led by noted author Geoffrey Moore. The book, Living on the Border, written by Moore, also appeared at the same time. We used this opportunity to form an alliance with the Chasm Group and Jamcracker. We went to the market to talk about how the concepts described in the book were exactly what was being done by Jamcracker.

So that was the launch pad. How do you keep up the momentum once it's launched?

First, you attract the "early adopters." These are the guys who are willing to stick their necks out because they want to try something new. Next you cement yourself into major alliances with big brand names. This enables the end-user to see that the product has legitimacy. People will feel that with these large brands involved they can trust the solution and the company. This builds confidence in the mainstream buyer. You don't make much money in the early stage, but only in the mainstream.

How does one then go about scaling the market?

Marketing scalability is very simple. At this stage you get into viral marketing. How do you leverage every one of your partners - technology, product and channel partners? You try to convert your suppliers into channel partners and channel partners into suppliers. In short, you are trying to create an ecosystem wherein the differences between the suppliers and customers or the channel begins to blur. That's when word of mouth starts to work. This approach was utilized very effectively in the consumer world. Now we are trying to use it in the business world.

Was the same approach used at Exodus?

Absolutely. With Exodus, we first went to the early adopters who were category killers, like Yahoo, Ebay and Hotmail and made them our key customers. Then we went after the enterprises and created alliances with the likes of Sun Microsystems, Compaq and several others so that we could go to the large enterprises and tell them we could offer a credible, full solution. This strategy worked very successfully. Once we satisfied the dominant players in various markets, we essentially leveraged our initial success and went after the mainstream market.

Would it be a fair assumption to say that, with Exodus, by the time you had a robust solution there was a tremendous demand for the services, while at Jamcracker you are still in a phase where you have to spend a lot of time and effort on market development?

Absolutely! We entered one phase of the market and migrated to the other phase in Exodus. We entered the early adopter's market that didn't have much infrastructure. Exodus' solution for customers was a large expense and also their cash register. As a result you are also hoping for the success of all those people. So when eBay and Inktomi became successful we became successful too. The timing was perfect.

You have always emphasized the importance of timing.

Things do not happen by accident; you have to position them. Chances are, if your gut feeling is good, you effectively position and accelerate your business, which is very important.

After you have successfully launched and captured the market in the U.S., the next step was to globalize? What was your globalization strategy?

In globalization there is always a dilemma. Should you do it alone or partner? There are three possible strategies: acquire, start a Greenfield project on your own, or enter into a joint venture. We chose all three strategies, according to the particular market.

For example, Europe is a Greenfield market for ASPs. In a Greenfield market we could relate culturally a lot better in the UK than anywhere else. So it was easy to jump-start a Greenfield project in the UK. In a place where the languages and cultures are very different you go for a joint venture or an acquisition, as we did in Japan. The company must implement the appropriate strategy, taking into account the market dynamics and cultural factors of each country.

Why the names Exodus and Jamcracker? What was the thought behind the names?

Exodus stands for the exodus of communication from our data centers. In the case of Jamcracker, it was the name given in the early 1900's to a person who cleared log jams in waterways used to transport lumber wood.

With Jamcracker you seem to be "creating the wave versus surfing the wave." What are some of the challenges?

I think it is a function of your personality. There are some people who are more tuned to taking on a new concept and are hell bent on creating a market out of it. That is what creating a wave means. You are restless, you see several factors developing all around you, and you try to absorb them. At this stage there is no concrete data; you are going largely by your gut instinct. Later you can put data in place to justify why you are doing what you are doing. Surfing the wave is when you know you have started to move past what you call the proven thing.

Once you have penetrated the market, what strategy do you use for operational scalability?

I think the key is to recognize that you want to be scalable. It is most talked about, but least practiced. There are three approaches to consider: Do I develop a core product and then call in an army of people to customize it, offer a final product to the customer with minimal customization requirements, or partner with a company so that I can ensure scalability without getting bogged down by the issue myself?

> *The smart entrepreneur knows which revenue he wants, and is willing to give revenue to other people so that he can gain three times more.*

The problem for an entrepreneur is that he sees revenue everywhere and wants to take every penny of it. But the smart entrepreneur knows which revenue he wants and is willing to give revenue to other people so that he can gain three times as much.

What should the scalable mindset be?

The moment you move to a philosophical view of scalability, you create the process that enables scalability. The technology has to be scalable and the market segment must be scalable. Your sales people should be able to sell scalable products. Usually your sales people have a tendency to bring in every project out there so that it can be customized for them. How do you create the cookie cutter model? Think of it as a McDonald's. If you think of every business as a Mc Donald's, chances are you will be able to scale the business faster.

What about R&D in a startup?

In a startup there is a balance between trying to do it all on your own and leveraging your partners. The reasons are very simple. Leveraging will give you a lot more strength. First of all, a startup has limited resources, so you must know where you are going to put your chips. With respect to both Jamcracker and Exodus, the business model essentially required us to leverage our business partners' products. That is true for any successful company today. The entire solution offered to customers is made up of vendors and partners. What we do is leverage our partners so we can offer the customer a larger solution than what we could have engineered on our own. At Exodus, we leveraged on Inktomi and on Cisco for our R&D infrastructure.

Two days before Exodus went public you brought in Ellen Hancock as CEO. Why?

I liked her background. I was introduced to her by one of Exodus' board members. When I started to talk to her about Exodus' business model she caught on to what I was trying to accomplish within 10 minutes. Ellen has a big company track record; she is a long-time veteran of IBM with strong engineering and general management experience, coupled with stints at National Semiconductor and Apple Computer. In a nutshell, I was very impressed with Ellen Hancock's background long before I talked to her and I felt her operational experience would be invaluable in taking Exodus to the next level. Wall Street needed to know that Exodus had the right people to take it to the next level. As you know, one of the skills of an entrepreneur is to see beyond the near-term.

What is the downside associated with the startup life?

Failure. For every success there are probably 500 failures. People talk more about successes than about failures because people want to motivate others. You should learn once from a failure. If you fail repeatedly, you have a problem.

Kanwal Rekhi's mentoring played an instrumental role in Exodus' success. Can you comment on that?

Kanwal Rekhi is the embodiment of mentoring. To begin with, he is an extremely passionate individual who I believe was initially driven to prove himself and, after having achieved professional success on a grand scale, is now motivated to see that others benefit from his wisdom. Kanwal is known for being very blunt; he calls a spade a spade. His other great quality is his willingness to support you to the hilt, even at the worst of times. At Exodus Communications, Kanwal advised us on what specific markets to focus on, how to scale the business, how to execute fast and to do one thing at a time. Those were the key mantras that provided the foundation to the business. Later we diversified significantly, but during the formative years, focus was imperative and Kanwal emphasized it during every meeting.

What role has your family played in your success?

How much your family supports you plays a large part in your success. When I was 16 my father encouraged me to do stock trading. He encouraged me to take risks and never chided me for failures, in fact he wanted me to learn from my failures. He was a middle manager in LIC. He believed in his son. We were an extended family in Madras. I was brought up by my grandparents, the way it happens in India. They played a phenomenal role. They inculcated in me a strong value system. I was influenced by everything they did.

What is the most important strength that you attribute to your success?

When I believe in something I pursue it all the way. I do not give up on anything that I believe in, and I don't do anything half-way.

Vinod Dham

Intel, NexGen, Silicon Spice

Connecting the Dots

Vinod Dham is popularly known as "The father of the Pentium chip." He joined Silicon Spice in March of 1997 as their CEO. Silicon Spice was acquired by BroadCom in 2000 for $2 billion.

Dham spent 16 years at Intel, during which time he led the development of the Pentium chip. Leaving Intel soon after the Pentium hit the market, he joined NexGen, a chip company, as chief operating officer and executive vice president. NexGen was soon acquired by AMD and Dham found himself in the unique situation of competing head-on against Intel. As group vice president at AMD he played a powerful role in the development of the highly visible K6 processor.

This interview took place over three meetings. The first meeting took place at his residence in Fremont hills, the second at the Silicon Spice office with Dr. Anil Gupta, and the third was carried out in his car on his way to work on a Friday morning.

The meetings with Dham were like listening to a very well coordinated orchestra. He was in total sync, with the energy and excitement of a twenty year old. He is very people-oriented, candid and easygoing in his attitude.

We talked about the challenges and strategy behind the Pentium launch, the merger of AMD and NexGen, the disruptive technology at Silicon Spice and the importance of transparent communication. Dham shared his passion for the strategy of connecting the dots, from concepts to development to marketing to financials, all the way to the customer.

> *"In the technology sector, morphing is a given and the leader who can't steer the morphing will get thrown by the wayside very quickly."*

At Intel, was the product transition from 386 to 486 and from 486 to 586 roughly of a similar quantum?

The development of the 486 to Pentium was a significantly larger quantum. The 386 was an integer CPU; two other chips had to be integrated with it to do the full function. The 486 was a minor jump and basically integrated the three chips.

The Pentium was just not pulling everything together, it was taking the next big jump. Pentium was supposed to go not only into the desktop machines but also address the Unix market. It was not clear at that time whether Windows or Unix was going to dominate. You didn't just want to design a chip that was purely maximizing the Microsoft instruction set speed-up, but also addressing the Unix version of it. Sun's Sparc chip was Unix-based and if you were going to compete against them, you wanted to make sure you had that capability.

Another fundamental shift between 486 and P5 was that imaging and graphics features were becoming an important aspect of computing. With the rising popularity of computer games, which are basically images and graphics, the PC took the form and shape of a consumer appliance.

From 486 to Pentium, there was a fundamental change in the marketing approach. Intel marketed it and branded it like never before. In fact, at that time Intel's marketing budget was on the order of 40-50% of its R&D budget. That is quite a sizable number of dollars being put into marketing. Is this valid?

You are absolutely right; the biggest change was not just the technology but also marketing. Intel needed to convince consumers to buy a new PC. We were the first ones to advertise on TV, so Intel became a household name. When it was being branded, the techies and nerdy types thought it was a waste of money. We totally underestimated the power of brand. When you are a monopoly, the power of the branding is important.

Why was the chip named "Pentium" and not "586"?

Numbers cannot be copyright-protected by law. If there is a name that you trademark and copyright, then it cannot be copied. That's why the name was given, because we wanted a clear distinction from clone companies that were selling a similar type of product.

What were some of the challenges in developing the Pentium processor?

We were developing products at Intel at our own pace. When you are a monopoly you are not dictated to by market at all because you are creating it. You dictate your own pace of doing things. When we introduced the Pentium, the market was not ready to accept it. They were saying, "Hold it! We don't want the Pentium yet. We have to make some money too." Intel made money by introducing new processors, whereas the PC manufacturers made money by selling boxes with the older microprocessors.

The 486 processor was doing very well and the PC manufacturers were just beginning to make some money on the 486 systems. Normally, PC manufacturers take one to two years before they can build cost efficient systems, and by the time they did we had come out with the new Pentium processor.

Guess what is in Intel's best interest? To wait and let them continue running 486? Intel would have done so if there was a guarantee that there was no competition in the market, but along came Advanced Micro Device (AMD). Intel's goal was to stay one generation ahead of the competition. Now we were one generation ahead but our customers were saying they didn't want to be. The dilemma was how to convince the customers to buy a product they were not ready to buy.

So how did you make the customers buy the Pentium?

We went around the traditional players by creating new rabbits. The giants, Compaq and IBM, were not interested. We picked a company called Packard Bell to create the market. They didn't have new technology advantage over the other players and we used that to our advantage. We gave them the new technology, Pentium, and they ran with it. This started threatening the big PC players. The numbers started coming in quarter after quarter, and an unknown company was beating the established PC system manufacturers. That was how we got every PC system manufacturer on the bandwagon.

Another thing we used strategically to our advantage was the CD ROM, which was becoming a standard then. We came up with the PC home machine theme: It is user friendly, you can use CD ROM to listen to music and play games. We rallied independent software vendors and game vendors to develop games for this machine. Another huge challenge was that, overnight, we had to convince a world that had built 5-volt motherboards for the past 25 years to transition to 3.3 volts for the Pentium. Suppliers had to invest money in the production line. How could we convince them? We had to go on an around-the-world trip trying to convince them to change.

It was not only the hard work and the vision, but also the right blend of events that had to happen at the right moment. It was the overall strategy that transformed the Pentium solution into a compelling need.

Did Intel ever consider manufacturing the PC, and if so why?

The only reason Intel would have liked to make PCs was because of the fear that ultimately there would only be four computer hardware companies in the world. This is not unlike the automotive market- GM, Ford, Chrysler and Mercedes Benz compared with Sun, Intel, IBM and Compaq. In such a hypothesis, IBM would finally use the power PC, Sun would continue to use Sparc, Intel would be on the X86 and the entire competition would gravitate back to a vertical market. In such a case, to whom would Intel sell the chips? The Industry will be back to a vertical market, and there will be no horizontal markets.

We did 20-odd case studies with Andy Grove for a period of 6 months at Stanford University on companies such as Microsoft, Novell, and Motorola. The task was to identify the reasons these companies succeeded or failed and the last case study was: In light of all this, what should Intel do? Part of the conclusion was that logically Intel should never make PCs because it is a low margin business. Of course your revenues can become ten times more, but the profit margins would be only 15% as opposed to around 70% or more with the microprocessor. Why would Intel put a steel case around the processor and make money on the steel case? However, in order to sell more and to protect against that vertical market, Intel needed to build the PCs. So Intel began to build PCs only in small quantities.

The second issue was that no one was taking leadership in our business, the x86 business. Microsoft, Compaq and Dell were sitting on the sidelines and somebody had to lead the parade. So we took it upon ourselves to lead, to show the world how to do it.

Shifting gears to Nexgen and AMD. What is your perspective on their competitive strategy against Intel?

Fighting against Intel isn't an easy job, to put it mildly.

NexGen was a design boutique shop with very good chip designers but no business strategy. To some extent, they were quite naïve about what would it take to compete with Intel. Nexgen had a two-chip solution, a proprietary chip and a proprietary bus; therefore they needed a special motherboard, so a special PC needed to be made. How are you going to compete with Intel with such a strategy, for God's sake? We had to change the design strategy significantly. We moved to a single chip solution and used the same bus as the Pentium bus, so it would plug into a similar socket that the Pentium chip plugged into. Suddenly, you had a readymade infrastructure of a hundred million units to tap into. It was clear that if you do it and do it successfully there will be somebody who will put a value to it. That's what most startups do and that's exactly what happened in NexGen's case, with AMD finally acquiring them. With AMD, pricing was central to the strategy in competing against Pentium, a microprocessor that is faster and cheaper than a Pentium.

How did the alliance between AMD & NexGen come about?

NexGen had needed a fabrication (FAB) plant to build their product. A fabrication house in those days cost a billion dollars and NexGen wasn't even worth a billion dollars. NexGen needed to find a FAB partner, so we went to IBM, Motorola, Samsung, and Texas Instruments. I was so steeped in Intel culture that I did not think of AMD. I guess all those years I was anti-AMD. I had taken 20 days off in August and was traveling all over France by train. I remember reading an article that said AMD was in trouble and that they had a FAB in Austin which was idle. I also remembered from my Intel days what a liability an idle FAB house could be. Thus, while AMD had an idle FAB, NexGen had a product but no in-house FAB. I just put two and two together. It did not require a rocket scientist to figure that out. I came back from my trip and went to the CEO of NexGen and told him that NexGen should merge with AMD. We used our board member to connect us with AMD and the story we had was so compelling that we nailed the deal very quickly.

Let's switch gears to Silicon Spice. Is the business model based on creating disruptive technology?

Yes, we created a disruptive technology, a paradigm shift. We built a chip, an operating system, and software tools that allowed us to compile in C level a suite of applications, a bridge (aggregation of chips on the board), then built the board and an evaluation card. We thought that the world would not be able to comprehend the significance of what we had done so we went out and actually built a box, a Spice box, integrating all the pieces. In total we built seven different complex pieces, giving us an enormous edge over our competition. It becomes very difficult for the competition to do it all. My thinking was to make it very difficult for someone else to get in. The solution was complex for us; however, it was a very simple turnkey solution for our customers.

Most companies are happy just building a chip and then selling it. We built a great product, a complete solution for the customer. Of course, the downside to this approach was that a lot more money was involved in the development of the solution.

Generally, no company is alone in a certain market space, which means that you are competing either to be the first or to have the best features or the lowest total cost for the customers, or it is the best service that goes with the product or some combination of the above. In the case of Silicon Spice, what was the competitive landscape like? You obviously beat the competition, but presumably the competition must have been thinking along the same lines.

When we started, Texas Instruments had the largest market share. They are to the DSP market what Intel is to the microprocessor market. I had competed against Intel when I was with NexGen and AMD. Having worked at Intel for 16 years, I knew that the very strength of a large company, a behemoth, is also its biggest weakness.

Intel's strength was in building microprocessors. During my tenure, I knew they made several attempts to diversify into other areas. The motive behind the strategy was to have other products when someday the PC became less important. Money was not the problem; billions of dollars could be thrown, companies could be bought, engineers could be put into those markets. The fact is, they did not succeed for two reasons.

The first reason is the mind set. The mindset of the company always revolves around core competence. So at the end of the day if there is shortage of manufacturing capacity, the non-core businesses suffer at the expense of core business. A company that is a monopoly rarely gets beyond putting its resources and its energy behind anything other than its cash cow. All the other businesses end up getting only lip service at the end of the day. The best people are typically not assigned to manage them. For example, Intel has spent billions of dollars in the last few years trying to diversify into various other markets with little success. I don't care how much money they invest, unless they spend significant time and resources required to execute the overall corporate strategy it will not succeed.

I knew that the very strength of a large company, a behemoth, is also its biggest weakness.

The other thing that happens is that your thinking becomes very linear in large organizations. I was involved with 386, I had done 486, then Pentium, which was an extension of 486. What you do when you are linearly improving design is that you carry all the baggage and your thinking gets constrained into accepting some well-defined patterns that worked in the past. You never break away to a different space and say: Is there a totally different way of doing it that could be better than everything else we have done so far?

So I knew from my Intel experience that you need to be at least 10 times better than the competition to even get attention, especially if you are competing in a market with well-established giants, such as Texas Instruments. If your product is only 2 times, 3 times, or even 5 times better than the competition, it may not be good enough. The larger companies will drop the price temporarily and block you out for good. As an upstart, you absolutely have to have an earth-shattering edge. This was our strategy at Silicon Spice.

Strategy is a result of your total understanding of what's happening out there, what's happening with customers, what's happening with technology, what's happening with market trends. A convergence of all these factors creates a strategy.

Why did you decide to be acquired?

There were several reasons why we agreed to be acquired by Broadcom for two billion dollars rather than go public. Part of the reason was that in order to really create this disruptive technology we had to get it out on the street. The barriers to market entry were so high that no stand-alone company could have done it.

Another reason we went with Broadcom was to build credibility. Even though we could show that Silicon Spice had the competitive edge, there was lot of uncertainty. What if Silicon Spice ran out of money? What if it took longer for the market to develop and therefore ran out of runway before take-off?

At what stage did you think about approaching Broadcom?

I did not want to think of any alliance until I had "Silicon." They approached me prior to us having Silicon, when the product was taping out; however, I did not entertain any offers until the chip was stable. The valuation of a company is a function of product stage. Complex products are very hard to explain and comprehend, so the best thing is for them to see it all. They say a picture is worth a thousand words. They saw the picture and the deal was closed.

From Broadcom's point of view, the optimization for them would not just be to get Silicon spice, and not just get the technical people working in Silicon spice, but to get you. How does Broadcom get somebody like you to stay?

The reason why people like me stay is truly the excitement of making a difference, coming here and building a great company. At some point it is not the money; you go beyond that in order to make something as everlasting as the Pentium processor. My reasons for joining Silicon Spice were very obvious: a) I had done enough chips, and b) I was convinced that the microprocessor was no longer the limiting item in the ability of the user to have the total experience of going on the Internet. The entire thing had to do with broadband and connectivity. With the deregulation of the telecommunications sector, an enormous landscape had suddenly opened up and that's what brought me in.

To address the retention issue, people have to be retained based on a system of rewards. The rewards come in two ways, financial and having a work environment that is conducive to the employees meeting their short and long-term career objectives. Money by itself is not a motivator. It becomes an issue of how you are going to be treated in an environment that you are a part of and whether you feel what you are doing is meaningful to you. If those conditions are absent, you will leave.

In the digital era, business model and strategy become obsolete very quickly. How do you orchestrate morphing? How you recognize that your old model doesn't work?

We have morphed considerably at Silicon Spice. The real trick is not only recognizing when and how to do it but capitalizing on it very quickly. How you steer a ship with 125 people and take them along with you is an even bigger challenge; it is how companies succeed or fail. When you steer the ship in another direction you communicate your vision, and even before the ship moves you

> *In the technology sector, morphing is a given and the leader who can't steer the morphing will get thrown overboard quickly.*

begin to behave as though the ship has moved. It is all about leadership and execution. It creates a lot of constraints, upheaval, morale issues, doubt and fear. To succeed you have to keep focused and make sure everyone stays on board, stays dry and gets to the other side. In the technology sector, morphing is a given and the leader who can't steer the morphing will get thrown overboard quickly.

Switching gears to the corporate environment and culture, how did you create excitement at Silicon Spice?

Fundamentally, the engineers must enjoy the work and know they are going to succeed. Of course the team has to be smart, capable and the work environment people hired as their colleagues should be good enough for them to respect and to feel that they will collectively succeed.

Then you should have some trust in the leadership of the company, know that the CEO has done it successfully a couple of times before and can probably pull it off again.

At Silicon Spice we kept an open environment, which is a most fundamental thing, to be in touch with people and communicate with them. I had an open lunch hour on Fridays. The entire company got together and had lunch. We discussed the status of the company, like whether we were in the process of raising money or signing up customers, making some development schedules, announcing new products and demos at various conferences. For example, about a year and a half ago, I remember that things weren't going right and I debated whether I should I share with the employees some concerns about the company, as the process can be quite demoralizing. I concluded that they would rather hear depressing or demoralizing news from me than hear about it indirectly. I strongly believe that however bad or good the news is, it is important to share it with the employees. It helps build trust. Employees are smart; they know that things sometimes go wrong, but they should have the confidence in the leadership to pull it off and get the company back on track.

While at Intel I had the habit of taking all the pressure on myself in order to protect all of my people, which you have to do to some degree as a leader and manager. However, what I concluded was that if I shared the burden with my direct staff, they would join hands with me and help me pull it off, which I found to be very satisfying. When you work on a very, very complex program it sometimes takes two three years before you see success, during which time the team should be working incredibly hard. During that period of two or three years, how do you keep people motivated? There are daily setbacks and victories. We correct the setbacks and celebrate our victories. This keeps the ball rolling and the hope alive, so you keep the focus.

At the end of the day, it is critical not to lose focus on the two or three most important things: job zero, job one, and job two. Job zero is something we should have been working on yesterday; job one is what is really in front of us; job two is the next project. The team always wants to know beyond what they are currently engaged in, what is next and exciting, when their project is ready to go to the market. They can spend 80 per cent in the new and 20 percent in the old or vice versa, depending on the work. Keeping them excited is a very delicate balance and is critical. You have to keep the team excited and motivated to keep going forward.

I stay very much plugged in with my people and what's going on with them, whatever it is. If you do that, people are much more open. It is a win-win situation with the staff. The personal interaction with your team is a part of the leadership role that never gets written about. It makes a huge difference at the end of the day.

Any big challenges you have faced in the past two years at Silicon Spice?

When I came on board at Silicon Spice the team was relatively inexperienced in a number of functional areas. When I took over I found that the team had whiled away six to nine months experimenting with an idea that had attracted me to this company to start with. So there was this phase when we had to radically change the prototype to get to the end product. There was a dramatic change in the direction of the company from where it was to where we took it. The original design was based on a multi channel device and we completely erased those plans and morphed it into the voice area. This change in direction, both in terms of the target market and the architecture of the product, was dramatic. This was the biggest challenge we had to face and, looking back, I feel glad that we took the challenge. It was like taking a big ship going at 60 knots an hour and making a sharp right angle turn. Many people thought it would stop and sink. While we were changing the direction we communicated well, kept the team together and ultimately pulled it off. I am very proud of the Silicon Spice team for having succeeded under such circumstances.

How do you build a solid startup team?

Good people are very hard to find. There are plenty of people willing to throw money at you and a lot of entrepreneurs have great ideas. What ultimately makes the difference between mild success and great success is the caliber of the CEO, the senior management staff, and the product development team. For example, at Silicon Spice I knew the people I wanted to hire. I had a matrix that included the names of individuals with their areas of competencies and what their aims were. I then hired a headhunter and told him who I wanted and in which order. This can be a laborious job. It all has to happen simultaneously while you are working and raising money, but you have to be focused. I used to spend 30 to 40 percent of my time on hiring alone.

What role has family played in your success?

My wife has been very helpful in giving objective advice. As a CEO, everybody you turn to has some personal agenda. All the constituencies that you turn to have some personal agenda. For example, if I am thinking of selling the company, taking it public, or some other fundamental issue, before taking it to my staff or even the board of directors I have to prepare myself in my thought process. Who do I use as a sounding board? It is indeed true that it is often lonely at the top and sometimes the only person I can trust is my wife.

Your comments on Andy Grove, the Chairman of Intel?

If you don't connect the dots you cannot survive.

The biggest education in my life came from watching Andy Grove in action. He is a man who actually connected the dots, saw the big picture. I have always been fascinated by business strategy and Andy Grove is a master strategist. I was fascinated by his insight, how he connected the dots the way he did. I would go into a meeting, connecting in my way, and then see how he put the various pieces together and see what the difference was and where the difference came from, what the driving force was and what actually changed. A lot of people say Andy Grove is a great technologist, but in my opinion he is also a great business strategist, and that is what Intel is lacking today, someone who can connect the dots. If you don't connect the dots you cannot survive.

Desh Deshpande

Cascade Communications, Sycamore Networks

Davids and Goliaths

Gururaj "Desh" Deshpande is the co-founder and chairman of Sycamore Networks, Inc. Dr. Deshpande co-founded Sycamore Networks in 1998 with the vision of creating next-generation optical networking technology that will revolutionize the backbone of the public network.

Prior to co-founding Sycamore Networks, Dr. Deshpande was founder and chairman of Cascade Communications, a company he started in 1990. Between 1991 and 1997 Cascade grew from a one-person startup to a company with $500 million in revenue and 900 employees. In June of 1997, Ascend Communications acquired Cascade for $3.7 billion.   Before founding Cascade, Dr. Deshpande co-founded Coral Network Corporation in 1988 and was with the company until 1990. Before that, he served in various management positions for Codex Corporation, a subsidiary of Motorola, and taught at Queens University in Kingston, Canada.

Dr. Deshpande has garnered many top industry honors. In 1999, Red Herring Magazine named him one of 1999's Top Entrepreneurs. Dr. Deshpande was named the 1999 Mass High Tech All-Star in the telecommunications industry. Dr. Deshpande holds a B.S. in electrical engineering from the Indian Institute of Technology, an M.E. in electrical engineering from the University of New Brunswick in Canada and a Ph.D in data communications from Queens University in Canada.

Dr. Anil Gupta and I interviewed Dr. Deshpande via conference call. We found him to be soft-spoken and extremely articulate. He comes across as a butterfly with wings of steel. It was very clear that with Sycamore Dr. Deshpande is not interested in selling but in building a world-class organization like Cisco, and that's what's driving him this time around.

Dr. Deshpande details how Sycamore leveraged Cascade's (his earlier startup) carrier network customer base to build Sycamore and to compete with the likes of Cisco and Nortel. He describes the roles an organization's design and culture play in attracting and sustaining world-class talent and building great sustainable corporations. We discuss the product, technology, globalization, and competitive strategies utilized by Sycamore in order to become a leader in the optical networking space.

"We thrive on the challenge of outrunning big competitors."

In Silicon Valley, once you have been an entrepreneur it's virtually impossible to work for somebody else. Some people become serial entrepreneurs while many others become angels or venture capitalists (VCs). In your case, Sycamore is your third venture. Clearly you seem to have taken the serial entrepreneurship route. What's driving you to do that?

General Alan Michael, who is now in his seventies and has done many startups, once said to me, "Women give birth to kids, or life; the closest men come to that is through startups." I think there's a lot of truth to that. It's a very exciting experience when you start with a clean slate; you say you're going to do something and actually are able to do it. I think it's the excitement and the creativity that's really exhilarating about starting these companies.

After selling Cascade to Ascend, did you consider the life of being an investor or was it really not in the cards? Did you know you were going to do another startup?

No, the way I've planned my life is to set goals for three to five years and then, if I achieve them, everything changes. When we sold Cascade to Ascend I really had no clue what I was going to do. I did toy with the idea of just being an investor and being on boards and so on. In fact, I was the founding chairman of two companies. I liked mentoring, helping younger entrepreneurs, but after I did a couple of those, it just wasn't enough. On the other hand, there were a lot of serial entrepreneurs who did short stints at eight or nine companies. That's not really what drives me. In starting Sycamore I really wanted to build an institution, not just another hot startup. So I'm hoping that Sycamore will be alive and kicking for the next five hundred years and will be more of a substantial institution than a hot startup. When I look back at what happened at Cascade I realize how great a company it was. This time I need to create something that's not only better than Cascade but I also need to build something that's sustainable and long lasting. That was the motivation for Sycamore.

You said Cascade was a great company. What made it great?

We went from one person to a thousand people in six years and we may have lost only two or three people during that time. The turnover rate was very low. People wanted to stay. It was an environment where people felt really good. They felt like they were the founders of the company; they felt challenged; they felt they were contributing and creating something new. In a lot of ways that was how the company worked. Decisions were made based on the merits of the decision itself as opposed to who was making it. There was no authorship for any idea and there were not a lot of big egos. Obviously people were very driven and very focused. It was an extremely competitive market and we were competing with the toughest guys in the marketplace.

It's really mixing and matching all these capabilities - how to be polite yet firm, how to be a tough business guy and still be a nice guy. Many companies have a very hard time mixing those kinds of things. Both at Cascade and Sycamore it seems very natural.

The key to any company is its people. Now that you have made several people in your company wealthy beyond their dreams and expectations, how do you hold onto them and keep them excited as well as attract new good people?

Excitement is the key word. There are a lot of very good role models here in the company. Many of us were vested a long time ago, when Cascade went public. Most of us who work here made so much money in Cascade that we never need to work for the rest of our lives. A lot of people here get up in the morning, get to work at 6:30 and stay late, not because they have to but because they want to. There is a high level of excitement. Right now there are a lot of multi-multi-millionaires who have already cashed the amount. I still see a lot of confidence and excitement in them. There will be some people who probably just want to go and sit on a beach - and they should, if that's what they want to do. But I think for most people, after they have a certain amount of money it doesn't really change their lifestyle; things don't basically change much. I think a lot of the people are here because they want to have fun. It's a lot of fun! It's like building a castle; stone by stone, you see it grow, you see it come together. I think it's that part of it that really excites people. And we need to make sure that we keep that excitement and fun going.

When you say "fun", what kind of an environment are we talking about? Is it laid-back, as in several Silicon Valley companies?

Sycamore is laid-back in the sense that people don't work nowadays in suits and ties, but also it's very mild-mannered. People are aggressive, yet balanced; they have to be, otherwise they can't compete in this market. It's a family kind of atmosphere. Most of the people here put family as their number one priority. That doesn't mean that they don't work hard; they work extremely hard. It's just a nice, stable culture.

Would that be an East Coast (Boston Area) – West Coast (Silicon Valley) thing?

It's easier to build these kinds of institutions on the East Coast than on the West Coast. On the East Coast the culture is a bit more long-lasting; There is a loyal employee base and people are driven by long-term goals. In Silicon Valley I think it's gone a little too far in the other direction. I wonder if any good companies will get built on the West Coast now, since nobody wants to stay with an idea for any length of time. I've never seen a good idea develop overnight, where everything is successful in an instant. The first time there is a slight setback, everybody is gone, looking for another opportunity. That attitude will be hard for the West Coast in terms of building long-term, sustainable companies.

You've always been an East Coast guy. When you started Sycamore did you consider moving to the West Coast?

Not really, I think because our kids were born here on the East Coast. It's funny, I grew up in India and for me the West Coast and sunshine has a lot of attraction, but the kids can't imagine living without snow. It really wasn't an option I considered.

Let's shift gears. On the strategy front, if we think about the concept of cyber wars, or competitive wars in today's economy, one way to simplify it is to think of the wars of David versus Goliath, or a Goliath versus a Goliath or a David against a David. When you look at Sycamore versus Cisco, Nortel and so on, is it a war between a David and a Goliath? Is this the right way to categorize it?

This may have been true to begin with. We have the agility of a startup but at the same time we have the experience and foundation of a fairly large company. What differentiates Sycamore is ambition - the fact that it's going to be a Goliath, though a different kind of Goliath. It's only a two-year company and we're already up to 650 people, with lots of revenue and customers. That's something unique about Sycamore. We have one and a half billion dollars in the bank. So I don't see us as a startup. I want to compete with Cisco and Lucent, be bigger and better than those guys. Any time there's an innovation, a new technology that comes into the market place this rapidly, it's the Davids, the younger guys, who have the advantage. But considering the business we are going after, which is the infrastructure business, unless you have that escape velocity, unless you have the ability to build the distribution channels and so forth, you can't survive as an independent entity.

If the technology was, let's say, a self-selling technology, then a young star-tup really has no obstacle as long as the technology is leading edge. But if you have to build a pipe to the customer and also service capabilities that are critical for their business, then an existing Goliath has a huge advantage over a startup.

Yes. What I think will happen is that out of all these startups there'll be one or two that'll actually make it to the next gear of the game, which sort of becomes the central focus for a lot of the technology to rally around. Obviously Cisco does acquisitions and ends up playing that game. Nortel is doing fairly well; Lucent is fumbling but they won't go away. And then it is a question of which of these startups actually have the ability to stand up, cross the barrier and get to the same level as those big guys.

So in terms of distribution channels, how does Sycamore do battle with a Cisco or a Nortel?

Well, I think a huge advantage is the fact that we did Cascade. We couldn't have done Sycamore if we hadn't done Cascade. Cascade was probably the first startup company that sold carrier networks to all major service providers in the world. So when Cascade penetrated all these accounts, we already knew the CEOs and CTOs of every carrier in the world. As a result we had an opportunity to get into those accounts. This is not a luxury that a startup would have with maybe 10 engineers building something that's going to be a little bit better and cheaper

So you've proven yourself to be credible with the customers?

That's right. That got us in the door, though of course we have to continue to perform and prove ourselves and make it all work. But the fact that Cascade had such an excellent reputation with the customer base gave us the opportunity to build these channels.

In terms of Sycamore's advantage, does it lie in being the best technology provider or is it the speed with which you're able to bring the equipment to the customers?

I think it's the speed. But behind that is the technology strategy. All the technologies that we bring to the market place you can break up into two parts: soft optics and hard optics. Hard optics refers to the physics of the optics, that is, the ability to shoot the laser beam, filter it, amplify it, make it go as far as you can. Soft optics refers to putting all these components together into systems and then doing a lot of software on top of that in order to create a nimble connection. If you want a connection from California to Boston, you can get it right away and you have it as long as you want it and you get charged only for the time you have it.

When you say that you want to grow into a Cisco in 10 years and possibly even become bigger than them, how do you plan to accomplish that?

From a strategy perspective, you've first got to break up the job that you need to do into pieces. Within this new and exciting digital economy piece you can break up the network into three pieces. The first piece is where you convert all the information into IP packets. The second piece is where you take those IP packets and switch them around so that you send them to the right place. The third piece is creating pipes across the world so that you can go within a city, city to city, or across the entire globe. So if you break up the whole industry into these 3 segments, we are focused on just one segment, the connector which is creating the pipes, and that's a huge business. I think that's $30 or $40 billion a year business, which is all done the old way. Now we're trying to convert it to the new way, which will possibly penetrate up to 15% of the market over the course of the next four or five years. It's still a huge business, a multi billion dollar business. It gives us a framework that allows us to just focus on that part of the market. Of course, to play that market you need maybe five or six technologies and we need to be number one in all of them. That's a big enough sandbox to build a substantial company.

So it's also a sustained opportunity?

Yes. It's a large enough opportunity, but a very focused one. I think you can break up the architecture of the network so that if you're the best in one particular segment, people will buy that piece and not demand all of the pieces. Within that piece, which is a very large piece, we have to stay current with everything - acquisitions and so on - because each of those segments will then fragment into another ten, fifteen or twenty segments. We have to stay on top of each of those little segments that get fragmented. That's where we'll need new startups, new acquisitions, and so on.

Would it be correct to say that the flexibility Sycamore offers its customers to come on and come off is coming from soft optics?

Right. The strategy is in the optical networking system today. Look at Corvis, for example; it's really dominated by physicists. And each one of them is trying very hard to gain a competitive advantage in the market place by making the light behave a little bit better. That comes from hard optics. They work very hard and come up with a laser, a filter, or something that makes that part of it work a little bit better; but to me that's a short-lived advantage.

It's very much like the computing business was 15 years ago. When you look at Honeywell, Unisys, Perry, or Univac, all these guys thought they would be able to compete in the computing business by coming up with better processor chips and better memory chips, whereas the processor chips got developed by Motorola and Intel. The same thing is happening with the optics systems. All the hard optics, valued hard optics, construct the components and those components are going to be a huge market with JDS Uniphase, Corning and so on. There are at least 100 startups with close to 5 billion dollars in that business, so the guys who do the components have to absolutely focus on the components and be the best in what they do.

I don't want to invest in components at Sycamore. We have a lot of good Ph.Ds here, at least 40 Ph.Ds in the optical domain. When they come up with a good idea, we call up some of these guys and say, "Hey, here's a great idea; can you go make a component? And by the way, when you have the component done we don't want an exclusive. We want you to sell it to everybody." We don't want to get stuck in a proprietary corner somewhere. We want to use the mainstream innovation in hard optics but be able to bring it to the market place very quickly. As time goes on, the amount of soft optics that you need to run this mission-critical applications will continue to increase. That is, you can't just take a product, put it together and sell it to the market; it needs to be manageable, it needs a lot of automation. So as time goes on we're going to continue to build on assets in soft optics.

What's happening in communications and what happened in computers, the switch from hardware to software, seems quite analogous

Right. We are the Microsoft plus Dell of the optics business. And JDS Uniphase, Corning and all those guys are the Intels and the Motorolas. We have a very differentiated strategy from that of say, Nortel, that makes the lasers, or Ciena or Corbis.

So there is indeed a technology difference in addition to just the speed with which you bring it to the customer?

Right, the reason we can bring this to the market place this quickly is because of the strategy.

Is it the Dell part that gives you the speed and the Microsoft part that gives you the soft optics focus rather than the hard optics focus?

That's right. In this particular business, unfortunately, the two businesses have to be together; because you can't just make the hardware and run somebody else's software. So say four years from now there is a bank of new lasers which come along. We'll be able to get that out to the marketplace in three or four months, because we already have all the software we need to take that innovation and just plug it into our piece. We're building all our software so that it's extremely well architected. Now the guy who comes up with the new laser wants to get into the business; he's got to innovate and come up with all that software. So when you look at Corvis, Ciena and others like them, every time they come up with a new product they redo all the software; they don't see that software as a key asset.

So in a way the software becomes sort of a proprietary channel to the customer.

That's right, it's the software that actually touches the carrier customer because that's how they manage the product. The network management, the operating center, the customer interface, all the training, all of that is software. What sits behind it is the light part of it, which gets better, faster and cheaper as time goes by. But everything else will remain the same. It's like the Excel spreadsheet which after 286 will work on a Pentium 500, a 1000, or whatever. So that's the strategy.

In the optical switching industry, vendors are moving towards providing total bundle solutions and customers, of course, expect the total solution. In that process companies either create or assemble that bundle by developing the technology in-house, by buying it or by creating an alliance. The question is, what strategy do you use and why?

Well, it's a question of whether you want to own that market or not. If you want to own the market, then acquisition is the only way. For example, creating the pipes or filling the pipes. Creating the pipes is a business. Filling the pipes is an alliance. The more people fill the pipes, the better it is for us. But we need to own all the technology that's needed to create the pipes.

With Cascade and Sycamore, the underlying technologies have changed quite a lot; however, your knowledge of that market domain and your customers are the same telcos. Was this your strategy?

Right, I'm fortunate that I am in a field which has these sort of big waves, waves that have lasted for a very long time, so you can keep the marketplace and the customers the same and not get caught up in that wave. You have to be able to stand back from it and be able to take an objective view so that you can catch those waves and not defend a wave too much.

70% of all Internet traffic was on Cascade switches. How were you able to gain such a big market share? Did you apply the same strategy at Sycamore?

Well, you know it's being very focused on a particular market segment and being the best at it. With many of these markets there's a lot of hype; it attracts a lot of people and then along comes another hype and people just go away and move on to the Next Big Thing. They don't have the attention span required to stay back and compete and build the business. These are things that we are very good at because we believe in this business. The key point here is that there is a big difference between just developing the technology and building a business. At Sycamore we not only have to create a technology but we have to figure out a way to put our technology onto the network and get our carrier customers to create a business. So it's not only about technology. What we really do is work with our customers to help them define our services and create a range of services that they can sell. In fact, we help them market it, because we have to create that pull. That's what we did at Cascade and that's what we do here at Sycamore.

Again from the strategy angle, is it essential for a business model to keep morphing? Looking at Sycamore, has the business model in any significant way evolved or morphed in its two year history?

Not really morphed. I think the overall goal of creating a connected world is a sustainable mission. I find that about every 6 months we have to come up with a new initiative. That part of it I think we have to continuously reinvent. It's amazing how little companies can set the tone for the whole market place. We introduced Intelligent Optical networking in December, 1998. Obviously we're a young company with zero revenue, but it's amazing that within 2 years everyone is in Intelligent Optical networking now. Obviously we had to move on from there, we had to move on to the next space. So every 6 months we try to come up with a new initiative which drives the market place, the employees, and the products. We try to offer a new opportunity to the customers, offer more services and so on. We're constantly building our overall mission.

When you say "every 6 months", what triggers the recognition that you have to move on to a new initiative, or is it just periodic?

I think it's partially periodic, but that's not carved in stone. When you reach the point where you've done what you set out to do and want to move on to something else, you must have built up enough new, fresh ideas to make that move possible. That seems to happen naturally about every six months, but it's not a hard and fast rule. I really like building companies where people's skills are very broad; I came from a very technical background but I'm also good at marketing and sales, manufacturing, and finance. At the end of the day they all involve common sense. The broader you are the easier it is to iterate a lot the strategies in your mind. I believe that the only way to create a strong company is by having the thinking of everybody in the company become broader and broader. That's what I find exciting about building this institution. If you work at Sycamore it will not be with the scenario that Desh will think of all the strategies and everybody will go along with it. At Sycamore, everybody in the company is thinking and planning. It's almost like you can't tell who came up with the idea; it just rises up and sort of ripples across the company. If it's good, it sticks; if it's not, it dies. I believe that having everybody in the company think about these issues is what makes the company so vibrant.

That's interesting. Would we be right in understanding that if more people in the company are multi-disciplinary, and thus of a higher bandwidth, then there would be, on a cumulative basis, a far greater iteration of strategic ideas than with people who have narrower specialties?

Right. Number one, it gets you a lot more ideas and number two, it protects you from stupid ideas. That is because people are outspoken; they won't say, "That's not my area, maybe I shouldn't be talking about it." That's a part of the culture that I find exciting. It keeps the energy and excitement going; everyone has to do new things every year. This is what we refer to as broadening people's skills. Instead of having huge marketing departments and engineering departments and software and hardware operating independently, I think it works better to put together smaller groups of people who have both the authority and the responsibility to go out and win market share.

What is Sycamore's organizational design strategy?

We have small groups that work together. Within the group you have hardware, software, manufacturing, and marketing, so they interact with each other. This is opposed to having five hundred people in software in one department and five hundred people in hardware in another department. We take ten software, five hardware, two manufacturing and three marketing people and put them together. Then we tell them to go out and win the market.

What kind of people do you seek when hiring at Sycamore?

> *In business you have to solve the most relevant problem in the simplest way.*

As in every broad company, there are people at Sycamore who have absolutely no academic degrees, yet are our key architects. There are no hang-ups about degrees. It's just the capability that matters. A nice thing about a high-growth involvement like this is that there is so much work to be done that anyone with the ability to assume leadership, take charge and get things done is very welcome. When they walk in, people are very happy to have them around because there's just so much to do. In a high-growth environment you don't have those territorial battles that go on in other companies. There is no hang up on degrees; people don't need to have a Ph.D from M.I.T. or anything like that, because there are a lot of bright people with no degrees at all. In fact, a lot of the Ph.Ds are disqualified from startups. I'm a Ph.D myself. What a Ph.D allows you to do is be a good researcher. You have to find the most obscure problem, one that nobody else in the world before has ever solved, because that's how you get your credit. In business you have to solve the most relevant problem in the simplest way. So relevance becomes the most important piece. Now if you can keep your eye on relevance as well as be able to deal effectively with both with complexity and simplicity, then you can really win big time. That's the great thing about Sycamore; we have Ph.Ds and a lot of very high-powered thinkers, but they haven't lost their common sense approach to problems.

An argument is made in today's Internet world that companies need to be born global. Do you agree?

Yes! You have to be born global these days for two reasons: first, because the markets are global and second, because the talent is global. I think a good, strong company has to be a global network of like-minded people. That's part of the reason I started Tejas in Bangalore and am hoping we can do this in every part of the world. You don't need big buildings and all that anymore; you just need good people. Somehow, with high tech it doesn't matter where people live -Finland or Sweden or India; they all seem to talk the same language and it's pretty easy to get them all synchronized.

In terms of access to customers, has it been just as easy for Sycamore outside the U.S. as in the U.S.?

So far it has been, even though it takes time to build the infrastructure. You have the big account and you have to build that network somewhere, but if you look at our customers we probably have more international customers than domestic. Also the markets are getting very aggressive. Previously you developed a technology in the U.S. and then you debugged it and five years later you took it global. The global market resisted that technology in every possible way. They had their own strategy and they thought that they had their own unique, proprietary way of building the national network. But today everyone wants to part of the global economy, so they need the same technology. The barriers have come down and almost all countries invite us into their markets. This has made it a lot easier to adopt a global strategy up-front.

What skills do you see as necessary for success in a global economy?

You need the ability to adapt and learn, and you must have the initiative to go out and look for things. The curiosity factor is important, because things are moving so fast we can no longer just learn a thing and then use it for the rest of our lives.

Continuing on the strategy front, there are two areas where you are pushing the envelope simultaneously: the concept of concurrent product and market development. Can you elaborate on this?

You know, with markets developing so fast and the technologies developing so fast, you need a very rapid feedback loop. Market changes, technology changes, so things that were once impossible become possible and the way people use technology changes rapidly. You have to keep a very tight, constant loop between market and product development. And when you have a short development cycle it gives you a better chance to crack that market.

You started Cascade in 1990 and Sycamore in 1998. What's the difference in starting up a company now?

I think the environment is a lot different, but more than that, I am very different. When I started Sycamore I obviously started with a lot more confidence, a bigger idea, and more ambition. Now I don't have to go through a lot of the messy things that were necessary in the earlier days. Cash was so scarce that I had to optimize every little thing - which chair to buy, which table to buy, all that kind of stuff. Nowadays I don't have to. The opportunities are so big that I can stay focused on the opportunity and can afford to move a lot faster. That's because 1) I've have a lot of experience and I don't waste a lot of time on silly things, and 2) there's a lot more money available.

So "time to market" has become more critical now as opposed to technology?

"Time to market "is always critical but you can afford to spend money on it a lot more now. In 1990, if you got a few million dollars it was a lot of money. You had to be very careful about how you spent that money so that you could go to the next checkpoint to get more money. But now money is so easy it doesn't matter whether you spend one or three million to get to the check point.

Sycamore had one of the hottest IPOs, with a huge market valuation. Has Sycamore's soaring valuation set unreasonable expectations? What kind of Wall Street pressure do you face in such a market?

I really don't feel extra pressures as a public company. The fact is that we are trying to build Sycamore for the long term. Obviously it's a very competitive market and we have to fight every day to get our share. At the same time, everything is being done in the context of building something for the long term.

Now let's switch gears to teamwork. It's well known that Daniel Smith (Sycamore Co-founder) and you are a hit team. What makes it work?

I think it's the fact that both of us believe in similar things. We were drawn back into the entrepreneurial arena because we thrive on the challenge of outrunning big competitors. After I had laid out the Sycamore plans I reminded Smith how hard it would be to take on the entrenched incumbents and win. That was the hook and I knew I had him.

> *Basic trust is the most important ingredient for teamwork.*

I don't think its true that it's a techy-business kind of thing. I think that he knows as much technology as I do and I probably know as much business as he does. We learn a lot from each other. I think he's a very honest, very ethical guy. There's a lot of trust. You don't constantly have to watch each others' backs in terms of what the other guy is trying to do to you. Basic trust is the most important ingredient for teamwork. And since we work well together, that spreads throughout the company.

Disruptive technologies create waves of opportunities and these waves increase in magnitude and frequency. How does one spot these opportunities?

You need two things. In some ways you have to disassociate yourself, because you need some out-of-the-box thinking, but at the same time you have to soak yourself into the market to really get a feel for it. What makes a lot of these opportunities possible is that they penetrate deep into the society. Now in the bandwidth market you can change things if you make something ten times cheaper or ten times better or if you make the business cycle ten times faster. Typically you need that "10X" factor of improvement. If you have one dimension it's pretty good, but if you have all 3 dimensions you can build a huge company. So you look deep for the big opportunities.

Continuing on that train of thought, it has been said that the next 25 years will see the rise of the network economy. How do you see it changing our lives?

Number one, it allows people to create value from wherever they are and the reward for the value creation is independent of where you live. For example, within the globalization context, people who do work in India and create the same value as the people in U.S. will start getting paid the same amount. So value creation can happen anywhere in the world. You can tap into a huge global resource.

Another thing is that news travels very fast. Good news travels fast and bad news travels fast. Good news is created by excellence and so excellence will get unfairly rewarded. If something is good then the whole world will know about it and they'll all jump on the bandwagon. If someone screws up, he will get unfairly punished. Mediocrity will get punished. If you look at it from the macro sense it's good for the economy, because only good, efficient organizations will survive and mediocre organizations will get killed.

Won't there be a void?

Well, there's bound to be a lot of dislocation till the process stabilizes. So from a macro sense it's great, because productivity goes up, a lot of wealth is created, and inflation is kept low because of increased productivity. So you've got more money, no inflation and lots of growth. But the bad thing is that it creates a big digital divide. People who can keep up with all this stuff will do extremely well, but people who can't keep up will be left behind. That's the problem that the economy will create in the years to come and people need to be aware of the digital divide and find ways to deal with it.

How do we do this? Do you see a solution in the near term?

I think I do. Number one, there is a lot of wealth created with this new economy. Number two, the technology itself that helps create that wealth can be used as a tool to bridge the divide. Call it education, motivating people or bringing them up to speed. The traditional educational system is just too slow, with the framework of classrooms and teachers and all that stuff. But hopefully this new technology will become pervasive enough and good enough that we can use it as a tool to solve all these problems. So I think the new wealth and the improvements in the technology must be put to good use.

We are quoting you here: "The Stars have lined up; there's never been a better time, so make the most of it." Focusing on India, because a lot of Indians are dreaming of this opportunity, what's your advice to them? How should they make the most of it?

Well, number one, they must realize that it's a global economy. The benchmark that they should set for themselves is the global standard. It is not enough to be good in Delhi or Bangalore or Bombay; you've got to be good globally or you will get wiped out. I think setting benchmarks that are global is very important. And then having a conviction and a dream that is large and ambitious can build sustainable businesses. If you have a small idea, maybe it will be bought by somebody, but that doesn't create an industry. So Indians have to learn to think big, think global and build sustainable companies. In the process there may be a lot of failures. The higher you try to jump, the more you shoot for, the more the chances are for you to fail. That shouldn't be looked upon negatively, as India often does. Culturally, people in India are not used to dealing with failure. That's the biggest lesson that Indian businessmen have to learn from the Silicon Valley.

Is this because here in Silicon Valley, if we have a failure we learn from it, and before you know it we are back on our feet?

Not only that, the venture guys will fund you even more if you've failed once and have learned the lessons! Of course it's a question of why you failed. If you failed because you never really worked, then obviously you deserve to be punished, but if you failed because you took the wrong gamble, then that's OK. I think overcoming the fear of failure is probably the biggest thing that India needs to learn in order to really venture into this new world.

Now we are going to switch to the personal side. Why did you move from Canada to the U.S.A.?

In Canada I worked with Motorola, but it was like a startup. We started with twenty people in a garage shop. And after four plus years, we grew to about four or five hundred people. So it was like a startup, and when I got a taste of the startups in '84 I decided I wanted to do a startup of my own. Unfortunately you couldn't do that in Canada because there were no venture capitalists then. That's why I moved to Boston. It took me about 3 years to get my green card and I used those 3 years to familiarize myself with sales, marketing, manufacturing - all those different things. So when finally I got the green card I decided to do a startup. I teamed up with another gentleman and then left my job. That was like jumping off a cliff! It was a risk, but a calculated risk. We had saved enough to keep going for 18 months. Startups were something we really wanted to do.

Going down memory lane back to Coral, you have said: "It was the toughest decision I ever made (leaving Coral) and it was the toughest lesson I ever learned." Can you elaborate?

My partner and I worked together for six to nine months on Coral before we were able to get the seed money from the venture capitalist. We closed a four million dollar round with very prestigious venture guys. So that was a dream come true, right? What else do you want? But unfortunately, within 4 months my partner and I had a difference of opinion about how we should build this product. I believed very much in "time to market" and we were trying to build a product that was in competition with Cisco. It was going to be 10 times better than Cisco. But as we started getting into implementation, it turned out that building a product five times better was a piece of cake, eight times better was kind of hard and ten times better was very hard. But my partner said, "Desh, give me two more weeks and we can crack this problem." Two weeks went by and we were at the same place. Another two weeks went by - same place. So we disagreed on how we should move forward. I felt the best thing would be to just let him run the company and that I would leave. That was a very tough decision.

The lesson learned was that when you go through failure, suddenly your comfort zone and tolerance get a lot bigger. Your threshold for pain is a lot higher and you realize that it really isn't as bad as people make it out to be. I think that was the biggest lesson. One becomes significantly wiser and tougher as a result.

Is it true you left the company (Coral) with $26? What's the story here?

What happened was that I left Coral in May, 1990 and started Cascade in October, 1990. The other person just kept going on the same track. Two years later Coral got sold to Synoptics for 15 million dollars. That's when I got my share of the check - 26 dollars! In fact I had to take a capital gains loss because I had put in $300 to get my share and I got a check for $26.95.

Do you still have it lying around somewhere? Is it framed, as we have heard?

Yup! Absolutely. Every time I get cocky about Sycamore or anything else, my wife always points to the picture and says, "You're the same guy who did this!" That keeps everything in perspective.

How do you maintain your balance while juggling several balls in the air? Work, family - how do you do it?

I think you have to believe in your priorities. For instance, if I get a call from my son saying, "Dad, I need you to come to school", I just do it. It's very clear in my mind that that's priority number one. It's demanding and it takes time but it's important for the family to know that they are priority number one. The fact that they know that allows me to actually spend time at home without having to be home every day. I think these priorities have to be very clear in your mind.

What's a typical day for you?

I get up at 5.45 a.m. and I usually leave home at 6:45. I get to work around 7:30. I work until 7.00 or 8.00 before returning home and spending time with the family. If I'm traveling, I'm gone from Monday through Friday. I usually spend the weekends at home. We have 2 boys, 14 and 16.

Tremendous pressures must be associated with entrepreneurship. What are some of the sacrifices you have made?

I personally don't see them as sacrifices. I mean, it's a game that you like playing and you just play it, even in the hard times. It's funny, other people look at it and say, "How could you sacrifice so many things?" But if that's what you like doing then that's what you like doing, right? So I don't really think of it as a sacrifice. In fact people who feel it is a sacrifice shouldn't be doing it. It's got to be a game that you really enjoy.

What are some of your hobbies?

Mostly I spend a lot of time with the kids. They're at an age where we do a lot of things together. I don't do skydiving anymore. I just did that a couple of times a long time ago. I play tennis and chess.

Who do you look up to?

Lots of different people in different areas. For values, I look up to my parents. They are in their 70s but are still pretty active and involved. My wife has a tremendous value system. A lot of the people at work, even though they come from different cultural backgrounds, share a similar value system. I mean you can read the Gita and you read about karma yoga, but you actually see people practicing it here. To me, that's pretty impressive.

What makes you tick? What drives you?

I just like creating new things, coming up with big ideas, ideas that are bigger than what I thought was possible and bringing them to fruition.

If you look at the 80/20 rule, what's been the one key to your success?

I think just hope and optimism. Things don't get me down. Lots of things go wrong but somehow I seem to have a very optimistic attitude toward life. I can see the bigger picture. It might be a little naïve but that can be an advantage.

Looking back, do you see any mistakes and say, "Oops! I missed that one."?

Not really. Life is a journey. It doesn't matter what path you take as long as you're having fun along the way. So one of the things I have done well is that if I stop having fun with something I just change, like quitting Coral. If I take a wrong path and things just aren't working out, then I can find excitement in changing course and taking off on another branch. I'm pretty happy with the way things have turned out. I think of it as a game that you play, and whether you win or lose doesn't really matter.

Of all the things that you've done in life, what do you pat yourself on the back for most?

I think it's the relationships that I have. Sometimes people build businesses but they build them at the cost of a lot of other things. Fortunately for me, I haven't run the business at the expense of all these relationships. I enjoy my colleagues, my family and my friends. To me this is very satisfying and I draw a lot of energy from it. I come to work and I see a lot of smiling faces and that's very energizing.

You've said: "If you get lucky, don't forget others; remember your roots." How has this applied to you?

It sort of goes back to the digital divide. I think you've got to figure out a way to help the guys who can't make it on their own.

In what way are you sharing your success with society?

> *I think education is the key to unlocking the potential in every human being.*

The educational institutions in the U.S. are very, very strong because of the connection with their alumni. I'm hoping the institutions in India can start doing that because a lot of them have very successful alumni. My wife and I, in our own humble way, have started a program with I.I.T Madras and it seems to be coming along. We've indicated that we will give them five million dollars a year for twenty years. We hope to build that into an initiative where the institution starts connecting back with the alumni and alumni can become intellectually and emotionally attached to the institution. That would be good for both the alumni and the institution. If that concept works, I'm hoping we can extend it to lots of our institutions. I think it is a very powerful way to build self-sustaining private institutions, as happens in the United States. I think education is the key to unlocking the potential in every human being.

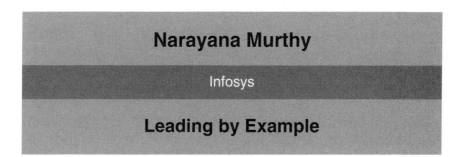

Narayana Murthy

Infosys

Leading by Example

Narayana Murthy founded Infosys in 1981, along with six other software professionals. Today Infosys is acknowledged by customers, employees, investors and the general public as a highly respected, dynamic and innovative company. In March 1999, Infosys Technologies became the first India-registered company to be listed on an American stock exchange (NASDAQ: INFY).

Mr. Murthy has received several honors and awards. He was listed as one of the Top Entrepreneurs of the Year by *Business Week* and was *Business India*'s Businessman of the Year, the Indian corporate world's most coveted award. He is a member of the Asia Society's international council and the board of councilors at the University of Southern California School of Engineering. He is also on the Wharton Business School's Asian executive board.

Mr. Murthy obtained his bachelor of electrical engineering from the University of Mysore and his master of technology from Indian Institute of Technology, Kanpur.

Mr. Murthy, Raghu Batta and I talked in January, 2001. Even though the interview was conducted via conference call, with Murthy several thousand miles away, he held our attention at all times. Mr. Murthy has a soft voice that is filled with authority. We enjoyed the conversation immensely.

In this interview, Narayana Murthy categorizes the evolution of Infosys over the past twenty years. He explains how he was able to develop an organization in India with a global mindset and culture necessary to compete in the new economy. He sheds light on Infosys' competitive strategy to strengthen its position as a leader in the service software domain. He discusses his leadership style and the various challenges he has faced along the Infosys journey. Toward the end he makes an interesting comparison between the Silicon Valley and Bangalore (the Silicon Valley of India) and provides key pieces of advice to budding entrepreneurs in India.

"Our fundamental philosophy is to synergize the organizational objectives and individual aspirations."

Looking back over the last 20 years, how do you categorize the different stages in the evolution of Infosys?

Stage one was what you might call the pre-liberalization or pre-economic reform stage, between 1981 and 1992. Government played a very critical role in the growth of the company. The speed of decision-making in the government was very slow. We had to go to Delhi for every minor approval and almost no decisions could be taken in the boardroom. It was during this period that the country was more or less closed to outside investments in technology and industry. For example, it could take us between 6 and 24 months to import a piece of new technology. Traveling outside India was also very difficult because we had to get approval from the Reserve Bank of India. Opening of offices outside India was very difficult. Equity was not a viable financing option because we had an officer called Controller of Capital Issues who had to approve the premium at which you could have your IPO. He always looked at the past data and gave a very low premium. As a result, you had to give away a lot of equity to raise a little bit of money. In addition, a number of high tech multinationals did not operate in India because they were not allowed to own 100% of equity. As a result, IBM walked out of India in 1977 and most of these multinational companies operated through their agents in India.

Stage two was when the government of India decided to liberalize economic reform. Once these reforms kicked in the speed of decision-making was increased. When compared to the 6 to 24 months it would take to import, say, a Sun Sparc station, today we don't need to go the government for approvals at all. In addition, with capital account convertibility, we don't need approval from the Reserve Bank for travel or for opening offices, hiring consultants, for example. The government also abolished control of capital issues, thereby allowing the company and its investment bankers or lead managers to decide on the premium for the IPO. This made equity a viable financing option. Then of course, by allowing 100% equity to be held by high tech multinationals, we saw the entry and return of several multinationals such as IBM. Companies like Microsoft and Oracle, almost every high tech, started operating in India.

Stage three really started when companies like Infosys realized their need to become global companies. I define "globalization" as producing where it is most cost effective to produce, selling where it is most profitable, and sourcing capital where it is cheapest, without worrying about national boundaries.

Now we realized that, as a corporation which truly embraced this concept of globalization, our customers were primarily in the first world. Since all our developments take place in India, we knew we had to go a step further. We had to get ourselves listed on a stock exchange outside India, preferably in the United States. That's how stage three got started, when we got listed on NASDAQ in March 1999. That allowed us multiple opportunities to enhance the awareness of the corporation and to enhance the corporate brand equity among prospective customers and prospective employees. It gave us a much wider investor base and created a hard currency-based stock option plan for employees outside India. Finally, it allowed us to perhaps use ADRs as an acquisitions currency.

Stage four is really one of becoming much more multi-cultural. In other words we have to have local people selling Infosys in each marketplace. We have to have a much higher percentage of local people in front-ending our efforts in terms of delivery of the software. We have to reach the level of corporate brand equity that Infosys has today in India in all the major markets we serve. We have to go toward much higher end-to-end solutions in terms of dollars and in terms of person-years.

India tends to be a "seller-focused" market, whereas in the U.S. the customer is King. Is Infosys developing a global mindset to cater to the global customer?

In fact, we are developing a global mindset. We compare ourselves in everything to the best in the world. We do not say that we are happy being the best only in India. Infosys has been voted the most admired company in India among 7,500 listed companies in several surveys published in Business Today magazine. We look at well-known companies like General Electric, Microsoft, Hewlett Packard, Sun Microsystems, and Sony to benchmark ourselves in various dimensions of operation - whether it's in the area of finance, disclosure, corporate governance, attraction and retention of employees, stock options, quality, or acceptance of new technology- in the area of growth. In every respect we benchmark ourselves with the best in the world.

Having experienced phenomenal growth over the last 10 years, what was the key strategy for Infosys to be able to scale?

When IBM came to India in 1992 a lot of people told me, "Look, the game is over for you guys because all these multinationals are coming and all your employees will desert you." There were three ways to react. One was to say that this was is our Karma; we had run the marathon but now we'd have to give it up. The second was to say that we'd go to the government and tell them to keep these multi-nationals out. I obviously didn't like this because I was the president of Nasscom between 1992 and 1994. I felt it was unconscionable for me to do such a thing. The third way was to say, "Let's find out what these multinational companies do to attract and retain people and see if we can emulate them." "Chance favors a prepared mind" is an apt saying. Around that time, all the liberalization effects were coming to fruition. We said we would give competitive compensation to our employees, we would create a work place much more attractive than any multinational could do, we would create stock options which, along with the normal salary, would be much higher than any multinational could provide, and we would have technology as good or better than any competitor could provide.

So I think the primary reason for our growth is that we opened up our minds and said we would learn from people who were better than us and we would compete with them on those terms. I think the ability to accept competition, to learn from competition and play the game with a positive mindset is really the strategy that has worked.

When did you first begin granting options to employees?

We have been giving shares since 1983, but I think we began on a major scale in 1994.

What are the core competencies of Infosys?

We have three major core competencies. First is our people's ability to learn a new paradigm of technology or business quickly, assimilate it and bring value to the customer. Next come processes. We must create processes for every new paradigm that we start, any new technology-based development, or new offshore software development; for example in the e-commerce paradigm, compression of cycle time. Third is the ability to embrace new technology, to deploy it and provide benefit in terms of the quality and productivity of our people.

We believe that as long as technology changes, as long as customer relationships change, as long as market preference and business models change, there is opportunity for Infosys. The only constant is change, which we welcome, because as things keep changing we have the opportunity to develop software. Even in the paradigm of packages, professor Michael Porter says, "Strategy is about becoming unique in a market place." If that is strategy, then every corporation has to create unique business tools, unique business models, and those will have to be reflected in the information systems. This means that even above a standard package you will have to create a layer of customization. So our business will always be there as long as technology changes, as long as market preferences change and business models change.

As a people-intensive organization, what is Infosys' organizational strategy?

In our line of business, the main assets are our people. If our assets walk out physically tired, it is our responsibility as leaders to make sure that they walk back in the next morning mentally and physically enthusiastic and energetic. They must look forward to spending 8 to 12 hours of productive time when they come to work in the morning. To do that, we have to understand what drives different individuals. Some people may want recognition; others may want to learn new things, make more money, or have flexible hours. I define "empowerment" as synergizing the organizational objectives and individual aspirations.

> *I define "empowerment" as synergizing the organizational objectives and individual aspirations.*

There is no doubt that Infosys has to grow at a certain rate. Once that is done we can look at how we can make the life of each individual in the company better and better. As long as people meet their responsibilities to their customer they are free. Our fundamental philosophy is to synergize the organizational objectives and individual aspirations.

Is your culture consensus- driven or is it driven from the top?

We are a consensus-driven organization. If you want to be a high-energy, high-aspiration organization you must come to a certain consensus. Having said that, let me also say that it is the leader's job to create high aspirations, because leaders raise the aspirations of people and aspirations build civilizations. So while consensus is extremely important, it is the job of the leaders to make sure that there are high aspirations and that there is consensus towards those aspirations. We have a group called the Management Council, consisting of about 45 people, over 50% of whom are less than 35 yrs old. The idea is that all these people can sit together, discuss and debate and then reach a consensus.

Over the last 10 years, Infosys has become a global Goliath. Several startups in India are sprouting up on a daily basis and trying to copy your busi-

ness model. What is your competitive strategy: Goliath versus David and Goliath versus Goliath?

I keep telling my colleagues that there are only four attributes of a corporation that will result in sustained success. These are speed, imagination, excellence in execution and a system that measures and enhances the rate of improvement. This is all. As long as our company embraces these four attributes we will continue to be successful. The day we stop embracing them, the day we take our eyes off these attributes, we will disappear like dew on a sunny morning. It doesn't matter that there are Davids and Goliaths as long as we do not take our eyes off these four parameters. I also believe that these four attributes will have to be demonstrated in every functional group in the company, whether it's finance, human resources development, software development, quality management, information systems, sales and marketing, planning, or facilities. In every department, in every function, people will have to show speed, they'll have to show imagination, they'll have to show excellence in execution. I believe that excellence is organic. We can't just say that we'll show excellence only in software development and in the rest of them we won't. That's why Infosys was the first company in India to articulate the concept of offshore software development and the 24-hour workday. Infosys was the first Indian company to provide quarterly audited balance sheets and income statements. Infosys is the first Indian company to incorporate a large-scale stock option plan. It was the first to create a large campus. It was perhaps the first company in the world to recost its balance sheet and income statement according to the generally accepted accounting principles of 8 countries: India, the U.S., Canada, the U.K., France, Germany, Japan and Australia. Look at our campuses anywhere in India and you will find that they are truly world class in every dimension.

Wouldn't this be your thinking as the leader bringing it to the organization?

No, I wouldn't say that. We are a group of people here. In the management council there are about 45 people and every one of them is committed to all the attributes I talked about. Certainly, as I said, it is the job of the leaders to raise the aspirations of the others. I don't think there is one single person in the company who can solely be credited with what we have achieved.

A few of your major customers- Nortel, Cisco and Lucent, have established offshore development centers, or ODCs, in Bangalore. Going forward, how are you going to retain these clients?

As long as companies like Cisco and Nortel recognize that we offer much better value for money, they will definitely continue to work with companies like Infosys. A company will continue to produce things in-house until the transaction costs are less than the market. The moment the external market becomes cheaper than conducting the same transaction inside the company, it will outsource it. But I think the trick of the trade is to make sure that these extraordinary customers of ours continue to find value in dealing with Infosys. If we do that, we will retain them. There is no insurance in this game, no guarantee. The only guarantee is the fact that you are willing to work harder and smarter.

In the evolution of a company you have different conflicts, particularly people's conflicts. How do you deal with these conflicts, having a team-oriented approach?

First, as far as possible we try to be transaction-oriented. This means that every new transaction is started on a zero base; that is we don't carry the biases from the previous transaction over to a new one. Second, we have collected a team of very smart, high aspiration individuals who know the transactions that they are going to win and lose. They have a very high level of self-confidence and are able to accept the loss of a certain transaction. Third, they know they are all working toward a common purpose. We truly believe that if we put the interest of the community ahead of our own personal interest we will be better in the end. Finally, we believe in confronting all thorny issues head-on. We don't believe in hiding issues under the carpet. We are open; we close the door, talk to each other one-on-one and then say, "Look friend, I think this particular thing was not right. This is my understanding, so let's sit down and discuss it so that in the next transaction we don't have any of these issues." Most of my colleagues and I believe in resolving issues whenever there is a difference of opinion. Of course, it should be done in a manner where nobody gets hurt.

Will Infosys continue to grow organically, or are you planning to diversify into other high-growth areas through acquisitions?

As far as acquisitions are concerned, we have looked at several opportunities. We have an acquisitions and investments group that is responsible for such activities. To date we have not come across a company that we would like to acquire. Remember, the companies we are looking at are all people-oriented companies. This is not the same as acquiring a technology with a small group of people and then bringing your strength of management into leveraging that technology. That is a game which Cisco has played tremendously well, but we are in a business where we have to bring together two masses of people of different cultures, aspirations, expertise, and hopes. This is not easy. We have been rather slow in looking at that on the issue of acquisitions. With respect to investments in other companies, we have made a few strategic investments. For example, we have invested in companies developing leading edge technologies whereby we can learn from these companies by being partners in software development, and where we think the technologies will offer considerable commercial opportunities.

If you look worldwide, Indians have very good credibility and are seen as having real brainpower. Is it really possible for India to create products and markets?

There have been several studies which have looked at why the U.S. is perhaps the premium place in terms of productivity, particularly in software. There are multiple reasons why Route 128 and Silicon Valley have had porous kinds of relationships, inter-company kinds of things. There is the confidence of the industry and academia, plus the high mobility of the workforce and the extraordinary competitiveness of the market place. There is the premium on innovation, and of course the venture capital availability. These are some of the things that have led to Silicon Valley and Route 128 being what they are. In India too, when we create an environment similar to that, I have no doubt that Indians will produce products which will be world-class. But, given the fact that the market place is not as competitive as we'd like and the environment is still not as conducive to innovation as we'd like, I imagine it will take a few years.

Other than environment, what major differences between Bangalore and Silicon Valley stand out for you?

Bangalore and Silicon Valley have commonalities in the sense that there are a lot of young entrepreneurs in both places who want to succeed. These young people are energetic, ambitious, and highly educated. The first difference is that cooperation between academia and industry is not as good in Bangalore as it is in Silicon Valley. Second, and more important, the porous culture that is pervasive in the Silicon Valley, whereby learning is transferred from company to company rather rapidly, is relatively non-existent in Bangalore. I think the competition, that is the collaborative and the competitive mindset, is not as strong in Bangalore as in Silicon Valley. These are the two major differences. Of course in Silicon Valley all the infrastructures such as legal, financial and HR that are essential for entrepreneurs, are much better developed in Silicon Valley than in Bangalore.

If I were a VC and came to India with $100 million, what would my strategy be?

Although we have seen a number of successful companies here in India, I would say there's really no place in the world like the U.S. with its success rate, particularly in Silicon Valley and Route 128. While venture capital is available in India today, the environment is still not as competitive, the premium on innovation is still not as high as we would like. I think it will take another 3 to 5 years for Indian companies to produce several world-class products and for this phenomenon to catch on.

What is your advice to the new entrepreneurs today? What should their first few steps be?

First, you must have a very good idea which has a very clear value proposition and can be articulated in a few sentences. For example, the product or service offered must either reduce cost, improve productivity or reduce cycle time.

Second, you need a market which is ready for such an offering. Unless you are introducing something which creates discontinuities in the market place, like Netscape's browser or the Palm Pilot, the market should be ready to adopt your product.

Third, you need to put together a team, a group of people who have a mutually exclusive but collectively inexhaustible set of skills and experience. And the team must have a common vision, a common goal, a common mission and a common value system. Finally, you need finance.

In Silicon Valley we had HP as the beacon of light for aspiring entrepreneurs back in the 1960s and 70s. Infosys is in a similar situation today in India. What role are you playing?

People who have started their own companies are our ambassadors to the outside world. We have been a very open company in terms of sharing ideas and information with the outside world and even with our competitors. We believe that in the end, the only way we can keep the innovative spirit of our people is by driving innovation ourselves rather than having our competitors doing it. That's one. Two, we truly believe that the only way India can solve the problem of poverty is to have hundreds and thousands of companies as good or better than Infosys. To that extent, I think we are very open in providing any help to any set of entrepreneurs.

What guidelines should a foreign company, a U.S. based company for example, adopt when conducting business with an Indian company?

Whenever I conduct a transaction with our vendors I use the following guidelines: 1) the vendor should provide the agreed quality product on the agreed date at the agreed price. 2) The customer- that's Infosys- should pay the agreed sum on the agreed date and, in arriving at the price, should make sure that the vendor has a decent margin so that he can become stronger and stronger and can provide better service. Finally, both parties have to make an effort to make all the transactions pleasant. I would say that while some companies only provide good value for money, no customer will benefit in the long term by reducing the whole game to one of a commodity game. I think companies have to look at the basic strength of the company in terms of its people, its commitment to processes, its commitment to technology, its investment, its infrastructure and then arrive at a value-for-money model rather than just going for the cheapest player.

If you look at the current college enrollment trends in India, most students are pursuing computer science. If this trend continues for another 10 or 15 years we may not have people with strong expertise in fundamental disciplines; for example, mathematics, physics, mechanical engineering, and chemical engineering.

I agree with you. I share the same concern. The solution is not to prevent people from studying whatever they want; I firmly believe in freedom of choice for the individual. My solution would be to increase the intake at I.I.Ts; let's enhance the intake at the Indian Institute of Science and other colleges, regional colleges, and science colleges. We are a country of a billion people so let's triple our intake at all these places. Let's produce more mathematicians, more chemists, more physicists, more electrical engineers and more civil engineers so that we will have good people for basic sciences, for building power plants and bridges as well as becoming good IT professionals.

You're a man of very strong principles and ideals. In all our research leading up to this interview, that comes across loud and clear. What does it take to be such a person?

I think it's important that all these things become second nature. You should not even feel that you are making an effort to be what you want to be. It should be effortless. Once you do that, I think it's very simple.

You said that your role models are Gandhi and Lee Quan of Singapore. Why?

> *I have always admired both Mahatma Gandhi and Lee Quan Yew. Both of them shared one very fundamental common characteristic; both led by example.*

I have always admired both Mahatma Gandhi and Lee Quan Yew. Both of them shared one very fundamental common characteristic; both led by example. They walked their talk. Whatever they said they would do, they did. Mahatma Gandhi, as we all know, led the freedom movement in India by using nonviolence. Lee Quan Yew was instrumental in leading Singapore from what was a Third World country to a First World country. I think this is an important lesson for all of us in the Third World. Both also showed that if you subordinate your personal interest in favor of community interest, in favor of the country's interest, that you will be better off in the end. To me these are very important lessons.

What role have your parents and family played in your success?

Certainly, our basic mindset is molded primarily by our parents, brothers and sisters and the immediate family as well as by our teachers. To that extent, I think my father has taught me a lot of good things such as the importance of hard work, keeping commitments, being determined. My mother has taught me to honor values such as honesty, integrity and kindness. My teachers have taught me the importance of teamwork, striving for excellence and following one's dream.

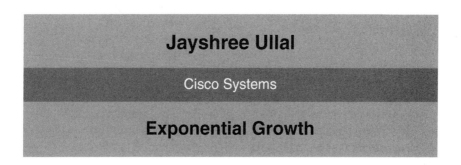

Jayshree Ullal

Cisco Systems

Exponential Growth

Jayshree Ullal is vice president and general manager of the Enterprise Line of Business at Cisco Systems. She joined Cisco in September, 1993 as vice president of marketing for the Enterprise Line of Business, following the acquisition of Crescendo Communications, Cisco's first acquisition. During her tenure at Cisco, under the leadership of Cisco's CEO John Chambers, she has grown the LAN switching business from zero to seven billion dollar run rate, reaching the number one market position. She has also successfully integrated many acquisitions for Cisco, including Kalpana, Grand Junction, Granite Systems, Class Data and Selsius.

Before joining Cisco she was the vice president of marketing at Crescendo Communications from 1991 to 1993. Prior to that she held management, engineering and strategy positions at Ungermann-Bass, Advanced Micro Devices and Fairchild Semiconductor.

She holds a B.S.E.E. from San Francisco State University and an M.S. in engineering management from Santa Clara University.

Dr. Anil Gupta and I met with Jayshree over a cup of coffee at Hobee's, a well-known health food eatery in the Bay Area popular with the Silicon Valley crowd. Jayshree comes across as a friendly, highly intelligent and energetic woman. She is an industry mover who combines a unique understanding of marketplace needs with a wide knowledge of up-and-coming technologies.

In our interview Jayshree talks about the challenges faced by Cisco during its first-ever acquisition. She defines the customer, market and competitive strategies she utilized to grow Cisco's Switch business to 5 billion dollars. She explains the importance of flexibility in product architecture required to meet ever-changing customer needs. Jayshree shares her organizational strategy for scaling the organization, retaining employees, and Cisco's star-tup culture even after its growth from a David to a Goliath. She comments on the attributes that make John Chambers, chief executive of one of the world's largest company, a visionary leader. Her passion and energy are brought to life through this candid discussion.

"Customer strategy is a thoughtful combination of technology strategy and customer requirements."

How did you begin your career?

After I received my bachelor's degree in electrical engineering from San Francisco State University, I joined Fairchild Semiconductor. I did process development and product development at Fairchild. From Fairchild I went to Advanced Micro Devices (AMD). This was a defining career move because at AMD I cut my teeth on various aspects of marketing and gained invaluable data communications knowledge. My job at AMD required me to identify new markets in the networking space. Once a quarter, I had an opportunity to present my ideas to AMD's management team. In doing so, the biggest thing I learned was to understand what the customers want today and to extrapolate that to what they will want in the future. Another thing I learned was the role that marketing plays in the success of a product. I also learned that you have to work continually to create and advance a market, because if you are not creating a market but just building a faster and cheaper product, it will be very short-lived.

How does one create that market?

There are three things required to create a market. First, you have to understand what the value is of the product you are offering. Second, you need to keep adding value to the product and finally you must differentiate your products from the rest of the herd. I strongly believe that the foundation for all of the above is good product architecture.

Would it be correct to say that product architecture becomes important because, although customers are not clamoring for it today, the architecture must be capable of supporting future requirements?

Absolutely. The product architecture must allow for flexibility and change. One of the things that most companies are guilty of is placing undue emphasis on cost alone. I do believe that cost is very important, but if you lock yourself into being the cheapest product, chances are that you have also locked yourself into an inflexible architecture that you cannot change later, when you need to add more features. I would rather build a more flexible architecture up front and then come back and attack the cost factor during the second or third iteration of the platform.

Similarly, from a software perspective, I would rather build a scalable architecture up front. This may lend itself to a few more bugs, but then we can come back in subsequent releases and add features and fix the code, rather than trying to build the perfect software scheme. When you are in a new market, it's more about "I think I have a general understanding of what is required and I think I know how the customer is going to use it."

So the key point is that you go after the product and market segment, not after a technology segment. Technology is the back end of it.

Yes. That is a very good way to put it. A technology seeking a home may succeed, but a technology which knows its home will almost always succeed.

When did you get the startup bug?

I had done enough startup-type projects in the big companies. I felt it was time to try a real startup. I joined Crescendo, a LAN switching startup, in early 1992.

How did the Cisco acquisition of Crescendo take place?

One of our board members, Terry Eger, was a former Cisco executive and helped make introductions. I also knew the CTO, Ed Kozel. During one of our friendly chats Ed was bemoaning the void Cisco had in LAN switching. We introduced the Crescendo switch prototype, thinking Cisco would be good partner.

> *A technology seeking a home may succeed, but a technology which knows its home will almost always succeed.*

In those days, you didn't build a fundamental startup in order to be bought. By then we had already taken the company from zero to thirteen million in revenue. We had signed up customers such as Microsoft, had partnerships with Novell, Sun and Nortel. We were well on our way to becoming a high profile public company. It wasn't clear or obvious to us that we should be acquired. But one of the things I realized was that while a startup can indeed develop a technology, it does not have the vast marketing and sales reach of a large company. Cisco already had revenue of 600 million, a 6 billion dollar market capitalization and a very successful sales organization. They had the channels and the access to large customers.

What was the acquisition like?

I couldn't have felt more comfortable with this team of Cisco executives, many of whom I had known for some time. However, there was a feeling of discomfort associated with giving up one's identity. Although we were financially better off, when you do startups you don't do it only for money, you do it out of a certain passion and exhilaration and the money is only one outcome. Giving up our identity and integrating was one of the most difficult things to overcome initially. We were Cisco's first acquisition and we were the guinea pigs. The smartest thing they did was to tell us to go and focus on the business and product objectives. This took about a year and during this period they integrated all other functions such as sales and manufacturing groups of Crescendo into Cisco.

At first I was unsure whether I would really last at Cisco after the acquisition. Well! I've now been here for eight years. At that time John Chambers was head of marketing and sales and I credit him and Ed Kozel for empowering us and believing in the Crescendo team the way they did. Although we were all highly driven individuals there were all sorts of challenges we had to confront at Cisco. For example, Cisco's sales force did not understand switches; they only knew how to sell routers. The structure of the entire company, from manufacturing to sales, was oriented towards selling one single product line: routers. However, we overcame all of these hurdles, primarily because of the faith that Cisco's senior management had in the Crescendo management.

Were the customers for switches and routers the same or different?

Although there were a number of customers who purchased both switches and routers, they did not buy any switches from Cisco because, prior to Crescendo's acquisition, Cisco did not have any switching products. So customers procured switching products from our three leading competitors - Synoptics, 3Com and Cabletron.

We had to make the acquisition a success. We were fiercely focused and we worked hard on differentiating the product. I personally spent a lot of time with customers, influencing them and helping them see why our solution was superior. Meanwhile, our engineering team was focused on building that superior architecture and technology.

In the switch business, you were not creating a new market without any competition. The market existed, competition existed and customers were buying from somebody else; you had to go after somebody's breakfast, lunch and dinner.

Yes and no. When we introduced the Catalyst family of switching products in 1994 the total market for switching products was $100 million. We were fortunate to catch the market during the hockey stick growth phase. The following year the total switching market exploded to one billion dollars. However, we redefined the switching market as a family and system, not as point products. In fact, this is what the Cisco fusion architecture was all about. It combined the strength of Cisco routers with the performance of switching to provide a multiplayer solution. Today, switching is a 14 billion dollar market.

So redefining the market was more critical than focusing on competitors?

If we had focused only on competition we would have marginalized to price and lower gross margins. The competition was satisfied with a gross margin return of 50 percent, while at Cisco our targets were around 65-70 percent. How do you justify a 15-point difference in gross margin without having a key architecture difference? To support this strategy, my customer visits weren't all about technology, features and price; instead they were about "Let me share our roadmap and vision about how we can take care of you in the next three years."

Catching the wave was one good aspect and redefining the market was another. What were some other critical factors that helped Cisco dominate the LAN switching markets?

Another important factor that propelled our growth in switching was good luck and timing and slower execution by our competition. Our competitors' strategy was focused almost exclusively on price. They did not put enough focus on quality, performance features and product stability. Cisco recognized early on that we were selling good products and good solutions that made or broke the IT manager. This IT manager would rather pay 30 percent premium than suffer from any downtime.

Another key element was that we fine-tuned the product by working closely with customers. Even though some of our competitors were quite big they did not do a good job incorporating customer feedback. Over time, we noticed that customer requirements for specific features could be supported only in our architecture. That is when you know you have made a shift in the right direction. The first hundred million dollars and hundred customers was hard. The next hundred million to a few billion was more about the scalability of our infrastructure and cost reduction.

You have three types of migration: the migration path for the customers, the migration path for the sales and service people and the technology migration. The technology migration in some sense is easier, but the customer side is hard. How did you manage this during the course of the phenomenal growth of your business unit?

That was another part of my learning experience at Cisco. The product transition in taking an existing multibillion CATALYST 5000 business and managing its migration with two new product lines (CAT 4000/6000) is a challenging experience. You have to make sure that customers understand that the current product has value and at the same time present the value proposition of the new product lines. You must then provide a migration path for the customers in making the transition with minimal disruption. We had to create products and technologies that fit into our overall architecture. Customers don't want to rip off their existing infrastructure and replace it with a new one.

Startups don't have such issues because they are starting with a clean slate, while Cisco has to provide investment protection and show the customers that subsequent products are all tied to the same architecture.

You grew the LAN switching business from zero to a seven billion run rate. What was your competitive strategy, going from David vs. David & Goliath then, and now Goliath vs. David & Goliath?

In the early stages the market was small, so everyone was a David. Our strategy was to build "best of breed" products and then leverage Cisco's Goliath sales and customer position in the router market to drive switching sales. Essentially this was done by riding on the coat tails of Cisco's established router market and linking LAN switches to the sale. This strategy was executed flawlessly, and as a result we became the Goliath in less than 18 months. Once we became the Goliath, the strategy was a combination of better execution and good defense. Competitors were attacking Cisco relentlessly. It is a lot more fun to climb up a hill that is under your control than to stand on top of the hill and be shot at by arrows from all sides. Many of our detractors wondered if Cisco could keep innovating beyond the Catalyst 5000, Cisco's flagship switch at that time. We introduced the Catalyst 4000 and Catalyst 6000 and combined this with an overall architecture (Cisco Fusion, Cisco Assure and now Cisco AVVID). The speed of innovation was critical.

How do you see competitors like Juniper Networks or Sycamore?

> *Cisco is one of the best-run large companies of its size because of the entrepreneurial spirit it has, and in many ways we still function like a collection of many startups.*

We have managed to retain the entrepreneurial spirit of a Sycamore or Juniper, despite our size. To put things in perspective: Juniper and Sycamore are much smaller companies, with a revenue run rate of around 500 million in fiscal year 2000. In comparison, Cisco's revenues were 19 billion in FY 2000, with over 38,000 employees. However, in my opinion Cisco is one of the best-run large companies of its size because of the entrepreneurial spirit it has, and in many ways we still function like a collection of many startups.

During the growth at Cisco you have performed a series of acquisitions. What were the trigger points?

Trigger points for acquisitions have been driven by the tremendous growth of the switching market and the need to augment our mainstream products. For example, we acquired Kalpana and Grand Junction to complement our modular switching line with stackable technology. The acquisition of Granite was triggered by the need for cost effective Gigabit Ethernet technology. Class Data, our first Israeli acquisition, brought quality of service. Selsius delivered IP telephony.

Have there been instances when you chose not to acquire? If so, what was the secondary strategy there?

By 1999, we were the leader, having reached 50% market share with many billions in revenue. However, the upstarts were challenging us in various switching markets, alleging that our architecture and products were dated. We desperately needed to address this threat and we evaluated the two options - acquire another company or develop organically. Although we had made numerous acquisitions in the past to support our growth strategy, there are times when an acquisition may not be the best strategic alternative. If we acquired a layer 3 switching company, it would not have the Cisco IOS software. It would have taken us a year to integrate all of the software with existing services, so all the money put into acquiring the company would have been negated. Instead, we created an internal accelerated program to deliver a product in 12 months. Not only did the product ship in record time, but also the CATALYST 6000 is a flagship product, built by an outstanding engineering team and now generating revenues in excess of 5 billion dollars this year (2000).

Many people were criticizing Cisco for not acquiring a company to address this competitive threat, but the results show that we chose the smartest option.

What was your marketing and customer strategy?

At Cisco, the business unit's objective was to be the number one or two player in the market. This message was handed down without any ambiguity, so the marketing strategy from Day One was very clear: Help drive sales toward achieving a dominant market share in the LAN switching markets. The first year our LAN switching market share was 0%. Now at the end of year seven, it is more than 7 billion dollars, with over 55% market share.

A key tenet, both for Cisco and for myself, has been to stay close to customers; they can provide invaluable information, thereby influencing our product strategy. In return, the customers learn from our product visionaries, architects and implementers. If the customers are satisfied, your business has a solid and long-lasting foundation. If they are not satisfied, you have to get to the bottom of it, address all of their concerns and work to build a strategic partnership. Customers can often guide you on the long-term vision of the product and in some cases they have driven our acquisition strategies

A thoughtful combination of technology and strategy plus customer influence equals a winning product.

By definition, the customer is always right. My philosophy on customer strategy is this: A thoughtful combination of technology and strategy plus customer influence equals a winning product that reduces the risk of disruption and helps to nurture long lasting partnerships.

What has been your organizational design strategy?

The switching organization grew from 50 to 1000 people between 1993 and 2000. As always, hiring a topnotch talent pool is challenging. In the early days, we had an entrepreneurial culture, but as the organization grew, building a hierarchical scalable organization became imperative.

The market was growing so rapidly that hiring outside professionals with the right skills was challenging and often times almost impossible. Retaining entrepreneurial leadership is vital, so I tended to train, promote and build leaders from within to cultivate and retain key personnel. We developed four or five vice-presidents and ten to fifteen directors in our business unit.

Moreover, with the industry being nascent, my preference was to nurture and train managers from within. My view was that outside managers could not have absorbed the culture and technology of Cisco soon enough. We also augmented our employee base with leaders and engineers from various acquisitions. At the same time we continued our rapid hiring and pursuit of top talent.

In the past few years, with recruitment in the Silicon Valley region becoming increasingly difficult, we bolstered our staffing efforts by locating development centers in North Carolina, Massachusetts and (one that is very near and dear to my heart) the Global Development Center in Bangalore, India. My colleague Prem Jain and I were very keen on this. We forged key university partnerships with leading Indian technical universities such as IIT, BITS and leading Indian custom software development companies such as Wipro, HCL and Infosys. In August 2000 we announced the largest development center for Cisco outside the U.S. in Bangalore, India. Today this center employs 500 engineers and is expected to grow to 2000 employees in two years, with commitment of $200 million in investment.

What is your management style?

> *Strong teams with a clearly articulated set of objectives can accomplish seemingly impossible goals.*

My management style has always been open door and results-driven. I firmly believe that strong teams with a clearly articulated set of objectives can accomplish seemingly impossible goals. I also learned the importance of teamwork from my immediate boss, Mario Mazzola. He was very encouraging and supportive of my new ideas, even my occasional mistakes. Without trying new ideas you never evolve, grow or learn. Cisco culture rewards decision-making and results. It doesn't matter if you make some wrong decisions; the worst thing you can do is to sit on the fence and be indecisive.

We understand that employee turnover at Cisco is well below industry average. What are some of the reasons for this?

I think the overall employee turnover at Cisco averages around five percent. One reason for this is the obvious fact that employees have a lot of financial incentives to stay and continue to vest their options, which typically vest over a period of four years. Second, and more important, is the feeling of empowerment people receive at Cisco. Despite being a fairly large company, employees have autonomy at an individual level, a group level, and a business level. They see that what they are doing has a direct impact on the success and profits, the bottom line of the company.

I have found that the joy of succeeding and achieving results is a bigger motivator than even financial ones. Rallying the team to milestones, schedules, revenue, and helping them see their personal contribution to it was important. Success breeds more success and the financial success follows naturally.

What are your comments regarding John Chambers' leadership?

There are several attributes that make John a great leader. Fundamentally, he has a very strong focus on both the business and customer issues, both in times of crisis and of success. He is extremely driven, empowers his employees, is decisive, and most importantly, he knows what he knows and he knows what he doesn't know. As a result he is supremely confident about delegating responsibilities to his subordinates. He is also extremely encouraging to young leaders in the company and is very approachable. He really understands how to scale the business and the obvious benefits of the network effect. He sets very high targets for the business units, with the objective of becoming market leader in the respective categories. In summary, his leadership abilities are responsible for extending my original two-year commitment to work at Cisco, following the acquisition of Crescendo, to eight years.

What about yourself, what is your core strength?

I am results-oriented. I think people are the greatest asset to getting things done. Once I have developed the vision and strategy of where I want to be, then I can rally the troops to do whatever it takes to get it done. A true sign of an inspirational leader is when none of the people work for you, and you can still get the job done.

> *A true sign of an inspirational leader is when none of the people work for you, and you can still get the job done.*

What's next? What is on the road ahead?

There are times in life when you don't have to know all the answers to all the questions. This is one of those questions for which I have no exact answer. I have decided not to decide my road ahead. I have decided to try an experiment in balance. I was greatly influenced by my grandfather, who passed away a year ago, and of course by my parents and husband as well. When I was young, I spent many summers with my grandfather. He was such a simple man. It wasn't his home or his riches that attracted me to him, but his unconditional love. I have begun to realize that in the corporate world we are so focused and driven that we lose sight of other important dimensions. I wanted to take a break before my kids grew up and went off to college, so I am grateful that Cisco has allowed me this opportunity.

Another thing I am enjoying is mentoring startups. Having been involved with half a dozen companies, I have been mentoring the founders and other senior management staff in these companies. In doing so I have been able to attain a great deal of fulfillment and satisfaction and I feel that by mentoring, I am giving something back.

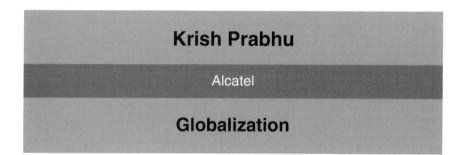

Krish Prabhu

Alcatel

Globalization

Dr. Krish Prabhu is the chief operating officer of Alcatel Telecom. He has played a key role in moving Alcatel toward the forefront of today's telecommunications solutions providers in the U.S. His vision and judgment have been instrumental in the recent acquisitions of several data networking companies, enabling the company to address the Internet infrastructure needs of Alcatel customers worldwide.

Dr. Prabhu began his telecommunications career with AT&T's Bell Laboratories, where he was a senior member of the technical staff. In 1984 he joined Rockwell International's network transmission division. After Rockwell's transmission unit was acquired by Alcatel in 1991, he served as vice president of business development and chief technical officer at Alcatel Network Systems, where he oversaw research, product development and business development activities. Most recently, he served as senior executive vice president of Alcatel Telecom, where he was responsible for the worldwide Internet and Optics Group. He is based in Dallas, Texas.

Dr. Prabhu has a Ph.D and M.S. Degrees in electrical engineering from the University of Pittsburgh and an M.S. Degree in physics from the Indian Institute of Technology in Bombay, India.

Ragu Batta and I interviewed Dr. Prabhu together one late afternoon in October, 2000. He has a loud, booming voice that resonates with confidence. It is a required asset for steering the operations of the 30 billion dollar Telco giant that is Alcatel. Dr. Prabhu is a very well-read and believes that history is a great teacher. The pace of the discussion was frantic. Dr. Prabhu was ready to go from question one.

In this interview Dr. Prabhu gave us a sense of what it takes to run a truly global enterprise. He described how Alcatel, in a matter of a few years, transitioned itself from a company with virtually no presence in the United States to now being a major force. He also outlined how Alcatel was able to become the dominant player in the telcom sector.

"The reward of entrepreneurship is the satisfaction that is gained in successfully scaling the walls or maneuvering around the road bump."

Alcatel has done a stellar job in the last two years. It's grown tremendously at an incredible speed and as a result has regained the attention of Wall Street. What led to this?

First, about four or five years ago Alcatel was a very difficult company for Wall Street to understand. It was a huge conglomerate. So first and foremost what we have done is to simplify the company tremendously by focusing only on the telecom sector. Five years ago, telecom accounted for only 40% of our business. At the end of this year (2000) telecom will represent almost 100% of our business.

Second, we have taken those assets that were not core, divested them and invested the proceeds in acquiring companies, mainly in North America, to the tune of 17 billion dollars. So in a certain sense we have changed the company around through acquisitions.

The third thing that has helped us improve our image is our profitability. Our profits were at an all-time low in'95. They deteriorated significantly from'92 to'95. The operating profit as the percentage of revenue, the ROS, had dipped below zero. We are back to 7-8% this year and on our way to 10%. Going forward, what you will see is better ROS. Consequently, the market now recognizes that our earnings are in line with our peers, especially the ones that they love, like Nortel and others.

Lastly, as a French company we have really taken a very American approach vis-à-vis dealing with the market. For example, we now publish quarterly reports and provide good financial guidance to the Street. Except for the profit warning in Sept'98 we have met or exceeded all the earning projections given to Wall Street every quarter. So that has built a certain level of credibility with respect to the management and the market.

Has growth in some very important markets contributed to enhancing the image?

Yes, especially in DSL, where we have established a leadership position. Also, in the optical space between submarine and terrestrial optics and optical components, we are among the leaders. It's still a small game; there are not too many players out there. Cisco is still a new player in both of these markets. So in the cohort areas of infrastructure, DSL and optics, we have established a leadership position.

Alcatel has successfully morphed to become a global leader focused in tele-communications. How did a company the size of Alcatel, with such diversi-fied interests, go about taking such a giant leap?

We did sell off a lot of our non-core businesses. First of all, we had a stake in something called GEC Alsthom which was in power plants, electric high-speed trains, major projects of that sort. Along with GEC, we took that whole entity public and we still retain a share in it, though we don't manage it. Then we had the engineering business that did general engineering, so we divested that. We also had a whole lot of other interests in publishing and transport, even in wineries - some very good wineries for that matter. We were a cable operator in Switzerland. So we've divested, we've sold all of those assets.

This year we are doing an IPO of our copper cable business. We are the world's largest user of copper, by the way, in our energy and data cables that use copper. So we are divesting; we are doing an IPO of that entity. Essentially, we have taken anything that was non-core telecom and basically divested it or sold it.

Must have been a hard thing to do to push this plan forward, given that Alcatel is headquartered in France where the labor laws are a lot more stringent than in the U.S.?

Well, this speaks well for the things that the company has done. You're abso-lutely right in saying that the labor laws are more stringent in France, but the company has worked with local authorities to manage this smoothly. You should also not forget that in European countries and even in the U.S., in some industries there are tax incentives and concessions given to manufac-turers to set up certain types of industries. So to come in when times are bad and basically say, "We'll shut this down" is not easy. What we have done is divested a number of interests by selling them to someone or floating them as separate companies, resulting in a win-win solution for everybody. It was tough, but it is to our credit that we managed to do it by working closely with the local communities.

Alcatel chose to acquire a presence in the U.S. by mergers and acquisitions. Why did you go this route?

The U.S. has 40% of the world market and 65% of the influence in terms of equipment purchases all over the world. U.S.- based service providers participate in other regions of the world, and in terms of new service deployment and new technology adoption, the U.S. is typically a leader. We felt very strongly that if we were not a key player in the U.S. we could not be a key player on the global scene.

Alcatel really came about by the merger of a French company, C.I.T., and the American company, I.T.T. I.T.T was not allowed by charter to do any-business in the U.S. That was the charter of A.T.T and A.T.T., by charter, couldn't do any business outside the U.S, which was the charter of I.T.T. So in a certain sense we were considerably handicapped. Because we had no presence in the U.S. we had to acquire that presence and then grow around those acquisitions. Therefore, our only strategy for establishing our presence in the U.S. was indeed to acquire it and grow around it.

With Alcatel being a global company, were there any geo-specific (Asia-Pacific, Europe and Americas) strategies that you had to employ in order to be successful?

I think one of our key strengths is our reach. We are in 130 countries with local offices in all of them. That's probably larger than any one of our competitors - Nortel, Lucent, Cisco or Ericsson. Probably Siemens has a comparative reach. Even Ericsson is not in all these countries.

In the Asia-Pacific region there are some countries that are naturally inclined to be lined up with American suppliers. This is technically the case in some of the Southeast Asian countries. Then there are other countries that generally line up either with a European supplier or an American supplier, depending upon the political climate. China is well known for doing that, whether it is airplanes, cars or telecom equipment. So in the Asia- Pacific it's a little bit more linked to the political environment in the individual country.

Our strategy is a little bit different in Europe. Since it's our home base, we have a significant competitive advantage over the North American telcos. The strength is in the numbers. We can generally attend to our customer service needs with the right amount of "feet on the street." As long as we have technological parity between the players I think we can win at the end of the day.

In the Americas it's an all-out battle, largely based on technological strength and in some cases on local presence. And a lot of what happens in the United States today holds true for South America because U.S. operators are now entrenched in every major South American country.

Alcatel has used an American management approach of openness. Going forward, do you see this as becoming the norm globally?

It's not just openness, but a way of doing business - quarterly financial reporting, giving guidance, executing that guidance, alerting the analysts if you think there may be trends that will take you away from your guidance. All these are aspects of normal behavior today for companies that are trying to maximize their market cap. And you can see similar practices being adopted by the other European telcos, such as Nokia and Ericsson. So my sense is that Alcatel is not only there, it's the only way for the company going forward.

The employee skill set requirements for the global workplace have changed dramatically. How are you restructuring the Alcatel work force to compete in the new economy?

Retraining people to address all your skill needs for tomorrow is not really an option. The technologies that are needed in the post-Internet world are so different from the technologies that were needed in the pre-Internet, manufacturing-dominated world. Contract manufacturing is a classic example. We have several factories we have sold to contract manufacturers. The employees of those factories are now employees of the manufacturers and their customer base is far wider than when they were inside Alcatel. This is clearly a win-win situation that allows us to hire people on the service side and on the technology side that we so desperately need to compete effectively. And I think the only answer to this is through some retraining wherever feasible; this kind of flushing out and flushing in what you need. I really believe the companies need to constantly keep doing this to stay on top.

How do you address the multiple requirements of your global customer base? How do you ensure consistency? This must be a huge challenge.

Yes and no. Let me give you an example. Today we have one source of technology for ADSL, one business unit with its own line of suppliers who make sure that the product is ready for shipment to customers in over 70 countries. In each country, what a customer sees as the face of Alcatel has to be consistent and similar. There are two challenges to this. On one hand, there are regional differences or local differences, country to country. So to have a local presence is very important because we know what the Spaniards want in Spain, what the Italians want in Italy or what someone wants in Uruguay. On the other hand, the technology is indeed a global one. There is no reason to believe that this technology needs to be different in any country other than minor adaptations, but that is just in the noise level.

So in a nutshell, we have a global source for technology and we have local presence to take care of our local customers. In a certain way the problem of consistency is better handled by us because what the customer really wants is consistency over time, not necessarily consistency over space. If I am a customer in Uruguay, I don't really care what Alcatel is doing for customers in Italy. What I want is to make sure that I get my technology needs identified: a) Can I rely on Alcatel? and b) Will Alcatel deliver on its commitments?

As you stated earlier, Alcatel has been acquiring companies in rapid succession. What are some of the challenges in integrating the acquired companies?

I think the biggest challenge is one of integration, but not only integration. Cisco says that they mastered the art of acquisition and that they have a machinery in place. I would not argue with them because their results speak for themselves. But at the same time I believe that Cisco also has its share of problems. For example, the customer may be unhappy because the various technologies that were acquired don't quite fuse together. In addition, the ability to scale the solutions to support large networks so that millions of end users can operate from these technology platforms also poses a significant challenge. This is especially true when you try to acquire and then integrate the disparate solutions.

Integration and scalability of point products acquired from various companies is one of the significant challenges. Small companies are developing point technology solutions with basically zero constraints. They are trying to develop something from scratch, do it better, do it bigger and or faster, but the problem of scale is quite different. The solutions not only have to interface with legacy systems but also scale up, because ideally when you roll out new solutions, the systems should scale to support millions of users.

In one of the articles about the science of integration, you were quoted as saying, "First, clearly articulate what our mission is together; second, define what their role is in Alcatel; third, work with them to make sure that the role suits them and is something they wish to cherish." Can you elaborate on these steps?

I think the formula that is outlined in those steps is really the formula we would like to pursue. I'm not saying that we have pursued it in each case but if we were to adopt a blue print it would be very much along the lines of what you said. For example, we had acquired a Remote Access Server company called Assured Access Technology in March 99. They had a platform that we didn't have in our company and collectively we could identify what their role would be. By the way, I don't know how the people feel about it in Milpitas today and I'm sure that there is always some disenchantment with anything you do, especially because you are working for a little company. There is a little bit of burnout, there is a little bit of cashing out and there is a little bit of itching to go do something new. While it's always fun to give birth to a child, it's not always fun to raise one. There are these kinds of problems that one encounters when you have given birth to something and now it's your job to make it big, make it grow. Anyway, in Milpitas today we have almost 200 people; when we acquired Assured Access there were around 70. Now we have defined a role for this group. Collectively, the role is well understood as to what they will be doing. It's not easy. No one said that it would be easy to take a technology and make it grow ten or hundred-fold, but that's what we want to do. The challenge is for the two cultures to melt in some way so you can achieve your goal of realizing that collective vision. To take this particular example, the biggest problem is in the integration phase. On the one hand, Assured Access needs to integrate into Alcatel so that they can use the full power of Alcatel, which includes 130 countries. On the other hand, Alcatel needs to give Assured Access enough autonomy so that they can do what they have done very well - to innovate at a very fast pace. And those are to some extent parallel and conflicting constraints. So this is not an easy problem. However, I think at the end of the day we can draw a line where the acquired company gets as much autonomy as possible while at the same time it uses the channels of the acquiring company as effectively as possible.

There are key differences when you're acquiring a large company versus a small company. With a small company it's pretty much the end of the road; with a larger company there may be a sense of failure. How do you turn these situations into successful M & As?

Well, people in these small company are often mercenaries. We have seen that in small companies that have been around for three or four years. People who have gone to three or four startups will come in; they know when the battle starts, they know when the battle ends. In their minds the battle ends when they cash out. I'm not saying this applies to everybody. There are a few who say, "I really like this technology. I think I can grow this to a 2 billion dollar business by being within Alcatel. Boy, that's the challenge I want to embark upon."

On the other hand, we have also acquired companies like Newbridge or DSC that have been around for fifteen or sixteen years, having grown their business from startup to becoming public to achieving revenues of one to two billion dollars. Then they hit the wall. Quarter after quarter there's no growth; the stock first tumbles, then basically craters. Employee stock options are worthless. Somehow they need to find a way of getting money out of their existing stock, which results in an acquisition. Certainly, this sequence of events may contribute to a certain sense of failure.

The way you turn both situations around is to again go through a three-step process: 1) Clearly articulate what the mission statement is, 2) Define their role in Alcatel and 3) work with them to make sure the role suits them and is something they will cherish. Then they get pumped up because they are wedded to their ideas and as a result have more strength. It's almost like having a big army behind you, being part of this big company. The new guys coming into the company take some time to develop that. And until they do it's the job of the acquiring company to make it happen. Once that happens I really believe that things fall into place. But until that happens, whether it's a small company or a big company that you have acquired, you have to deal with it appropriately.

Given the number of acquisitions by Alcatel in the past 18 months, do you have a formal integration task force that is used to integrate the companies acquired by Alcatel?

The integration task force works well when the companies acquired are small. For example, Cisco has successfully demonstrated the effectiveness of using an integration task force. On Day One, employees of the acquired company receive Cisco T-Shirts, a Cisco e-mail address, and so on. This works well when integrating 100 people into a 15,000-25,000 strong organization. When you buy a company that is 10,000-strong it's a little bit more like consolidation. I don't think a single task force will suffice, especially if you're doing these two types of acquisitions. Then we have done something different with one of our acquisitions, Genesys, which is a third model. Genesys is a call center software company located in the Bay Area. We gave them a lot of flexibility and they now operate as an independent subsidiary. The sales channels are highly synchronized and coordinated with the parent company; other than that, Genesys is really operating very much like an independent company. Since the acquisition Genesys' revenues have gone up substantially because they really are leveraging the global reach of Alcatel's sales channel. Obviously, we cannot do this with every company we acquire because then you become a loose conglomerate of all these acquired companies.

How would you categorize the culture of Alcatel?

The culture in Alcatel is not a homogeneous culture by any means. It is very much a heterogeneous culture, mainly because of who we are. When you look at Alcatel and its culture, is it one culture? The answer is that at the level of putting the customer first or at the level of having a certain approach dealing with market, you can have a homogeneous culture. But clearly, because we are so strong locally and yet are driving technology as a source globally, we will have subcultures within our homogeneous culture.

What is Alcatel's global manufacturing strategy in the new economy?

We've leveraged off the contract manufacturers (CM) and we're going to have one integration plant, per Geo. An integration plant is a plant that will integrate the output of other plants. So if I get something built by a CM or a supplier anywhere in the world, they ship it to the integration plant. I assemble the final product, integrate it and ship it to my customer. This has most definitely increased our flexibility as well as our ability not to carry a lot of fixed cost. As business ramps up or down you have a lot more flexibility, because you just have an integration plant that is sized to meet the needs of your customers. It can spread out an overhead over a large number of customers in a region. But what you are basically doing is leveraging through contract manufacturers' volume, board level production, and that kind of thing. This is a model that the computer guys use quite a bit. Cisco has used this model quite successfully.

Also, the contract manufacturers who are global can use volume economies to their advantage because they are supporting multiple customers. What hasn't quite been perfected is all of us linking our designs for contract manufacturers to secure components in volume, therefore further reducing costs. There are still a lot of unique designs from all of us. This is true for Nortel and this is true for us. We don't really worry too much about doing our designs in hardware so that we can really drive the components volume up, especially at the contract manufacturer's level. It's quite conceivable that eventually hardware will become extremely standardized, in which case we'll all become software service companies.

Are you planning to employ the incubator model which was successful at Newbridge (which Alcatel acquired in June, 00)? What are some of the challenges to implementing an incubator model?

I think the incubator model gives you the option of playing a little bit in the entrepreneurship world. However, I believe there are a number of issues and questions that are not well understood. For example, employees may believe that a person working in an incubator has better prospects for generating wealth as opposed to a person working in the parent company. This can lead to instability, with people not wanting to work in the parent company and instead wanting to work for the incubators. We saw this instability in Newbridge. There was some disenchantment and the parent company was losing people to the incubators, mainly because the incubators would have a better payout.

So we are thinking about adopting the incubator model for products that are peripheral and complementary to our core business so that the incubator has a specific role vis-a-vis the role of a major unit. Inside Alcatel most major units complement one another. For example, we do a lot of DSL in Raleigh and a lot of ATM in Ottawa and a lot of optics in Dallas and in France. Thus the business units complement one another. It would be OK for us to have incubators around these major centers, with activities which are somewhat complementary to the core activity of each center.

You have established very aggressive growth targets. What are some of the drivers of this growth?

We are in a few very high-growth markets - optics, broadband and networking - and to the extent that the market is growing, we can continue to ride that growth. Down the road, this growth will stabilize. We have seen decent growth in our enterprise business as well as in our service provider business. In terms of our additional growth strategies, it might be worthwhile for us to look at acquisitions targeted towards growth of top-line revenues as opposed to filling technology gaps.

One of the things that Cisco does very well is make acquisitions that really improve their top-line revenue growth. Although the companies acquired may be small, often perceived as only technology acquisitions, the fact is that their acquisition strategy is driven more on how it impacts their top-line growth.

Is your sales organizational design based on both large and small customers? This was under debate. What strategy did you eventually choose and why?

What we initially did was organize the North American sales channel into two sales divisions, with one focused on large customers and the other on small customers. This was mainly because of the dynamics in decision-making between the two sets of customers. This did not work to our advantage and we soon concluded that the transition from small to large customers was difficult to manage. You have small customers that started out as small one year but the next year became relatively large. Quest is a good example. What we have done now is reorganize the sales force in North America more by region, by country. So you have one for Canada and one for the U.S.

Today there are around 100 large service providers worldwide who matter to equipment vendors the size of Alcatel, Nokia and Lucent. Do you foresee any change in this model?

I believe that there are a lot of parallels between the telecom world and the auto world. You have Goliaths in the auto world, just as in the telco world. I do not believe that there will be large number of Ciscos happening down the road. For example, in the last 20 years in the computer software and hardware markets, we have seen the emergence of only a handful of behemoths: Sun, Microsoft, Oracle, Intel, Dell, Compaq and HP. In the telecom world, my feeling is there is no reason to believe that these Goliaths will die and that there will be an emergence of new Ciscos. People talk about Redback, Juniper and Sycamore as if they are all going to be like Cisco. I don't believe in that model myself. I believe that what will happen is that down the road these guys will hit a revenue or a growth wall that results in a decline of their stock price and it may stagnate for awhile. It happened to a number of companies - for example, Bay Networks, 3Com, and Cabletron.

So my sense is that there will be a Goliath versus Goliath competition. The laws of physics will decide how much you can really compete effectively with one another. There are about six companies in the telco arena with revenues of about 30 billion dollars each, with a global presence. These are Nortel, Lucent, Nokia, Erricson, Alcatel and Cisco. Next year Cisco is going to reach 30 billion, if they keep on their growth track. Of these six companies, some will do very well in terms of working with small startups and getting that innovation into their channels effectively, servicing their customers, improving their global presence and growing their business faster than their peers. This could lead to some consolidation, with one Goliath acquiring or merging with another. For example, in the auto industry a few years ago, there was Chrysler, AMC, Ford and GM. Now they are down to two. I think the same situation will come about in telecom. You will not have three or four U.S. players; you will be down to two, and you won't have two or three Europeans, you'll be down to one or two. I cannot imagine what will happen in Japan. My sense is that the Goliath versus Goliath battle will continue. The startups do play a very important role, but there is no way a Juniper will be able to develop the global distribution and service, operational scalability, and support capabilities of the top six in only a few years.

You are a leader of a global company, with an established track record. What are your comments on global leadership as an important requirement in leading a company in today's global marketplace?

I believe that all companies today are looking for people who have an international blend, who can appreciate what it takes to develop the business internationally. For example, take a guy like Clarence Chandran of Nortel. Clarence used to run Nortel's Far East businesses. I believe that anybody who has worked in an international setup will be critical to a global company. So Nokia cannot necessarily be thinking only about Finns to run its business, and Erricson cannot be thinking only of Swedes to run its business. In that sense I believe Alcatel has shown some leadership in nominating me, in basically looking at me, regardless of where I come from.

My sense is that the global citizen who understands what it takes to really make the business a global business, understands the sensitivities and the cultural aspects of dealing with customers in different parts of the world, will be the one who will emerge as the leader of tomorrow's big corporations. Companies who allow such leaders to thrive and move up will succeed; the others will pay a price for their narrow-mindedness.

Who are your mentors and how did they influence you?

That is a question that no one has ever asked me before. I would not refer to them as mentors per se, but certainly as role models or people I looked up to and learned a lot from. Because of these people there are certain things that I do differently today because of my association with them. Clearly one was my first boss in the U.S., Arun Netravali, president of Bell Labs. I worked with Arun for 3 years and in fact he recruited me to Bell Labs. I learned a lot from him, particularly in terms of analysis, looking at problems, trying to see if the problem has been sufficiently resolved, and not beating it to death. One must not waste too much time, but still address all aspects of the problem so you can move on. These are things that Arun did very well.

At Alcatel, two individuals, Serge Tchurk, Alcatel's current CEO and Jo Cornu have influenced me in many ways. The one thing that I learned from Serge is to be unfazed by a problem. He is a very tough guy. No matter however difficult the problem is, Serge remains unfazed. I'm very impressed with the way he handles the toughest situations. For example, in September of 1998 Alcatel had a profit warning; the stock crashed 40% in a single day and there was a lot of bad press. I went with him to brief a number of Wall Street analysts. The analysts were livid,

> *No matter how difficult the problem, there is always a good solution.*

wondering why the profit warning came so suddenly; there were all kinds of crazy allegations about why we withheld the profit warning to close our DSC acquisition. I watched Serge handle the situation. He always stuck with what he knew he had done right. Basically, he believes that no matter how difficult the problem, there is always a good solution. One needs to focus on the solution and not get overwhelmed by the problem. I saw this over and over again because I worked with him very closely.

Then there is Joe Cornu, also from Alcatel, who was my predecessor. One of Cornu's strengths is that he is very good at distilling input from a large number of people who have disparate opinions on particular issues. This is very useful, especially in a global company. There are employees from all over the world trying to protect their constituency, and to be able to zip through all that and get to the bottom of what is important and at the same time get everyone's buy-in is a true asset. It is a very difficult thing to do and Jo Cornu is a master at it.

What's a typical day at work?

Well, I usually get up around 5:30 in the morning. Then I come into work around 6:30 or 7:00. This is partly because I might have conferences with Europe and that's about the prime time in Europe. That's usually over by about 10:30. The rest of the time before noon is usually spent with customer calls or something or the other that relates to customers. Early afternoons are usually spent attending to matters more internal to the companies.

In what areas do you spend most of your time?

At this point, my focus is on strategy, visiting high-level customers, increasing shareholder value, growing the business and growing the image.

Things are changing on such a short cycle time today that it's hard to predict what's going to be out there tomorrow. What are your comments on the future? Where do you think the niches are going to be?

Well, one thing I can say is that the present is very exciting and the future is going to be even more exciting. We are quite blessed to live in this day and age. With such technological changes taking place around us, given our profession and our background, we are lucky to be right in the middle of making these changes happen. It really is quite remarkable. However, at the risk of oversimplification, I feel that a majority of the entrepreneurs today appear to be driven largely by money. With such an attitude it would be interesting to see how they handle the situation when they hit some road bumps. One of the rewards of entrepreneurship is the satisfaction gained in successfully scaling the walls or maneuvering around the road bump.

On the other hand, there is no better time to become an entrepreneur than today. The entire infrastructure is in place to be exploited and that's really a great opportunity at this time in human history. We're going to transform the world in the same way it was transformed during the Industrial Revolution. The difference is that it took three hundred years then and it'll probably only take us twenty.

What impact did your upbringing have in shaping your value system and beliefs?

This is a very good question but it's very hard for me to answer because there is no doubt that the moral and ethical fabric of which a person is made up eventually goes back to his earliest days, to the time spent with his parents. All I can remember is that we were a very typical Indian family. I was one of 5 kids. I was actually the fourth kid, the middle kid. We were a solid middle class family. It was a very happy childhood and both my parents put family ahead of everything else.

I think that support from the family is invaluable. Support like that is very, very important because it is not guarded or reserved; it is unconditional. My wife has been very supportive of my career and she has supported me 100% in terms of what I have done up to this point. I feel that we are very blessed in that regard.

What skill stands out that you can correlate to your Eastern and Western background?

Well, I believe it's a combination of skills. It isn't as simple as being able to compute faster than the next guy. I certainly believe that it's important to analyze problems and, as part of that analysis, be able to look at certain things a little bit faster, a little bit better than the next guy. In my particular case, I am aware of an acute sensitivity to dealing with people. I don't necessarily mean my peers or my superiors but rather those who are subordinates. I mean that in more than a hierarchical way. I have an acute sensitivity in dealing with them, a way that I feel is responsive to their needs. You may refer to this as having good interpersonal skills. I believe that the cause of my success has been the support of this particular constituency. It's not my peers or my superiors, but the guys underneath me who have been my strongest supporters. To me, that is a very important aspect of managing large organizations. The people in your organization must feel very good about you as the person at the top of the organization.

What are your hobbies?

I like to read a lot. I'm actually catching up with a broad range of reading that I haven't had time for in the past 10 years. I like to read a lot of history and a lot of fiction. I'm going back and reading some authors of the late 19th and 20th century. One of my favorite authors is the Argentinean, Jose Luis Borges. I am catching up on his fiction because he's really a marvelous author and has inspired a generation of new writers. The other authors I am reading are Thomas Mann and Franz Kafka. I am also quite interested in history. I subscribe to the New Yorker. I read the New Yorker from cover to cover because I really enjoy it as a magazine. Between reading and my kids, I don't have much time for anything else.

Now you have all this success. What are the downsides, sacrifices and pressure levels?

I think balancing between your personal and professional life is always a tough act and that balance is critical, because your family pays a price for it. I have clearly noticed in my twenty-year career that during the first ten years I was spending a lot more time at home and in the past 10 years I have been spending a lot more time away from home. To me, that is not a very healthy situation. Personally, that is the biggest sacrifice. I think outside of that it isn't all that bad, but the biggest sacrifice is that your family has to give you up and to some extent you have to give up your family.

In my first ten years I used to do a lot of things that were just for my benefit. Now I really don't have time to devote to things that I would view as being for my own benefit. To me the time you spend with the family and the time you spend with yourself is really compromised because of the success you have had.

What's the driving force behind your success?

That's a tough one, but I'm largely driven by the fact that I want to win and I want to win very badly. I guess really, for one reason or another, we all like to win in whatever game we are playing. This is not because there is a trophy that I covet, but just the fact that the game gets so intense sometimes and I get very focused on winning. To a certain extent, one should also have some fun playing the game, but at the end of the day it's because I'm a very competitive guy and I want to win as much as the next guy.

Rajat Gupta

McKinsey & Company

Global Leadership

Rajat Gupta heads the world's leading management consultancy, McKinsey & Company. The firm occupies the number one spot on the list of students' preferred employers, and has done so every year since 1997. It has been called "the world's most influential consulting firm" and is known for its client impact, superior talent pool, and strong culture of meritocracy.

Rajat Gupta began his career with McKinsey in 1973. In 1981, Gupta became the head of McKinsey's Scandinavian office. On returning to the U.S. in 1990, he ran the Chicago office until his election to Managing Director in 1994. He holds a degree in mechanical engineering from IIT, New Delhi and an MBA from Harvard University.

Rajat Gupta is a globetrotter. I knew up-front that it would be a challenge to connect up with this very busy man who manages a talent pool 7,000 strong in 43 countries. These interviews were conducted through a series of phone conversations at various venues. The first discussion took place on Gupta's way home from Dallas in his car. The second was held while he was stuck in traffic in New Jersey and the third was conducted while he was on his way to the Asia-Pacific.

Gupta is an aggressive listener, takes his time to formulate his thoughts, and speaks sparingly. During the discussion he offered his views on leadership, culture, organizational strategy, mentoring and the meritocracy system. We talked about what it takes to establish a global mindset and how companies today should adapt to change. Finally, he shared his passion for his brainchild, the Indian School of Business.

"Leaders are typically able to see most things in both a raw and integrated fashion."

When companies are faced with challenges and seek external help, one of the first names that comes to mind is McKinsey. Why?

No one hires McKinsey & Company to preserve the status quo. Our personal commitment, our passion, is to help our clients achieve positive change. This has been our goal since our founding nearly 75 years ago, when our firm created the profession of modern management consulting.

Our fundamental mission is to enhance the performance of the companies we serve through working on truly integrated issues of concern to top management. We work on improving the overall performance of the company. We work on organizational issues, strategy issues, enhancement of operating performance, and mergers and acquisitions. We work with the company to figure out what is of critical importance, and we hold broad-ranging discussions on what will improve the company's performance.

For example, questions we might ask in the organizational area: How does a fast-growing startup company scale up to the level of a global company? What are the organizational challenges? In other situations, such as entering a new market or making acquisitions, we look at integrating the two organizations. Then there are issues relating to strategy in a competitive market place. For example, how do you sustain and build value and competitive advantage? How do you enter new market segments? How do you create growth in a company? What kind of investments should you make?

I'll give you an example. Today I was meeting with the board of a company, and we spent over two hours talking about the key challenges they were facing. There were three or four, and one was the intensive search for talent. It was a knowledge-intensive business so we dealt with such questions as how to attract the best talent and how to retain them and how to motivate them? This was one big challenge. This company happened to have a very high market capitalization which was based on a huge growth record over the past several years. How does it continue to generate such growth? Does it do so organically, through internal growth or should it consider some acquisitions? What are some of the risks? Should the acquisitions be large or small? The third topic of discussion was how to migrate up the value chain. How can they broaden beyond primarily providing contract software? So you start with a broad set of questions and then focus in on specific issues. The next step is to launch the effort.

Having been at McKinsey for over a quarter century, what in your opinion are some of the fundamental reasons why companies fail?

As you know, the only thing that's constant is change itself. The market, technology and products are changing rapidly to keep abreast of the changing trends of globalization, deregulation, and so on. Such an environment creates both threats and opportunities.

Companies fail because they get a bit too calcified and don't move fast enough. An organization that manages to continually reinvent or restructure, to adapt to the changing environment, stays ahead of its competitors and successfully exploits new opportunities. If you accept the impermanence of excellence, if you assume you are good and take things for granted, you slide fast.

Change is very difficult, but if you make it a way of life, it is not as dramatic as it seems. It is a constant set of decisions you are making, and sometimes not making a decision is the right decision by itself. As you know, it is always easier not to make decisions and stay where you are. I don't think companies that change a fair amount go through much trauma. It is just that the culture is of questioning, reinventing and moving on. If you have that kind of culture in a company, it is not any more traumatic than staying still.

Once McKinsey has recommended a solution to the client, how do you ensure its success?

It is dependent upon how broadly and how well the change program is being communicated. Part of it depends on whether there are champions and advocates for the change within the organization who are highly regarded, and how passionate they are about the change. Part of it is having a compelling rationale for it. By paying attention to detail, by paying attention to people and by constantly communicating, you can make it go a long way.

How do you measure McKinsey's impact on clients?

We have a two-part mission statement; one part is to have an extraordinarily positive impact on our clients and their performance and the other is to build a great institution.

When I give a report to my partners on how the firm is doing, it invariably starts with the quality of the relationships with our clients, the type of work we are doing for them, and the kind of impact we are having. In assessing the quality of relationships I ask questions like: Are we serving the leading institutions? Are we serving them on the most central issues, and are we improving their performance as a result? Are they, over time, becoming a leader in their industry? These are all client-oriented metrics.

When we look at our partners, we evaluate what they can contribute toward building a great institution. That has to do with ideas, with people, and with how we manage ourselves.

In terms of ideas, we ask: What is your contribution toward the state-of-the-art thinking on management? Have you done some original work? Do you have an external reputation for that? Do you write and publish? Does that enhance the reputation of the firm?

On the people side, we may ask: Are you a good mentor? Do people want to work with you? Do you connect with them? Do they look to you as a role model?

On governance, we examine a person's capabilities in building a practice, being an entrepreneur in a new geography, running an office, or being on one of the committees that runs the firm.

This is very important to us, and we spend an enormous amount of time ensuring that McKinsey is truly a meritocracy. It is fundamental in attracting good people and ensuring that the employees have faith in the system and a desire to work for McKinsey. We tell them that if they are good and make the right kind of contributions they will be recognized and will do well. There are no politics in the organization, and we have a peer evaluation system. Another very important value is what we call "One Firm." One Firm means that we are all in this together. There is no intermediate level of profitability on which we measure and reward people. It is one partnership. What you would refer to in the corporate world as divisional profitability and incentives based on your division's performance does not exist here at McKinsey.

What strategy has McKinsey implemented for globalization and growth over the past few years?

That is a very broad question, and there are many different ways to answer it. First, we look at ways to establish a global presence. We have 84 offices around the world. Five or six years ago, we had maybe 40. We look at globalization as a huge opportunity, and consequently we have established ourselves in every significant economy in the world. That is one part of the answer. Another part is that we have shifted our focus and moved into the new economy in areas such as technology, e-commerce and web-enabling businesses. We've shifted our practice significantly, with approximately forty percent of our work focused in these areas.

Our strategy has been unique in that we are such a people-intensive, knowl-edge-based organization. Our assets are completely based on knowledge, ideas and people. We have not grown by acquisitions or joint ventures. Our basic formula for expansion has remained the same. You need a committed group of entrepreneurs or partners within the firm who want to go out and start up an operation somewhere.

We debated for several years about whether to start an office in India. But it was only when two or three of the partners said they were interested in going there to open an office that we established one. They went to India and started hiring the best talent in the country. They then developed this talent in the McKinsey culture. The simple key is to hire the best talent wherever we go.

McKinsey has consistently exhibited revenue growth rates of 10 to 15 per-cent. Is this a planned strategy? Why not try an achieve a 40 percent growth rate?

It is not really a planned event. I have been here for the past 27 years. It has been 10 to 15 percent in each of these years. In no year has it grown more or less.

Our profession is people-intensive. It is not product-based. It depends on the quality of the people involved. If you want to grow an organization and maintain quality and excellence in its culture, you can attract and absorb only so many people and inculcate in them the values of the firm. It is an apprenticeship-based organization, wherein you learn by observing and working with others and in teams. So if we try to grow too fast, we lose quality and excellence and ultimately our most important asset, our reputa-tion.

How does McKinsey cultivate a global mindset?

First, we are a truly global company. Our customer base, our clients and ownership are all more global than any other company I know. Some may have global customers but may not have global shareholders or global man-agement. When I look at the nationalities represented on our board and senior leadership, when I look at the composition of our client base, it is basically made up of companies from all over the world. If you look at the composition of our senior leadership, you will see that they reflect 50 differ-ent nationalities. If you look at how our ownership is represented, it is again the same way. In a sense, we naturally come with a global mindset.

Here is where the concept of One Firm comes in. We have a strong culture of collaboration all across the firm and we reinforce that in every system we have. There is a very open architecture in the firm and there are no regional structures; everyone collaborates with everyone else. The teams that are formed cut across offices and highly networked organizations and so on. That creates the global mindset.

We also move more people around than any other institution I know. At any given point in time, 100 of the 700 partners could be on the move somewhere. I don't think any organization has that percentage of senior management on the move. There is no home base and there is no headquarters for the corporation.

What is the strategy behind the McKinsey cellular organizational design?

We are very much a self-governing firm. It is a worldwide partnership with a unique structure. I don't think there are actually any parallels of size and scale. We are organized along three lines: geography, industry and function. There are groups of partners who form a team to serve a particular industry, a particular geography or function. These groups of partners form what is called a cell. The biological analogy relates to its permeability. You can enter the cell or leave it. If it becomes too big, we subdivide. This process resembles the phenomenon of mitosis.

It is very organic in the way it develops. People decide to form a cell and then go ahead and form it. In that way it is a very fluid organization with no hierarchical structure, no regional structure. It is a very flat, non-hierarchical organization. This organizational strategy was implemented about three years ago. This type of organization is quite flexible; it provides a lot of

> *If you want to retain leaders you must give them the freedom to do as they wish, without imposing too many rules and structures.*

entrepreneurial energy. It helps in adapting to changing requirements. The other important factor is that we attract very high-quality talent. We are an organization of leaders and not of leaders and followers. Everyone at McKinsey & Company is a leader, an entrepreneur, and if you want to retain leaders you must give them the freedom to do as they wish, without imposing too many rules and structures.

The cellular system lets us have our cake and eat it too. We can maintain the village-like culture that takes advantage of size and scale. People can choose to join two or three out of eighty cells. There are over ten geographical cells, thirty plus industry cells, and around eighteen functional cells. So I could become, for example, a member of the automotive practice, the Detroit office and the operations functional practice.

How is McKinsey able to attract the best talent in this competitive environment?

We attract the best talent by convincing people that we can offer an environment with a culture they would like to be in. Of course, the rewards and remuneration will have to be good. Fundamentally, potential employees are attracted to McKinsey because they believe that the organization has a unique culture, is committed to developing and improving their skills and is truly a meritocracy. Almost everyone who joins McKinsey leaves the place better equipped, with a superior set of skills and a greater number of opportunities than when they joined.

The point is, we really concentrate on the development of our people. Fundamentally, the development of the people occurs on the job, in a team setting, through mentoring by senior people and through teaching. Formal training also has a role to play. We invest a lot in the formal training of our people; I would say that accounts for about 10 percent of training. However, 90 percent of the training happens on the job, through working with others and by having the opportunity to discover things for oneself. If you hire the right kind of talent and leaders they will want to push the envelope. It is two-way learning, because you learn by observing others. You will also learn from the mistakes you make. You have to have the room to do it; you try something and you learn. You should also have a safety net so that if and when things go wrong, someone will come to your aid. When you are in such a culture you learn quickly.

What are your primary areas of focus as the head of McKinsey?

One of the things that is very important at McKinsey & Company is the reinforcement of the culture and values of our company, and this is done in a lot of different ways. It is done through what I talk about, decisions I make, and by reinforcing debates in the firm about the set of values of the firm and what we stand for. Making sure that we maintain the meritocratic system and making sure that these core values constantly get reinforced through our day-to-day actions and creating the environment is a big piece of the job.

As the senior personnel officer of the firm I spend a lot of my time talking to my partners. We talk about their aspirations and the opportunities they have in the firm. I try to make sure they remain motivated and get the opportunity to do what they want to do.

Another big chunk of time goes into the involvement with external constituencies, whether it is working with clients or recruiting or spending time with the young people who join us. I spend a lot of time on campuses and visiting clients.

I also spend a fair amount time monitoring the status of the firm. We work through committees basically managing the profits of the firm, shaping the agenda for the board, shaping the agenda for various committees that are evaluating people and so on. Then of course I also spend time working on the future direction of the firm, strategy and things like that.

What qualities are essential for managing an organization such as McKinsey?

In a place like McKinsey you need to have a high level of trust with your partners and colleagues. Leading a partnership also requires strong listening skills and an ability to understand where other people are coming from. My leadership role is in many ways that of a servant-leader, in order to understand the McKinsey partners and how to move them forward, leading from behind rather than telling them, "I know the way; follow me."

Having interacted with leaders of all kinds, what in your opinion are some of the attributes of a good leader?

Most importantly, I think strong leaders have a vision of what they are trying to accomplish and are able to communicate that effectively throughout the organization. Leaders are typically able to see most things in both a raw and an integrated fashion. They are able to see what they have to do or what they are responsible for beyond the immediate; they see the broader context. In addition they have the ability to communicate, convince and relate to people. Essentially they are good communicators. Although leaders come in different colors and flavors, quite a few of them are very charismatic.

> *Leaders are typically able to see most things in both, a raw and an integrated fashion.*

Switching gears to the personal front, what makes you tick?

I am personally driven by the Indian philosophy of karma yoga. You are supposed to do what you think is right. Don't worry about the results.

Who are your mentors and what roles have they played in your life?

I have had different individuals influence me at various stages in my life. During my early years, my parents were a very important influence. My father was a highly principled individual. He was a Gandhian (one who believed in the principles set forth by Mahatma Gandhi) and was involved in the Independence Movement. He was a simple man of high thinking. I believe that both my parents imparted strong values and their life's philosophy has stayed with me.

My wife has also been a huge influence on my life. I have been married for 27 years. She has influenced me more than anybody else, in terms of our way of thinking and philosophy. She is also simple and compassionate as a person. I have learned very important values from her, things like caring for people. She suffers when others suffer; she suffers on their behalf. She is an extraordinarily caring person.

You are very passionate about the Indian School of Business (ISB, in Hyderabad, India). What is your vision and what impact are looking to create?

I think the world never has too many leaders. Education - graduate education and business in general- is about leadership in business. If you look at India, you see a strong need there for both managerial talent and leadership in business. As a country with terrific human resources, we need to get more productively organized. The entire objective is to provide a school that will develop such leaders. That is the general idea. It has been two to three years in the making, and now there are over fifty people working hard to realize this vision.

We have a strong collaboration with The Wharton School of Business and The Kellogg School of Business, both of which are among the top five business schools in world. We have terrific support from faculty members from both of these schools and elsewhere. Sumantra Ghoshal, who I believe is one of the best academic thinkers in the world, has agreed to become the founding dean. Taking on this responsibility for creating a world-class school is very exciting and rewarding.

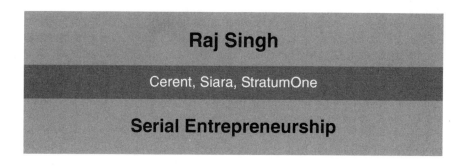

Raj Singh

Cerent, Siara, StratumOne

Serial Entrepreneurship

Raj Singh is the president of Comstellar Technologies and a general partner in Redwood Venture Partners, a venture capital firm he founded in 1997.

In 1992 he began a new career as an entrepreneur, starting InterHDL, a company involved in developing chip design software. Over the next few years Singh started three more companies: Advancel Logic, Fiberlane Communications (later split into Cerent and Siara Networks), and StratumOne. Cerent and StratumOne were sold to Cisco for over seven billion dollars. Siara was sold to Redback for over four billion dollars.

Earlier in his career, Raj Singh had many years of experience as an engineer in high technology companies, beginning with National Semiconductor in the early 1980s and including early entry at Cirrus Logic and Nexgen.

Raj is the co-author of a well-known book, *Digital Design and Synthesis with Verilog HDL*. He holds a BS in electrical engineering from Roorkee Engineering College in India, a post graduate diploma in mathematics from IIT Delhi, and a master's degree in computer science from the University of Minnesota, MN.

Raj is a serial entrepreneur, always on the prowl for the next new thing. Arguably, one may conclude that he finds the prospect of building a product from an idea much more appealing than the IPO. He is able to recognize his strengths and his limitations and, acting on this, creates one company after another.

In this interview, Raj Singh discusses the reasons behind his interest in serial entrepreneurship. He describes how he is able to move from one field of technology to another with such apparent ease and explains how he puts together top teams and builds great products. He talks about his role as a venture capitalist. He shares what he has learned over the years from the various entrepreneurs who have crossed his path. Finally, he tells us what he feels are the key steps necessary to build a successful company.

**"I look for the strengths in people and
not their weaknesses."**

*With InterHDL, Advancel, Fiberlane (Cerent, Siara), StratumOne, Roshni,
Redwood, and now Comstellar you have obviously taken the serial entrepreneurship route. Was that a conscious decision on your part? At what point
do you know you've finished your involvement with one company and move
on to the next?*

It's a natural progression that comes out of my style of working. I don't plan
these things; I don't say I'll do twenty companies in the next thirty years –
or even one company, for that matter.

When the senior management team has been on board and executing with
full steam for one year and the company is running like a well-oiled
machine, that's my signal to leave. You should leave a company at a point
where it is fully self-sustaining so that your departure doesn't cause disruption.

A company goes through phases and each one has a different leadership
requirement. There is a product development phase, then a market establishment phase, then a revenue generation phase. The skills required for this
range from being creative to being operational. Some people are creative
and others are operational; a few are both. As they go along they morph
themselves, adding to their skills. Some people can scale all the way and
some can't. To be successful you need to have the right person for the right
job.

So it's situational leadership. The moment you know that in the next phase
you're running out of your bandwidth and your limitations are going to stop
you from making the best contribution you can make, that's the best time to
get out and let another person take over.

*Since you have invested so much time and effort in building the team, the
product, and the company, how do you disengage?*

If you are success-driven, you can remain detached and objective, but if
you're ego-driven you're attached to the need to have your name be a part of
the success of the business. I am success-driven. I care about the success of
the entity itself; I enjoy the process. But when I feel that things are moving
away from my area of expertise, I start to run out of steam. As soon as that
happens I begin to look for a replacement so that I can eventually leave the
company. In situations like this, it's very important to keep your ego in
check.

You moved from such different domains. How do you do it?

This is my personality type. Some people are good at learning more about the same thing on a continuous basis and growing with it and some are good at learning new things. I'm very good at learning new things. When I am thrown into something I don't know much about, my faculties are immediately engaged. But once I have learned it I don't have the taste for incremental learning. I can only go for the quantum leaps. The incremental steps don't excite me, so I disengage.

I spent many years becoming an expert in EDA space. I wrote a book on Verilog HDL and then I suddenly made this transition into building communication systems. Because it's new, it excites me, like EDA was new. Before that I was doing electrical energy software. Before that, I was involved with real time software; before real time it was something else.

My learning is at a pictorial, architectural level. Beyond that I don't learn. I don't want to know what goes inside sonnet frame - how many bits and bytes there are. I don't want to know what it carries or how it is packed. For me, communication is like road transportation with a truck on the highway. In the truck you have boxes, and in these boxes you have bags and in these bags you have onions and tomatoes. How the truck moves at high speeds is what I worry about, not what is in it and how it is packed.

So when you built the transition, say, from InterHDL to Fiberlane and you were actually designing products, were you an active contributor to the product design itself?

Executive and technology roles are very different. You need one person for one job and the right person for the right job. The technology part of the business is very intense; execution of a startup company is also very intense and if you have the same person doing both, chances are that things will fall apart. In my case I put together a team with the right person with the appropriate technical background. I'm more of the macro idea generator and I leave the details for the technologist: he knows the market. At every company I've done I have always had a technologist with me.

Business is nothing more than common sense coupled with experience.

In my InterHDL days I was less of a technologist; even though I knew the technology, I was more of a CEO. Eli Sternheim, on the other hand, was more of a technologist and less of a CEO. Same thing at Advancel; I was the business person and CEO and Jay Sethuram was the technologist. I don't want to be a technologist at all. I am excited by the applications and the impact of the new technology more than the fine points of the technology itself.

When you started companies like Cerent and Siara it was still an emerging market. Wasn't it a big challenge to be able to determine what was required by the customer?

I draw upon what has happened to other industries in the past. All industries go through the same phases – they have very defined phases. By analyzing the changes they had to go through, I can learn valuable lessons that I can then apply to the telecom industry.

For example, from the computer industry we can see how the workload increases. No matter what you design, it's already going to be overloaded before it hits the market. You put out a processor and Microsoft has already developed software that's capable of consuming all the power it has. This happens in telecom networks also. The load on the network is increasing due to continued increases of data and voice traffic. As a result, the network is choked up and one has to determine where those choke points are. Opportunities exist in addressing these choke points in the network. Basically, one needs to take a big picture view of the evolution of the network and what problems might arise, and how they can be solved.

So you had a fairly good idea by the time you started Cerent that this was going to happen?

When an opportunity arises, something clicks in your mind and you have to go after it. When you go after it, you apply everything you know from experience and keep morphing as you go forward. There's another way to do it, and that's to spend a lot of time, really focus in on a problem and work hard to find a solution. Everyone has his own approach. You just use the experience that you've gathered and if it looks right you say, "Common sense says this will work." Business is nothing more than common sense coupled with experience. You use your intuition and you link that up with the experience you've built up. Intuition, common sense and unconventional wisdom are all important things to have. Unconventional wisdom is your own way of doing things. If you follow conventional wisdom you might conclude that a certain thing cannot be done, but if you follow unconventional wisdom, you know that there are alternative ways of doing things, many different paths you can follow.

> *Conventional wisdom is good for operational matters whereas unconventional wisdom is required for innovation and disruption.*

Common sense will get you to the starting point and unconventional wisdom will allow you to make things bigger or better or different. Some people think that there is only one way of doing things, and if they don't do it that way, they will fail. But others can see that there are alternative approaches. They might fail or they might succeed. Either way, it's worth a try. Conventional wisdom is good for operational matters whereas unconventional wisdom is required for innovation and disruption. An engineer will use a conventional approach because he doesn't want to fail; he has to finish the product and there are certain prescribed ways of doing it, so he follows the pattern. But to grow a business you need a more unconventional approach, otherwise you will only scale linearly.

What were some of reasons behind the phenomenal success of Cerent and StratumOne?

In the case of Cerent box, which is a systems box, we needed a lot more people from the telecom industry. That's why my VP of engineering came from DSC Communications, because he's qualified to find people for the relevant tasks and is able to guide his team. In the case of StratumOne it was silicon, so I said that the engineering people have to be from the computer industry and the CTO has to be from the telecom industry. It was a different combination.

So those two decisions contributed to the success of the companies in terms of product. It was the combination of the technologist from the telecom domain and the supporting engineers from the computer industry that made the whole difference. For this kind of approach you have to think in an unconventional way.

What is interesting is that all along you have really stuck by your intuition and gut feeling.

Despite the fact that it is all high-tech and high- risk I am always driven by my intuition and my gut feeling, not by what someone tells me. I can consult people and take their advice into consideration, but I will do what my gut tells me to do. I also know that the moment I stop doing that and take decisions based on other people's opinions, I am bound to fail, because my next decision will also be governed by them and soon my intuition will be out of the picture. Once that happens I will be a puppet in the hands of other people. The belief system within oneself is very critical. To be a successful entrepreneur, there is no other way.

236

So, when an entrepreneur starts a company he should not start out with the conscious intention of getting acquired. If he takes that decision up front he'll make all the wrong decisions going forward. But in reality, when VCs fund companies they are funding the company based on the exit strategy. Isn't this a contradiction?

When starting a company, if you take the decision of being acquired as the sole exit strategy, it can inhibit your thinking. Your end result should be success, which means that the product must first be developed and then revenue must be generated. When this is the focus you will take the right steps to ensure the company's success. Ultimately, a company may find your product or technology attractive and acquire you or you may decide to take it public.

The major difference between planning for an IPO or for an acquisition is the size of the sales and customer support team that you will require. Thus, you will invest accordingly to make the transition to going public.

You are entering these new domains and are able to attract the best folks in them. That must be a huge challenge.

My book gave me my first break by providing me a lot of visibility. We began to be known in our industry and gained some credibility. Our credibility helped us start our first company- InterHDL. My credibility increased with each success and this has helped me attract the best folks and build the best teams.

What qualities do you look for in people?

Fundamentally, I look for suitability to the job, trustworthiness and some degree of enthusiasm. I look for the strengths in people and not their weaknesses, because the weaknesses can be easily surmounted.

What culture do you inculcate in each of your companies?

Fairness. Treat your employees in a fair way. Be fair in stock distribution. John Chambers said that he could not find any problems with the stock distribution plan of Cerent when Cisco acquired it.

Also quick decision-making. I confront people and share my views with them. One must be fearless. Some people want to play the safe game and go by the rules. I don't. In the interest of the company I am always willing to take a stand.

Over the years you have interfaced with several entrepreneurs. What have you learned from them?

I have watched and learned from the top entrepreneurs, continuously expanding my knowledge.

From Suhas Patil, I learned perseverance. He went through several difficult times but he never gave up. He kept going until he was successful. From Prabhu Goel I learnt how to do business. From Atiq Raza, I learned that if you take care of your people they will take care of you. From Thampy Thomas, I learned to go for the rocks and not for the pebbles. From Prakash Bhalerao I learned skills towards execution. Anything that is unreasonable will not fly. You have to ask: "Will it be reasonable all the way?" If yes, go for it; if not, you will hit the wall in the future and pay the price. From Raj Parekh I learned how to make complex things simple. I learned how to orchestrate. A proposal can be accepted or rejected based on how you present it. For example, you have to capture the attention of VCs during your business plan pitch in 30 minutes or less. You have to be able to excite them. It's all orchestration. From Vinod Khosla, I learned to have a passion for whatever I do. I learned how to make quick decisions and to support the people I back all the way.

You worked at Trilogy, Cirrus Logic and NexGen. What did you learn at these companies that prepared you for entrepreneurship?

I joined Trilogy following my short stint at National Semiconductor. At Trilogy I developed an algorithmic simulator for chip design. Trilogy was a vibrant company where everyone had their goals and objectives well defined. It was a good transition because although it was large company, the work environment was similar to that of a startup. I found the environment challenging and exciting. I was there for three years and learned about organizational design and the importance of a synergistic work environment.

Then I joined Cirrus Logic as its sixteenth employee, working for Suhas Patil. At Cirrus Logic I learned how to interact with senior management, to communicate my point of view and engage in discussions involving contrary viewpoints without being offensive. This eliminated the fear of communicating with the top brass.

After about two years at Cirrus Logic I joined NexGen as its ninth employee, developing and designing their logic design tools. I was there for six years and it was a great learning experience in terms of working with the best and brightest engineering team.

You co-wrote the book Digital Design and Synthesis with Verilog HDL. How did the book come about?

While working at NexGen, a friend and colleague of mine, Eli Sternheim, mentioned to me how difficult it was to learn Verilog HDL from the manuals. That sparked the idea for the book and we decided to write on this subject. Verilog was a proprietary language of Gateway Design in Boston, an electronic design automation company started by Prabhu Goel. When I broached the idea of writing the book to Prabhu Goel, he was very encouraging and agreed to license the Verilog language to us. I then discussed the book project with Atiq Raza, CEO of NexGen, and he agreed to give me three months leave from work to write the book. We wrote most of it in three months and published it under Automata Publishing Company, a self-publishing company, since no publisher would pick up the book. It is very gratifying to note that it became an instant success and has continued to sell around 2000 copies per year since it was first published in 1991.

Switching to your role as an investor, what role do you play in the companies with whom you have invested?

I try to understand their management processes and find out if they are well staffed and well managed. I pay a lot of attention to the business plan and the means employed to execute it. To execute, they need to have enough resources, both in terms of money and people.

You must be inundated with business plans. Walk us through the process that culminates in a decision to invest in a particular company.

I receive more than fifty business plans per month. Usually the plan is reviewed by an associate who has the relevant background. We first look for the strength of the team. The team members will be assessed for their management experience, technology competencies and market knowledge. We then review the product and its architecture to assess the feasibility of the solution and how the solution stacks up against the competition. Then come the financial details such as money required during various stages of the funding, the revenue plan and so on. If the plan meets our selection criteria, we call in the team for a presentation. If we are impressed with the presentation, the partners then meet to discuss the proposition.

Essentially, we analyze the risks and challenges associated with the evolution of the company from conception all the way through taking the company public and beyond.

With all this experience and knowledge what is your advice to the young entrepreneur?

Here are some key steps that I feel are important for building a successful company:

Build critical mass in the company as soon as possible The most important thing in the formative years is to find a few good people to do the job. The 80/20 rule applies here: 80% of the work is done by 20% of the people. A company is like a human being – made of many different cells with each cell having a specific function. And just like the human body can fall prey to a handful of cancerous cells, an entire operation can be brought down by a few bad employees. The value of talented people cannot be estimated on a spreadsheet.

Build a company from the top down. Hire the top managers and then empower them to build their own team and run their own departments. This leads to two things: It gives the manager a sense of ownership and instills loyalty in the new-hire.

Have the right chemistry and communication. It is very important to hire the right person for the job. I strongly recommend hiring known people through a personal network. You know the good and the bad side of the new-hire and that eliminates second-guessing.

Be over-capitalized. These days, the time-to-market window has shrunk by a large factor. A systems company, be it software or hardware, needs to have beta product out in four quarters after funding. A silicon company needs to do that within six quarters or they might miss the window-to-market. To be able to achieve these goals a company needs to be over- resourced in both money and people. I apply a margin of 25%. Raise 25% more capital than you need; hire 25% more people than you have planned for and take 50% more space than you need. No matter how carefully you plan, Murphy's Law will always apply!

Consider dilution versus building values. I never worried about diluting the company as a result of raising more capital than necessary. Instead, I worried about how I could use this extra money to build value in the company. In a startup, cash is king and in a properly managed company, value-addition takes precedence over dilution.

Be generous with your stock options. The more stock you give the employees, the more you get out of them. A generous stock-option plan enables the company to hire more talented people who will help enlarge and improve the company.

Know your limits and be a good manager. Good management is not about motivating through fear but about getting more out of people by having the right chemistry coupled with a dose of humility. If you can't do something, hire someone who can. If you are running out of steam, find a replacement before it is too late.

Work effectively with your board. It is important to know why a company has a board of directors. It is their job to monitor the health of the company and provide both preventive medicine and corrective measures before it's too late. In a startup they are both the mentors and the monitors. It is important for a CEO to keep them informed. A CEO gets into trouble less for poor performance than for poor communication with the board. Clarity, completeness, accuracy and brevity are key factors.

Get input from your customers. The technology is only as good as the customer thinks it is.

Aim high and look at the big picture. Focus the goals on the company's roadmap. Execute at full speed or the competition will take the market away from you. As an entrepreneur, I always wanted to build a company with large goals. I focus on an achievable subset of the goals and develop a corresponding operational plan to execute them.

How are you giving back to the entrepreneur?

During my entrepreneurial journey, when I ran out of money in the Advancel days, a well-known entrepreneur wrote me a check out of the blue to keep the company alive. I am now doing the same- supporting hard working entrepreneurs in their time of need. It gives me immense satisfaction to be able to do this. Hopefully when these entrepreneurs are successful they will continue the tradition. An entrepreneur once called me to say that he had put his house on the block in order to ensure that his company would keep going. He had done all that he could do. It was time for someone to help him, and it was my pleasure to do so.

In what way are you giving back to the community?

I am offering part of my wealth and experience. I have a dream of creating a venture fund out of my personal capital, the returns of which would not come to me but would instead benefit select charity organizations in the U.S. and in India.

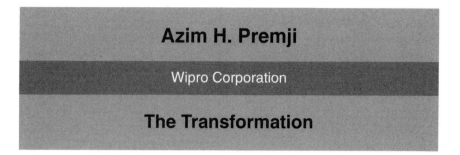

Azim H. Premji

Wipro Corporation

The Transformation

Azim Premji took over the management of Wipro Corporation in 1966 at the age of 21. Under his leadership, a $1.5 million company that had been focused on hydrogenated cooking fats has grown to a $625 million (in year 2000) corporation involved in services, technology and consumer products, with leadership positions in all areas. Mr. Premji is a role model for young entrepreneurs across the world. He has successfully integrated India's entrepreneurial tradition with professional management based on sound values and uncompromising integrity.

Premji has received several honors and awards. He was listed as one of the Top Entrepreneurs of the Year by *Business Week* and was *Business India*'s Businessman of the Year, India's most coveted award. Mr. Premji obtained his bachelor of engineering degree from Stanford University.

Raghu Batta and I interviewed Azim Premji in February 2001.

In this interview Premji catalogues the evolution of Wipro over the last twenty years. He outlines how Wipro is developing an organization and a mindset to compete in the new economy. Premji shares the strategy behind Wipro's diversification into areas such as IT, medical systems and consumer care. He discusses the company's quality initiatives, such as Six-Sigma, for developing best-in-class quality products. He explains Wipro's competitive strategy against the emerging Davids and existing Goliaths. He stresses the role of ethics and honesty in Wipro's success. He lists those things that India must to do to become competitive in the new, open economy and provides key pieces of advice to budding entrepreneurs. We end the interview with a closer look at the personal side of this intriguing man.

"The future is not what happens to you, but what you make of it."

Several of the ventures you have started over the years have hit the number one spot in terms of market position. You are the market leader in health care, fluid power and IT. Is there any common thread in your strategy that propels you to such leadership positions?

The most important thing in strategy, in terms of a new business, is focus. One should focus only on those businesses which give you an opportunity to become the market leader. If there is no opportunity either in terms of the competitive scenario or the extent of investments you're willing to make, do not enter the business. Once you have made a decision to proceed, go after it with single-minded determination. Be willing to commit resources, build teams and create competitive differentiations in order to be able to achieve that goal. This must be your mindset if you are to drive forward your vision for the organization.

Wipro's IT business has experienced phenomenal growth. Can you categorize the evolution of Wipro's IT business?

Between 1966 and 1975 our primary focus was to professionalize the company and Think Big. We were a very small company, put together in an arbitrary manner. Very early on we realized that the right people would make all the difference in making a business great. We put forth a major effort, spent personal time to track, attract and induct young professionals. We went to leading universities and management institutes in the seventies, when the practice of campus recruitment had not started in India, and sought out people from leading competitors. We transformed a company that had been managed by devoted people who had risen from the ranks by adding a fresh set of people who were capable of looking into the future, a set of people who could build the organization from the ground up.

From 1975 until the end of the'80s we supplemented our traditional business with high technology growth businesses. We went into the domestic IT market in 1980 when IBM exited India, and built an outstanding domestic business which stood apart from the competition.

In the'90s we used our expertise gained from the domestic IT business to build a global IT business. Our market valuation today really gets its strength from our IT business, with a significant amount of it coming from the global side.

Wipro diversified significantly in the'70s and'80s. What were the trigger points that led you to diversify specifically into fluid power, consumer care, IT and GE Medical Systems domains?

The first trigger point was when I came onto the scene in 1966 –67. We were a very commodity-based organization; even the edible fats business was primarily transacted through wholesale outlets and distributors. The first trigger point in that business was: "How do you come closer to the customer?" Closeness to the customer in the consumer business means really working much closer with the retailer, who then dispenses the product to the housewives. We changed the product strategy from tins which were wholesaled to smaller packs sold to retail outlets which had a much stronger brand following. Another trigger point was a shift in business distribution strategy from selling semi-branded commodity products to selling a more intensity-branded consumer product, distributed primarily through retail rather than wholesale outlets.

The trigger point to get into Fluid Power was a bit of an ad hoc decision. We wanted to diversify and we were looking at various projects. An opportunity came up and we went into a business where we thought that competition would offer us the chance to be number one. We saw tremendous growth potential in Fluid Power, as it supports the infrastructure industry, and chose Bangalore because of its research institutes and precision engineering industries, for this new business venture. Wipro's diversification into Consumer Care in the eighties played a vital role. The business's consistent profitability provided us with the financial strength that facilitated further diversification of Wipro into Information Technology and Healthcare Technology services.

Our refinement of strategic thinking was really exhibited from 1980 onwards, when we realized that our major thrust should be toward information technology. We systematically evaluated opportunities in information technology and went into a business spearheaded by microprocessor-based minicomputers.

The diversification that we made into IT, both domestic and global, was a well-thought-out plan. We wanted to be in a business that had high technology because we saw entry barriers based on technology. We wanted to be in a business that generated large after-sales revenue on an installed basis. As a strategic consideration, there are better operating margins in services as compared with products because there is more intimacy with customers. There was much more customer differentiation in services than there was in products. That was very much a part of our plan. The steps we have taken in building the service content of our product businesses systematically bears out that fundamental thinking.

We went into the Medical Systems business for three reasons. First, there is a lot of similarity in how medical systems and computers are sold and serviced. There is an extremely strong commonality of rhythm between the two businesses. The medical business offers a great opportunity in the after-sales service market, as does the IT business. We thought that service market would be very profitable, which it has turned out to be. So it is a combination of high quality products requiring high quality selling, followed through with a large installed base of a highly profitable service business similar to computers.

In addition there is a very high degree of transferability of key talent across the two businesses. Apart from common functions like human resources, finance and materials, where you can transfer people more easily, when you can also transfer people from research and development, manufacturing and purchase, I think it's a strong confirmation of the similarities of the two businesses.

It was also driven by the fact that we were partnering with a global leader like General Electric, who had invested and is continuously investing in training, in best practices, and in very powerful new initiatives. This was a tremendous opportunity to learn from a business that was in rhythm with our existing businesses.

What are Wipro's plans for diversifying in, say, 5 years?

We have no present plans to diversify. Our business is primarily IT in the domestic and global market, with an increasing thrust toward the service side of the business and continuously going up the value chain. We continue with our consumer care and lighting business because we have a sentimental attachment to it and it is also very profitable.

Switching gears to ethics, one underlying message projected both by Infosys and Wipro is that of ethics and honesty. Is the ethical and honest approach a competitive advantage in India today for Wipro?

Ethics has played a large role in our success. This too was a Think Big tactic. When people believed that big business was not possible in India without compromising ethics, we practiced what we believed, conducting our business in an ethical manner which proved to be very effective and, I might add, quite strategic.

Today ethics has become the cornerstone of our belief system. It gives a sense of clarity, purpose and pride to the employees and the customers and fosters up-front communication between them. We have found that by practicing within a very strong ethical framework we are able to achieve a high quality of interaction with our customers and our partners in terms of trust. Most importantly, it has instilled in the employees the right way of doing business.

Ethics has become of major differentiator for us as an organization, and it gives three very important side benefits. The most important benefit is great pride, character and "muscle tone" in the employees. The second benefit is with the investors because it reflects strict frameworks of governance and transparency. Because of this, the stock market values are soaring. The third benefit is that it reduces transaction costs. So there is a commercial value to it rather than a loss. Of course it necessitates better planning, because some actions, by using ethical bypasses, can get done faster.

Today Wipro has a global presence, including an office in Silicon Valley and a global customer base. How is Wipro developing a 'global mindset'?

We are a very successful company today in the global marketplace but we are still far from being a global company, because the composition of our key management is still not global. I think that is the acid test of a global company. I think what you will see over the next year or two is much more hiring from within the domestic areas where we operate. For example, in Europe we will recruit from the local talent pool and hire Europeans; in the U.S., we will recruit Americans. The strategy will be to hire management locally rather than having Indian managers trained to operate in global geographies. For example, in July of 1999 we recruited the CEO of our global IT services business from the U.S. and he operates out of Silicon Valley. This makes sense, as the United States constitutes 65 percent of our global business. In the area of acquisitions in our IT services business we will possibly acquire, in phase one, an American company and perform a systematic integration of management positions. This will help provide senior and top management with global experience and will further the global mindset of our organization.

Obviously your organization is a key asset. How do you stay ahead of the curve?

First, in a high growth situation you always have to recruit very high-quality people on a continuous basis. Our recruiters and our senior management who are involved in recruitment have been well trained to seek people who are not only technically competent but who have leadership potential and a strong value belief set. So the first step is really in terms of quality of recruitment, to which we pay a great deal of attention.

Second, we make a very large investment in training people, not only in the technical aspect of the job, but in the value aspects of Wipro. We train people in terms of managerial leadership and in terms of how to work in teams. About 7 percent of our total expenditure on compensation and benefits is spent in training and induction. This is a lot, even by global standards. For example, we send top executives to programs at Harvard Business School. From this year onwards we will be sponsoring eight or ten people in a one-year management program at the Indian School of Business in Hyderabad. We plan to give them a year off at full salary. We think that the Indian School of Business will most closely emulate a global environment, as compared with other Indian business schools, because it is oriented towards that environment. We also continue to send employees in increasing numbers to various global programs. We encourage employees to attend global training programs conducted by General Electric in India, which has a global composition of people. We also sponsor our employees in programs run by global organizations in India.

Third, we have established high standards of leadership because at the end of the day, mentoring and leadership determines the quality of the second and third line.

What steps have you taken to ensure the highest standards of quality?

We had complied with ISO 9000 and TQM quality processes in all our varied operations. But to become a global company we knew we had to do better than the competition and benchmark beyond the best-in-class. After evaluating various methods we chose the Six Sigma Quality initiative. Six Sigma was a measurable tool that meshed well with our culture and thought processes.

In the first operating year (1998-99) of the Six Sigma initiative across Wipro Corporation we achieved a savings of one million dollars; in the year 2000, total cost savings were four million. When people see results their conviction grows stronger. These savings are impressive and the opportunities to increase them are enormous. But it is the cultural change across the organization in terms of customer orientation, increasing reliance on data in decision-making and the teamwork which results from Six Sigma that excites us the most. When we started, most of our processes were at Three

> *When people see results, their conviction grows stronger.*

Sigma. By March 2000, we had achieved Four Sigma and by December 2002 we aim to be Six Sigma in most of our key business processes. We will measure our progress on this journey by the yardstick of customer satisfaction.

In our software business we adopted the quality initiative of Software Engineering Institute, USA, for excellence in software processes. In 1999, all three of our software businesses - Wipro InfoTech's Enterprise Solutions Division, Technology Solutions Division and Wipro GE's Global Software Operations - were assessed at SEI - CMM Level 5, the highest level of certification. That made us the first service company in the world to achieve this standard. This a unique achievement and shows our commitment to quality.

The Government of India has recognized our quality initiatives by awarding us the Excellence in Electronics in Information Technology award for six of the seven years since the award was established. These certifications and awards are a testimony of our commitment to quality.

Let's switch gears to competitive strategy. Wipro has become a Goliath in the past few years. Infosys is another classic Goliath. What is your competitive strategy against the Goliath?

There may be a few Goliaths in software services from India, but you must appreciate that at the end of the day the total Indian exports of IT services, even at six billion plus this year, will account for under 2 percent of the global market share. In many ways the Indian Goliaths really do not compete with one another in the global market space. The market is so large that we often target customers that don't overlap.

At Wipro we have strengths that differentiate us from Indian and other players in the global IT services market. First, our focus is significantly stronger on the technology part of global IT services. More than 50 percent of our revenue comes from sectors such as telecom, networking, and global support. We are the clear leader in this sector when compared to any competition. Second, we have invested significantly in quality through the initiatives of the measurable tool of Six Sigma, and through SEI CMM, the global Software quality standard. Overall, our quality processes are deeper and more mature. Third, we have a very strong base in our domestic IT business. Because of our predominant brand in India we do much more end-to-end projects here in India than software exporters would ever get an opportunity to do. We have transferred much experience from the home base into the global IT market space in services.

What other countries do you foresee as becoming your primary competitors? China, for example, is supposedly investing tremendous amounts of money and resources in an attempt to emulate the Indian model. Ireland and South Africa are also getting into the game. Do you see them as a threat going forward?

Ireland is actually now becoming a potential customer, rather than a potential competitor. China will probably be the most serious competitive threat for two reasons. One, there is a national program in China to focus on IT service exports. Two, the volume of engineers that they produce is competitive with India. The present reality is that China, both in terms of quality of technology and quality of their present management abilities, is several years behind India. But we will continue to study China as a potential competitive threat.

I do see Hungary and Poland as a competitive threat, but in terms of numbers, not as great as China. Wipro's experience gained from the domestic IT services market, our commitment to quality and our technology strengths are clear differentiators that will give us a competitive edge in the global IT services market.

India now seems to be opening its doors to multinationals. What should an Indian company's strategy be to stay alive and competitive?

The flow of multinationals into India is going to increase, because multinationals now see India as a mainstream market. They realize that the European and American markets are not going to grow more than 5 or 6 percent a year, so if they are aiming for double digit growth rates, they have to be present in countries such as India and China. They have to be present as a mainstream strategy, not just on an experimental basis. So the quality of competition of multinationals will be far more serious in the future than it has been in the past.

My advice to companies in India is to make very sure that the business that they are entering or the business that they are in has something unique to offer which can sustain competitive differentiators. As multinationals have a far greater financial force, Indian companies will have to focus and build a critical mass around the business to be globally competitive. Indian companies must enhance efficiencies to meet global competition at a level that is totally different compared to the pre-liberalized era. And we must build better customer relations. Unless a company is globally competitive in whatever it does, it cannot survive in India for very long. You'll see the next major shakeout in India take place in the small and medium scale sector, and that will be driven by competition from China, because the import tariffs are being reduced.

When I look back, I realize that Wipro was not blessed with the abundance of resources that many multinational corporations have. What accounted for our success was integrity, unshakable self-confidence and a concerted effort to beat the global competition. It took relentless work to achieve this and a determination to acquire world-class processes, develop world-class teams and attract world-class leadership. Wipro's success is testimony to the fact that if you get your fundamentals right it is possible to succeed in India and compete with the best companies of the world.

How are you positioning Wipro for the future?

To succeed in the next fifty years we must have a powerful brand identity and world-class quality. Our entire corporation is geared up today to add value to the Wipro brand and to deliver quality to the customer. After considering our fundamentals, we have systematically changed our focus from the organization to the customer. Our future is charted by our core values - human values, integrity, innovative solutions and value-for-money. These values manifest themselves through our new corporate identity, a unique symbol with a Rainbow Flower and a positioning statement: Wipro Applying Thought.

What about your failures? Any lessons learned?

Our biggest failure was our diversification into finance. We had started a global company in financial services which we finally closed down about two years ago, taking a major write-off. There was a limited number of customers for the finance business and we did not adequately understand that sector of the market. That can probably be categorized as our largest single failure.

The lesson learned was that you cannot enter a business where you don't have a serious enough commitment to build leadership. As a result, you don't put your resources behind that business; you don't consider that the business is adequately powerful and you therefore become a dribbler.

Another lesson I learned was about the complexity of business. If you enter a competitive situation as a latecomer and are not able to build any strong differentiation beyond a temporary wave of large profits, you cannot build that business.

What is a typical day for you and what are some of your focus areas, both external and internal?

I typically work at home from about 6:00 to 7:30 in the morning and am at the office at 8:30. I usually leave the office about 7:00 p.m. I catch up on my reading at night. I make about 5 annual overseas trips, each of approximately two weeks. About 60 percent of my time is devoted to employees and customers.

Today I am a facilitator at Wipro. My key role is to anticipate the future and continuously raise the bar to meet new challenges. I don't believe in wide-eyed thinking without taking the requisite action to constantly drive people in the organization to meet new challenges. I feel that vision and action are absolutely complementary.

It is important for me to understand the pulse of the organization and culturize the organization in terms of growth. I think the biggest challenge is how to maintain the integrity of the culture of the organization. If you are increasing your workforce by 40 to 50 percent annually, how do you maintain continuity of culture and the strength of that culture?

What role has family played in your success?

The legacy my father left me was the importance of values. What initially began as a personal practice of values later came to make eminent business sense. My parents inspired me to use the values of integrity and humanity in conjunction with ambition in all aspects of personal and business dealings. My wife and children have been very supportive in my quest to grow Wipro.

Whom do you admire most and why?

I admire Mahatma Gandhi for what he achieved in India in terms of restoring a sense of pride and national spirit. He built a movement that was able to instill a sense of nationalism and pride in a constructive manner. It was very, very difficult in those days.

I admire Jack Welch because of his remarkable leadership and his ability to identify key initiatives in the organization that really differentiate it from the rest of the global competition. He is able to see through the success of those initiatives with single-minded devotion. This is quite remarkable and really sets him apart.

What did you learn from your days at Stanford University?

Stanford inculcated in me the competitive spirit, the engineering discipline and methodology, and the fire to benchmark with and beat the best.

What is your advice to the new entrepreneurs today? What should their first few steps be? In other words, what should the startup strategy be in India?

I would say this to ambitious young people: Hard work is the most critical ingredient of success. There is no debate about whether you need to work smarter or harder. You have to work both smarter *and* harder. And the hard work must be towards a purpose. You have to identify a purpose that inspires you, challenges you and gives you tremendous satisfaction to pursue. Then pursue that purpose with a single minded, determined, unwavering perseverance.

> *The future is not what happens to you, but what you make of it.*

Never, never stop learning. What is important is not your existing knowledge alone, but your ability to keep refreshing it dynamically. In this era of the Internet it is necessary for ambitious people to equip themselves with leading-edge technology. And accept the certainty of uncertainty. Things no longer happen in a linear, predictable manner. Use your imagination. Sometimes experience creates fixed patterns that get in the way of imagination. I learned long ago that the future is not what happens to you but what you make of it. Do not wait for opportunity to come your way. Actively search for opportunities and grab them when you see them. Develop the art of influencing team members and always play to win. Learning to persist in the face of bitter disappointment is the key to success.

What keeps you going? What makes you want to come in to work every morning?

There is a very simple answer. Ultimately, the race is with yourself.

Sabeer Bhatia

Hotmail, Arzoo

Morphing in Internet Speed

Unable to repress his entrepreneurial spirit, Sabeer Bhatia left Microsoft in 1998 to found his second major Internet venture- Arzoo (meaning "passion" or "heart's desire" in his native Hindi). Bhatia co-founded Hotmail Corporation in 1996. As president and CEO, he guided Hotmail's rapid rise to industry leadership and its eventual acquisition by Microsoft in 1998. Today Hotmail is the world's largest e-mail provider, with over 150 million registered users.

Bhatia's visionary contribution to the Internet revolution has earned him widespread acclaim. His many awards and accolades include 1997 Entrepreneur of the Year, awarded by the venture capital firm Draper, Fisher Jurvetson. He was named to the "Elite 100," Upside magazine's list of Top Trendsetters in the New Economy. He was the recipient of the "TR100" award, presented by MIT to the 100 young innovators who are expected to have the greatest impact on technology in the next few years.

Bhatia received a bachelor of science degree with honors from the California Institute of Technology and a master's degree of science from Stanford University.

This interview was conducted over two sessions. The first was at Bhatia's apartment in San Francisco, with the focus on his first startup, Hotmail. The second, conducted with Dr. Anil Gupta, focused on his second startup, Arzoo.

In this interview Bhatia talks about how, as a result of a change in the business climate during 2000, he managed the transition of Arzoo from a B to C player to one that became a global network for real-time technology solutions and support for corporate technology applications. He explains the various phases of the morphing and the challenges he faced in doing so. He also discusses how he negotiated his Hotmail deals with the VC and Microsoft.

"If the General does not believe that he can win the war, then it does not matter if his army is the world's best."

Mr. Bhatia, your first startup, Hotmail, was a phenomenal success. With Arzoo, your second startup, you hit the center of the dot-com bubble. When did you realize that your business model was out of date?

Arzoo went through quite a radical shift. Even the market we were going after had completely changed focus, and if we had not morphed I don't think I would have a company under my belt today. The entire consumer Internet piece completely fell out of favor. People in the past year had made some big bets on this entire space and found that there is very little money in real terms to be made out of consumers on the Internet. The B to C story of the last few years has really not proven itself. The first test was during the Christmas season of 1999. People started noticing the numbers and realized that somewhere along the line the business model was broken.

What were the trigger points?

There were several triggers that led to a de-commitment to the existing business model. The first indication for me was that it was very difficult for me to raise money in the Business to Consumer (B to C) model. When I spoke to venture capitalists in November 1998, they were very hot on the idea and I stuck it out because I didn't want to incur a dilution in the company. I wanted a certain valuation. Had I dropped my valuation much lower I would have easily been able to raise twenty to thirty million dollars in November, 1998, because the market was really hot. I did not foresee that the market would cool off. I didn't have any hard numbers to back my plan, but in this game you really don't have numbers when you start out. You have to run with an idea or a plan based on instinct. That's why everybody funded these B to C companies to the tune of fifty or sixty million. Everyone was predicting it was going to be big.

Had you agreed with the VCs on valuations and taken the money, would that have been a good thing?

It probably would have been a bad thing, because I would have committed a lot more resources and investment dollars into pursuing the older business model, which today is totally defunct. You just cannot make money in the B to C market. I would have committed much more in terms of dollars and resources to pursuing a business model that would not, in the long run, have succeeded. So the very first inkling that the business model might not work dawned on me in January or February 2000, because I did not get funding, though in February 2000 I finally did get a term sheet for twenty million from a VC firm.

Another trigger point was that earlier this year, around March 2000, when many of our partners began announcing that they were going to shut down their stores and go completely out of business. That was a big red flag. It was really the first solid proof that this whole market was not going to work. I went into a period of reevaluating. I think I had to convince myself first, before I spoke to the management team, because you can't demoralize an existing work force. It was during this period that I came to terms with reality. I spent four weeks thinking: Is this something that I really want to spend the next four years doing? Can I really make this work? In a startup, it's not just the next three or four months that matter. It takes four years of your life to build a startup. I was very fortunate the first time, when I did everything in two years from start to finish.

By April 2000 I knew I could not commit any more money. I was convinced that I would not be able to execute according to plan, and to top it off, the stock markets continued to display their dissatisfaction towards the B to C e-commerce model.

Is it imperative that the founder, the CEO, be a believer in the business model and have enough passion to communicate his belief to others?

Absolutely true, especially in a startup. You have twenty people on the team and usually two or three people are running the company. If the General does not believe that he can win the war, then it does not matter if the army is the world's best. Given that, how do you de-commit to yourself first?

You have to be completely convinced. You have to really go through a process of deep thinking, deep evaluation and re-evaluation, and be completely convinced that you do not believe the model will work. You try to see the future before someone else does. That's what an entrepreneur really does, right? You try to create something that is useful that has never existed before. When you reach that point, you have to convince yourself that this model is not the right one to pursue. Sometimes in doing so, you also have to look and see what else you can do. Is there an alternative? Is there some transition path? Or are you so convinced that this is really not going to work and you're going to have to shut the company down?

In some areas, like specialized chip development where you have committed an enormous number of resources, there is no such thing as transitioning into something else. You don't re-invent, for example, if you have already launched a service, such as Hotmail. Assume that it already has a million customers, but now, a few years into the game, you believe that the business cannot make any money because the customer services are all free. At this stage, if you want to morph the company it becomes very difficult, almost impossible, for you to say, "Well, I'm not going to do Hotmail, I'm going to do something else," because you already have customers, partnerships and relationships with companies that will all be affected. Fortunately, at Arzoo we did not have consumer partnerships or relationships that we had established. All we had was partnerships with maybe fifty or sixty commerce vendors and, with a majority of them, we didn't need a hard sell to convince them that we were going to annul the contract, because a number of them were also going out of business.

The next step really is to convince your senior management of your new strategy. Hopefully, you have an open channel of communication where you can discuss very sensitive issues. For example, I asked questions such as, "Let's question our business model." My style is to convince people of my point of view as opposed to telling them that this is not going to work and thus we should stop doing this. The approach I took was to say, "Let's talk about it, these are the reasons why I think it won't work but if you can convince me otherwise, then we will continue to do whatever we are doing. Let's see if this is the right thing to do." Fortunately, everyone in my management team was convinced and they said, "You're right, we cannot make money continuing down this path." I had also by then presented an alternative for them. I suggested that since we'd developed a platform for information transfer, why not leverage the same platform to go after a market which has some potential?

During these discussions with the management team, did you have any sense of whether they had already reached the same conclusion or did you feel you had to convince them of the need for change?

Many of them had reached their own conclusions. Sometimes you find that people who work for you are more sensitive to market swings than you are. During the first quarter of 2000, Business Week magazine issued a front cover story saying that B to C was dead and that the next wave was Business to Business (B to B). By then a few of our engineers, being highly valued commodities these days, started leaving the company because they had been reading about the e-tailing industry having trouble.

Which means that the management team had probably come to the same realization that things had to change?

Right. It is easier for employees who aren't part of the management team to move on when they recognize that the company isn't making any progress. They don't feel the same responsibility that the managers do. There's not that much loyalty, especially in Silicon Valley. I can't speak for every startup or corporation in the world, but in Silicon Valley it is as if you are literally hiring "consultants" for a very short period of time. People have seen companies go out of business so often in their lives that it's now become a fact of life. One of the things that you're seeing out of this entire fallout in the dot-com world is the emergence of the age-old truth that nine out of ten startup companies will fail.

The problem was that in the last two years nobody had seen any dot-coms failing. Today, there is a huge fallout in this entire space. This is not a new phenomenon; it has been happening since the '70s. Large companies go out of business; DEC for example, was swallowed by Compaq in the late '90s and even Apple almost went bankrupt. There are countless numbers of storage companies that went out of business in the '80s. In other words, going bust is not a new phenomenon. Everybody knew that people were nervous and the market that we were going after was not going to be that big.

Arzoo morphed and started going after the technical knowledge market. Did you already have a vision in your mind about this new direction or was this something that emerged out of discussions with the team?

I think it was a combination of the two. Primarily we needed to look at how we could monetize the existing platforms. Soon after we said, "Well, since we cannot go after the product-centric categories, let's go after general categories and have people pay for information, make it a people to people (P to P) information exchange." However, the problem with that is that people don't like to pay for information and, especially with the advent of the Internet, they want to get it for free. So fine-tuning that model further, we asked ourselves what kind of content people were willing to pay for. The only kind of content that people will pay for is entertainment content, primarily adult entertainment, or one that genuinely solves a business related problem. Every company has legal issues, every company has technology issues, every company has HR and management issues. It seemed to us that the most lucrative of these four was really the technology issue because today there are thousands of corporations using technology to become more efficient in their operation. So we fine-tuned that whole model, not just to go after the technical area but also to consider how we could create this product so that we offered it only to companies, enabling them to solve their IT related issues. That's really how our current business model was born, out of those discussions.

Were you thinking in terms of technology platform and finding new applications or was this the only general direction that you evaluated? Or were there in fact two or three quite different directions that were in the basket and, at some point, you said, "Let's forget the other two and focus on technical knowledge."?

In our case the only difference was whether we should go after all markets of knowledge and knowledge exchange or limit ourselves just to IT. This was the major discussion.

It seems that a good thing about focusing on technological knowledge is that it becomes obsolete very quickly.

Yes! And there is a constant need for it. You have an engineer who might be great in Oracle 7, but soon Oracle 8 comes out; then that same engineer either needs retraining or needs to talk to some experts. Companies are constantly coming out with newer products and newer pieces of software, operating systems, databases, all of which make our value proposition quite compelling.

In this new model you have corporations as customers on one side and you have the individual experts on the other side. Do you act as a filter?

Oh yes. First of all, we filter the quality of people who become experts on our site. Only those whose resumes are completely verified by individuals in our company are allowed to become experts. Second, over time what we want to do is hire in-house super moderators to be the first line of defense for all the questions that come in; so every question that comes in is first filtered and verified as a proper question. Every answer that goes back to a corporation is also filtered through our own set of experts. Otherwise there is no difference other than the monetary component between us and a use net group, where people can post a question and get an answer, but without quality control. We tell our customers that we will ensure quality, we'll give them the best answer, we'll give the right answer, and we'll put a layer of moderation in between.

In terms of orchestrating the morph, how do you recommit after changing the focus of the company?

Ultimately, the CEO has to convince the whole company, including every employee in the company. The CEO must address the reasons why the existing business model will not work, the reasons for the shift to a new business model, why the new model will succeed, and finally some details about the transition. Ultimately the leader has to convey his belief and convince every employee of the company, either directly or indirectly, of the change in the strategic direction of the company.

Did you have to change any people in the management team?

Our VP of engineering left and a lot of people in the lower ranks left, which is not unusual. People believe in certain things, that's why they join companies. Conversely, they leave if they don't believe in the business model.

Is it true that morphing a company at a later stage of development is a much bigger challenge?

Absolutely, no doubt about it. Although the task becomes easier as long as the product or service has not yet been offered to customers. I believe that wholeheartedly. If we had already launched, spent significant amounts of money marketing and built a brand for ourselves, as most people want to, it would have been a lot more difficult. Then you would have to convince millions of people all over the world that Arzoo had become something completely different today.

Did any of the business model components from the "old" Arzoo carry over to the "morphed" Arzoo?

A number of technology-related implementations used in the old Arzoo model were leveraged into the new model. For example, the database platform was reused and the entire instant messaging platform that we had built was also successfully used. It was primarily the business model that changed.

Was that an early decision, to keep the core technology because that's where the bulk of the investment had been made?

Yes. We asked how we could use this technology for something else, rather than saying, "Let's pursue a new business model and develop a technology from scratch."

Most of the time, there is competition and no company is out there alone. If there is competition, what kind of a competitive strategy do you try to follow?

There is no company doing exactly what we are going to do now. There are companies that offer a platform for information exchange, but these are too generalized. They are spread too thin and there is no level of moderation; they are not built for corporate use. They are primarily intended for people-to-people information exchange. For example, Exp.com or Expertcentral.com are built so that individuals can exchange information. On the corporate side, none of these other companies have a layer of super moderation. Our whole focus and philosophy is to employ experts on-line, in-house and to enable people to get answers to all their questions. The sale is very much directed to the CIO. Our focus is not just techno-centric; we are going to scale that down to 6 areas of expertise, and will hire 6 super moderators in those areas. For all of those reasons, we are very different from anyone else.

They say no good deed goes unpunished and no good business model remains unimitated. If Arzoo has the best business model in this space, others will be out there, either shifting to your model or new people will be coming in. What is your strategy for staying ahead?

First of all, we have the first mover advantage. Also, there is no need to own the whole market space; that's the beauty of this whole thing. There are 600,000 to 700,000 corporations that use technology. We don't have to have each and every one of them as a customer. We will be profitable if we service fifty. Let somebody else take the next fifty. In fact, if people copy what we are doing, it's a validation of our mold.

Arzoo is your second startup. How is it different from the first one?

The market conditions are quite different now. Usually people say that it is easier with the second one; I think it's a little harder for me, given that I've had to change the business model. The market has changed; look at what has happened to the stock market in just the last four or five weeks (August 2000). It's a lot harder to raise money these days. Many companies are going out of business and at the same time it continues to be a huge challenge to hire qualified employees in Silicon Valley.

In summary, I find it is more of a learning experience the second time around than it was the first time around.

The content is different, the business model is different and the timing is different, but do things become easier because you are Sabeer Bhatia and you did Hotmail?

I think the only thing that becomes easier is the access to capital. Everything else remains the same. As you said, there are actually four things that are really required for a startup to succeed: technology, people, the market, and funding. Other than funding, everything else remains the same. At least in the United States, it's a very fluid market. Just because I have succeeded in the past does not change any of those three other fundamental risks. The market has changed on us; funding risk is not as high as it could have been if I was a first time entrepreneur. But now, given that the market conditions have changed, it's still a big risk and the other risks, hiring the right people and the technology itself, remain the same.

What are some of the mistakes you made at Arzoo?

You learn very little from your successes, but you learn an enormous amount from your mistakes. I made several mistakes at Arzoo and I am learning from them. For example, I hired the wrong people at the beginning. I hired a group of people who were not best qualified to do the job. I didn't do enough due diligence and research and it delayed the project schedule as a result.

Another key thing I have learned at Arzoo is that valuation does not matter. You've got to get the right players in. It is better to have a smaller slice of a much bigger pie rather than keeping the whole company to yourself.

What did you learn from the venture capital world?

It was a tremendous learning experience. VCs are very good for shooting through your business plan and drilling holes in it. They make you refine your business model.

The business plan kept improving every time. The business plan is really your means of communication. You essentially answer every question in your business plan. So when the VC asks you a question that you have not answered, the next time around you incorporate that answer in your business plan so that the second VC does not have to ask the same questions over and over again. People don't realize how important a business plan is. It is my idea of communication with someone I have never met.

It's well known in Silicon Valley circles that you are a great negotiator. What makes a good negotiator?

What makes me good is my ability to see through somebody and assess their need for what I am doing and my need for them. I think the best negotiating skills come when you can walk away from the deal and not worry about it; then you can come out way ahead. Your instincts should tell you how much negotiating

> *I think the best negotiating skills come when you can walk away from the deal and not worry about it.*

play you have. You always try to position yourself in a situation where you have tremendous negotiating advantage.

For instance, with Steve Jurvetson (of the VC firm Draper Fisher Jurvetson, who funded Hotmail), during our first meeting we did not have any negotiating advantage. Our alternative was to go with some other VCs who were willing to provide us $100,000 for a valuation of only $1 million. Yet I was able to negotiate a better deal with Steve because of one comment he had made. He said, "Had we given Yahoo the term sheet first, for investing $300,000 at a million dollar valuation we would have nailed the deal. Instead they went to Sequoia (a leading VC firm which funded Cisco and Yahoo), who gave them a 3 million valuation and offered Yahoo funding of one million. So 33 percent and a million dollars for it as opposed to 30 percent and $300,000." A feeling that they had missed a huge opportunity came across and I played on this sentiment to my advantage. I informed him that if he did not have a deal in place by 5:00 pm I would go to Sequoia. We finally got $300,000 for 15 per cent of equity, at a valuation of 2 million dollars.

While negotiating with Microsoft, it was three of you against eight of them. What did you take away from that experience?

Once again our leverage was information relating to how Microsoft could profit from Hotmail. The key piece of information was that Microsoft had a hell of a time providing e-mail to two million MSN customers. Even at Microsoft's internal network they had a tough time with e-mail. Users complained that MSN e-mail was always down. The reason they were having trouble was that the NT operating system was not built for a large user base. It was not a scalable solution. To be fair, NT was a better solution for the corporate market, where they had a maximum of a hundred thousand users, but was not built for the 10 million user market space. However, they could not use Unix because NT was fighting a war with Unix. How could they possibly admit defeat? We knew Microsoft could not do it alone, so they had no option but to buy us. By then Yahoo had already acquired our closest competitor and there was no one else who could give Microsoft what they wanted but us.

Once you sold hotmail to Microsoft you could have become an angel investor or a venture capitalist rather than do a startup yourself. Any particular reason why you chose to do another startup?

I am an active investor, with investments in a number of companies. I've invested in over 22 startups and I am co-chairman of one company. I wanted to start a company one more time and I thought there was a window to do something interesting and innovative. It is not part of any concerted strategy. I basically wanted to continue having fun and at this stage of my life running a company is a lot of fun.

Suhas Patil

Cirrus Logic, TiE

Mentoring Entrepreneurs

Dr. Suhas Patil is one of the best-known visionaries in Silicon Valley. He is an active angel investor in the Valley and a mentor to many entrepreneurs through the nonprofit organization, The Indus Entrepreneurs (TiE).

In 1981 he started Patil Systems and three years later joined hands with Mike Hackworth to found Cirrus Logic.

For several years Dr. Patil was an assistant professor of electrical engineering at the Massachusetts Institute of Technology (MIT) and later was associate professor of computer science at the University of Utah.

Dr. Patil received his B. Tech in Electronics and Electrical Communications from the Indian Institute of Technology, Kharagpur. He earned his master's and doctorate of science in electrical engineering from MIT.

Raj Baronia, CEO of IndoLink and I met with Dr. Patil at the Cirrus Logic headquarters. This was our first interview for the book. Though I had researched extensively for this interview, I was still quite nervous. Dr. Patil immediately put us at ease and began with kind words of encouragement.

Dr. Patil wears his experience well and has a presence similar to that of Albert Einstein. He speaks slowly and deliberately and is not at all excitable. He is known to be a very warm and helpful man and puts his heart and soul behind his words.

Showcased in this chapter are Dr. Patel's first few steps on his entrepreneurial journey. We talk in detail about how he transitioned from being a professor to an entrepreneur, examining the common elements between the two. Dr. Patil talks at length about the relationship of Guru and Chela that emphasizes a very close professional, emotional and personal interaction between teacher and student and the vital role it has played in the success of his company and TiE.

**"A niche today, an ocean tomorrow.
Those are the kinds of situations that
represent the best opportunities."**

*Dr. Patil, we would like to start this interview at the stage when you had
developed the VLSI technology and were seeking to take it to the next level,
to get it adopted and implemented. What triggered you to take the entrepreneurial route?*

Transition leads to the birth of new enterprises. These new enterprises may
have limited resources, but they carry a new vision of the future and have
advantages over established companies that are hindered by their conventional ways. But the important thing is that the change needs to be large
enough to create a market, which even if small today must be large enough
later. A niche today, an ocean tomorrow. Those are the kinds of situations
that represent the best opportunities.

It was my conviction that such a transition was about to occur in the industry. This change would be driven by the manner in which chips were going
to be made. There was definitely a transition point. The number of transistors on a chip were getting up to 65,000 and VLSI was looming on the horizon. It was felt that to place a large number of transistors on a chip we would
need design automation. Automation in those days was called silicon com-
plier and this was my field of expertise. It would change a lot of things - who
the designers were, and how the industry would operate. This was my
assessment of the scope of the technology and I had some inkling of the
business implications. I had already conducted research in this field as a professor but it had reached a stage where somebody had to adopt it and take it
further, and that's what I was seeking when I took the entrepreneurial route.

*You were a pioneer in your field. This was a new concept with no available
information on the commercialization of the concept. How did you conduct
the research and gather all the information needed to determine that this
was a viable venture?*

I had already considered that it might make sense for me to start a company.
I approached my close friends and used them as sounding boards. They
pointed out everything I needed to worry about; such things as: "Do you
have enough money? Can you attract funding? This is a new field; do you
really want to go out there?"

I was the first one in this field and there was no ready-made knowledge out
in the community. I found this knowledge in two places. The first was from
an incubator program at the university. The incubator would identify entre-

preneurs who would come and give a talk. I had been listening to them for a long time and started to form a picture of what was involved in building and creating a company. The second source of my knowledge and information were people who I knew and who I viewed as my mentors. Among them was Dr. Amar Bose, of Bose speaker fame. I had been his teaching assistant and had maintained contact with him. Then there was Dave Evans, who started Evans & Sutherland. There was Dean Brown, who himself went on to start three companies and was in charge of the incubator program at the company. I made appointments with them, ran my ideas and got a better understanding of what was involved and what I was headed for. Another important person was the senior VP of operations at General Instruments (GI) who had also started playing the role of a mentor. So I ran my ideas by him, to double check and understand the risks and the opportunities involved.

From all this research I synthesized that the market was ready. I realized that I had the knowledge and was indeed the world's best or among the best in this particular field of technology which would be the enabler of this change. I had no money of my own; my savings were hardly enough to initiate the kind of company I was thinking of. I was thinking of a hundred million dollar company. You may ask: why a hundred million dollars? Ten million would be too small a goal. One hundred million was a goal that sounded interesting, that was challenging; it was a stretched goal. But what you worry about when you start out is not the hundred million; you come down to earth and try and figure out what to do in the first year.

So how did you get the money for that first year?

At that time there was no VC money in Salt Lake City, so I went to the alternate source – corporate money. In this case, GI had shown an interest in the technology (VLSI) that I had developed for their internal use. I proposed to them that if they funded this research and development they could have the use of the technology. We also agreed that I would be free to do whatever I wanted to do with the technology and any revenue or proceeds generated from it would be shared with them.

I also requested working capital based on my track record with their research programs at the university. I obtained a $90,000 loan that was used as the working capital and a $360,000 contract for one year with a commitment that if everything went in the right direction they would follow it up with subsequent contracts. This was the basis on which I left the university to take the risk.

How did you make this transition from academia to entrepreneurship? Coming from a technological and academic background, did you find the business issues involved in running a company daunting?

Definitely; it was very challenging. The first thing I discovered was that the world of finance has its own terminology and this was all new to me. I had to learn these things in real time. Then there was customer interaction, deal making, and so on. I had to learn all this as I was building the company. My family has no business background, so I was doing all my learning at the school of hard knocks. But I think the best preparation for starting a company is a doctoral program. This gives you the clarity of thought and the pioneering spirit that is needed. The other thing that really helped was my experience as a professor. You also have to realize that in the American educational system, professors are raising money for their projects all the time. We write grant proposals for national science organizations and other funding organizations so that our researchers may have a stipend and pay their tuition. So I had been doing this already for almost a decade. I had been managing projects there with teams of 10 to12 people, so there was zero transition, in terms of management skills, from the university to a company.

How did you find the customers? How did you market yourself? What was the winning strategy?

If the customer need for a product is very, very great and there is no other place to find it, they are often willing to give you the money so that you can create something they can have for their own use. This also allows you to build a company around it. When you build a company around it, that technology will continue to be developed and the original company will not have the burden of paying everything in the future. I made use of this strategy of up-front customer financing. However, this was possible only after I had built credibility.

You now had the financing; what were the next few steps that you took to build the company?

Since this was not an established company, we literally started from scratch by searching for a place and looking for cheap furniture. All my employees were my former students; they were the only ones willing to take the risk with me. My team shared my vision and we already had a good established working relationship. What I had to learn, quickly, was how to set up the facilities and the financial systems. There is nothing complicated about this but since I had never done it before, I had to learn. For example, when you pay an employee you have to deposit the social security amount and other taxes you collect from the employee and your own contribution to that in a federal registry within three days. So the first thing I did after deciding to start a company - and indeed what any entrepreneur should do- was hire a good corporate attorney. The first professional to be hired on the job should be an attorney so that he can guide you on how to structure the company and also make you aware of all your obligations. Technical people usually don't have any idea about how these things work.

The second important thing is to have a firm grip on the ability to keep accurate accounts. I was fortunate in this matter. Since I had received a contract, GI sent their auditors to me and the auditors explained how I should set it all up. They provided up-front advice and the recipe for setting up the basic infrastructure.

Then we bought our furniture. First came a dining room table. You need a surface where several people can work together. I managed to get this from my home. All entrepreneurs are clever. They never pay full price for their furniture. We checked out newspapers ads and purchased furniture from auctions. This was the only time I ever went to an auction. So now we were in business.

In the Revolutionaries interview with the Silicon Valley Technology Museum you were quoted as saying: "Well, it was very nice in the beginning when the contracts were there. The hard times came when the contracts ran out and we had to make it on our own. And that is really where true entrepreneurship came into play." How so? Can you elaborate?

When we had a contract from GI, they were paying for everything. Life was easy. All we had to do was keep the technical work going and the funds kept coming. We had no worries about where the paycheck came from. There was a mutual understanding that the minimum contract would be for a two-year period. By the time we reached the second year, GI was experiencing slowdown and started cutting costs. It became clear that Patil Systems would be the first to go. At the same time, Larry Hill, our champion at GI, decided to retire. This added to the uncertainty. I had to talk the new guy on the block into supporting us for a few more months. We still had a certain amount of money but it would run out fast. So I called my team together and said, "Look, we don't owe anyone any money. We have some money left over from our previous contract. It is going to be very rough going forward, so we have to make a choice. We can either close the company and no one will come after us or we can decide that we want to build a company." I said, "As much as you wish to support me, it is in your best interest to find a safer place. Take your time and situate yourself." I asked them how they felt. The team said, "We've come so far and we are going all the way. We understand it may not be easy." I committed to them that I would always pay them before paying myself. It was a very crucial meeting.

I was not sure where the payroll was going to come from and I could not assure them that I could always meet it. The prospect of getting small contracts was there but it would not cover all our costs. It soon became clear that I needed to raise some money. There were no VCs in Salt Lake City and I had already started making calls to friends and family in an attempt to raise funds.

I was able to raise $380,000 from friends and family. Meanwhile, I had several small contracts for the development of chips. However, money that comes in dribs and drabs is not as useful as money that comes in one lump sum. You cannot sanely plan with sporadic funding; the focus is to just keep the torch burning.

By this time we had definitely decided that we were going to be a semiconductor company. Our product would be chips and not design automation. To do this we would need some serious money.

Is this why you moved to the Silicon Valley, to seek out VC funding to finance Patil systems? What were the immediate challenges when you moved to the Valley?

In 1984 I moved Patil Systems to Silicon Valley in California where the company was renamed Cirrus Logic Inc. It was a logical thing to do as the company's customer base was here. Within three months of moving here I was able to get venture capital. Venture capitalists like to invest in companies that they can get into the car and drive to, so to speak. The biggest challenge was to quickly establish myself here. I began by tracking down all my students, and through them I made more contacts. That was a challenge.

Cirrus Logic grew to be a major semiconductor company developing, manufacturing and marketing integrated circuits for personal computers, communications and consumer electronics.

You were the first president of TiE. What, in your opinion, is the purpose of TiE? What are its main goals?

> *The Gurus must be willing and able to give the time and energy necessary to make their disciples successful.*

TiE has three objectives: networking, mentoring entrepreneurs, and integrating with mainstream society. TiE's mission is to foster and support entrepreneurship. The Gurus must be willing and able to give the time and energy necessary to make their disciples successful. We want our success to be replicated many times over. This desire is at the core of our mission. Most entrepreneurs possess technical skills but lack financial, marketing, legal and networking strengths. We bridge this gap. I believe TiE is an effective way to channel the energies and ideas of its members toward a worthwhile purpose. My contribution has been to lead this effort, to put the program together, to structure it.

Shifting gears to angel funding, what do you look for when you invest in a company?

What I look for is what I call the "sparkle factor". I see it in people who are very alive with ideas, are inquisitive, thought provoking, and who welcome challenges. Even if they don't know enough, they have the courage to try. Beyond this, I look for the ability to formulate problems and to solve them. I look for the right attitude and the ability to engage interestingly with other people. Then it comes down to people. I look at the founders. Who is the CEO? Can they attract excellence? Will people want to come to work for them? I pay a large amount of attention to the team members, their skill and character and personality traits. Are these guys going to succeed, no matter what?

We also look closely at the products and technology to see if what is delivered to the market can, at least for the foreseeable future, provide a sustainable competitive advantage. In order to succeed you need a fantastic team, but at the same time, if you are working on an area which isn't going to yield a competitive advantage, you cannot build a company and you will not get funding. On the other hand, if you have a fantastic product and technology but don't have a team with the capacity to execute it, you are again not going to go anywhere. Similarly, if the team has the technical capacity but lacks tenacity and drive, it isn't going to amount to anything. If the team has all the above but does not have integrity and intellectual honesty, I still cannot work with them. So all of these things have to come together. You have to ask yourself, "With the right advice and support, is this team going to do it?"

If the answer is yes, then I participate with them. I give advice, I guide, and in certain instances, if appropriate, I give them money.

How do you mentor? What is your approach?

One has to nurture and mentor the entrepreneurs so that their odds of success improve. I was raised with the concept of guru/chela, which is very applicable in the Indian culture. Younger professional apprentices learn from master craftsmen. Silicon Valley is a wonderful place for this.

I am the coach. The way you guide a business is to assume that you are running it. What would I do? What would I worry about? I constantly try to understand what is going on and interpret the information. Then I make sure that the team understands the situation. Coaching involves raising questions, feeding information and motivating people to think. I encourage them to benefit from my experience. Here I utilize something I learned during my years as a professor. When you are advising a doctoral research, the student and professor meet every week during his theoretical or laboratory research and the professor is in constant discussion with this individual. In the industry today, this is called a one-on-one communication. Through this continuous communication there comes a point when the professor is able to understand what the student is experiencing. The professor is able see through the student's eyes, touch through the student's hands. The moment you have such an interaction you are able to understand fully what is going on and can provide better input. This is the sort of skill development that takes place with a good professor. This skill is exactly what is needed in guiding an enterprise. The entrepreneur starts out with an abundance of technical skills and energy and has to learn rather rapidly. Coaching involves bringing up, educating and fostering the learning of the person so that the speed of learning and efficiency becomes very, very high. By the end of this process, the entrepreneur becomes very skilled and now the role of the mentor switches from that of skill developer to that of consultant. When you see an entrepreneur fumbling you have to remember that twenty percent of things create eighty percent of the value, so you have to identify the twenty percent and take the hit on the rest. The twenty percent you do right is fine; the rest is of little significance. It is not a perfect world, you know. There are also many other things that are basically observations about reality in business that you can share with the entrepreneur. I try to provide the entrepreneur with the right perspective.

What skills do you see as necessary for success in the 21ˢᵗ century?

When things move and change so fast you have to learn to become an athlete. Athletic teams prepare and coordinate ahead of time, anticipating all situations, as there is no time to deal with them on the fly. This kind of approach is going to be vital.

You were one of the first few to set the stage. You are among the pioneers. What has been the key to your success?

I am a person who would rather listen, which I think is very important. You get more things done when you keep your mental faculties working very fast. The more you talk, the less you think. I have the ability to remain calm even when things are falling apart. I also have tremendous ability to focus to the point that I am sometimes described as being a little bit absent-minded. The energy comes more from focus of mind than from any arrogance about who I am.

What is your advice to all those aspiring young entrepreneurs?

First, you should be able to communicate well with the team. Second, you should be able to depend on your intellectual capital. Third, you must know how to find and recruit team members. Fourth, you must really understand the entire competitive landscape, and fifth, you must know your limitations.

Hatim Tyabji

VeriFone

Ahead of The Times

Hatim Tyabji serves on the boards of Ariba, Best Buy, eFunds, PubliCard and SmartDisk. Additionally, he serves as chairman of the board of the Datacard Group, sits on the dean's council at the State University of New York, and on the advisory board of the School of Business at Santa Clara University.

From 1986 to 1998, Tyabji was chairman and CEO of VeriFone, the transaction automation pioneer active in 110 countries. Prior to joining VeriFone, Tyabji held several positions at Sperry Corporation, the last one being president of information systems.

He holds a B.S. in electrical engineering from the college of engineering in Poona, India, and an M.S. in electrical engineering from the State University of New York, Buffalo. In addition, Mr. Tyabji also holds an MBA in International Business from Syracuse University and is a graduate of the Stanford Executive Program. He was awarded an honorary doctorate by the State University of New York.

I caught up with Tyabji at his residence in Los Altos Hills on a sunny Californian morning. Tyabji is a passionate man, filled with energy. He speaks from the heart about things that matter to him. One cannot help but respond to his enthusiasm. We discussed a variety of topics including strategies for survival in an economic downturn, the entrepreneurial mindset, the VeriFone philosophy and the reasons behind its success.

Note: A portion of this interview contains excerpts from Tyabji's speech at the TiECON 2001, Austin. Venkat Voruganti was kind enough to provide the transcription.

"The true power of growing any enterprise is 5 percent technology and 95 percent psychology."

Reflecting on the last three or four years, have we, in fact, lost our soul? Can you compare and contrast it with the 1987-88 downturn?

If you look back from late 1996 to recent times, you see an inverted dynamic. This inverted dynamic was a total aberration, born of a stock market gone mad. Entrepreneurs began to regard the capital markets not as a disciplining force but as the customer. That was the fatal mistake. In regarding the capital market as a customer, companies were created, hyped and sold with very little concern for attracting customers, with an intention only to create artificial wealth. The result was that many participants ended up wearing a set of ethical blinders, behaving in ways that seemed, interestingly enough, perfectly acceptable within the insular context. However, when viewed with a modicum of objectivity, the behavior was shortsighted at best. What we had was a bubble that I don't think we had seen before in high technology.

If you look at the enterprise, the ERP space, from a software standpoint and look at the last year or two, you see that CEOs of very large companies were under extreme pressure from their boards, who were asking: "What are you doing in electronic commerce?" They didn't have the foggiest idea what "electronic commerce" was. It made no difference whether or not electronic commerce was relevant to their businesses; they had to answer to their board. So they created vice presidents of electronic commerce and gave them budgets. These guys had to spend the budgets, so if any company came along that was applauded on the Street, they said fine and they participated and they became heroes. This was a world gone mad.

> *Entrepreneurs began to regard the capital markets not as a disciplining force but as the customer.*

This is much more than an economic downturn and the effect, particularly on high technology, has been infinitely more severe than anything that you saw in 1987-1988. I was out raising money for VeriFone at that time. The Dow dropped 512 points, so obviously I was extremely nervous. Percentage wise, it was massive, but within a week it had found bottom. Slowly but surely, in a couple of years it started to wind its way up. There was a fundamental level of sanity that existed at that point in time which eventually took hold. Today, April 8, 2001, the market has not yet found bottom. That's the real fear, not that we've taken a beating but that the market still hasn't found bottom.

The price/earnings ratio of the companies, and therefore the market valuations of the companies, had gone out of whack. This was not the case in the '87/'88 crash. This downturn really wasn't that difficult to predict, because you had a bubble economy that was obvious to anyone. But let's go back to '87; could you have predicted it? Not too many people predicted it.

How does an organization survive an economic downturn?

If an organization is focused on the fundamentals and understands that no company can survive without making a profit, then the approach is very different. What has happened in the last couple of years is that people forgot the word "profit". So you had absurd forms of behaviors. Markets are reasonably self-correcting. If you focus a company or reorganize a company to run on fundamentals and focus on making a profit, it is amazing what kind of discipline starts to fall in place. And this kind of discipline will be very helpful when you have to go through tough times.

I can tell you a couple of things that I have done over the years in several companies that have been extremely helpful. For example, we have always had a very global mindset. So if you have a global company and spread out across many areas, your ability to withstand a downturn is going to be much better. Right now the North American markets are almost at a standstill as far as high tech is concerned. But will that spread to Europe and Asia? I expect so, but so far it hasn't. So if you are solidly entrenched today in Europe and Asia your ability to be able to compensate is far greater. Today, if you are a U.S.- only company, you are toast. So that is one element which can be extremely important and helpful.

How can an organization actually take advantage of such challenging times?

It's a great time to hone the business. This is also a wonderful time to kill the competition. A downturn also gives you a chance to really sharpen your instincts and focus even more ferociously.

How do you see the story unfold in the next few years?

There's no doubt it will be grim. I expect that over the next 12 to 18 months the going will be very tough and a lot of companies will fall by the wayside. I definitely predict the P/E ratios will come down to where they should have been in the first place. Companies that have a low probability of being profitable will not be allowed to survive.

Let's switch gears to VeriFone. You established a unique culture at VeriFone that played an instrumental role in its success. Can you elaborate?

We put together a program called "Commitment to Excellence". There were three elements to the program.

The first and the most fundamental element was the VeriFone Philosophy, which has a set of eight precepts: building an excellent company, meeting the needs of our customers, recognizing the importance of each individual, promoting a team spirit, focusing on accountability in everything we do, fostering open communication, strengthening international ties, living and working ethically. This was the moral compass of the company. It was very clear from an ethical standpoint that if you were in VeriFone you lived your professional life according to the VeriFone Philosophy. And if you did not want to live your professional life according to that philosophy, then you should leave the company.

The second element was "Excellence in Thought". This was the strategic element underlying the philosophy.

And, last but not least, we had "Excellence in Action". We now had the philosophies and strategies, but they didn't make any sense if we could not execute and bring them to life. What we did in "Excellence in Action" was really very simple. We encouraged everybody in all of our locations around the world to share vignettes about where people have gone above and beyond the call. To go back to tribal societies, people did that by sitting around the fireplace and sharing stories. Well, we wanted to capture these stories so that when new people came into the company we could share these experiences with them.

So we put together this book with the eight precepts, with one precept per one page. But if you look at the book, you see it has not 8 pages, but 56. That is because the book is in eight languages. We were a global company and we were totally decentralized. It is not possible to ask your people to follow you if you don't make the effort to speak to them in their own language. One of the strongest elements of our global orientation was that we respected people's differences. Not only did we respect their differences, we took advantage of these differences. Not only did we take advantage of these differences, we celebrated them. Consequently we put together what in fact became a mini United Nations.

The implementation of the VeriFone Philosophy must have required a tremendous change in the organization. How did you create the change?

I was serious about these ethical issues. My people did not believe in it at the outset. It took me two years before they finally came around. At one point I was extremely frustrated because I felt that nobody was getting the message. I wrote a memo, partly out of frustration and partly out of desperation, and I sent it on my intranet. I think it really had the desired effect. It was a very heartfelt message that said:

"Life is not a spectator sport. As a VeriFoner, you are expected to live your life according to the precepts of the VeriFone Philosophy. If you disagree with these precepts, you have an obligation to speak up. If you observe actions that conflict with them, you have an obligation to take corrective action of your own. Sitting on the sidelines and complaining is patently unacceptable. I am counting on each one of you to continually be an instrument of positive change."

Let me share with you something that is personal. It is an experiment that I tried at home. I have been married for 32 years. It should be fairly obvious to you that I am very trainable. One of the household rules was that my wife's toothbrush was always on the right side of the sink and mine was on the left. That was the way it was for 24 years. Eight years ago I said, "Tyabji get some guts! Change the toothbrush from left to right." I got up very early, tiptoed to the bathroom, closed the door, and I switched the toothbrushes.

My premise was that if I was able to inculcate this kind of change at home, and if my wife was willing to accept the fact that after 24 years her toothbrush would be on the left and mine would be on the right, I could clearly take on the world! I have always believed that there is no reason to maintain the status quo in anything, including the conduct of human beings. Just try and change. Some things will be successful and some will be failures, but you will feel better for trying. I have always maintained that, whatever happens, I want to like who I see in the mirror; even if I am a failure in the classical sense, I will always walk tall.

I want to share a sports analogy with you, an analogy that I believe in very deeply, one that I have shared with many people over the years and that some people have taken to heart. It is about being able to overcome what appears to be insurmountable on an ongoing basis.

Roger Bannister, the English athlete, was a runner. In 1954 he broke the four-minute mile barrier. This was a barrier that had pushed back at man, holding the world's best runners at bay. Up until that point, nobody had run the mile in under four minutes. Bannister did that in May 1954. When asked how he broke the record, he replied:

"It is the ability to take more out of yourself than you thought you had"

Prior to Bannister's record, running the mile in under four minutes loomed as a psychological and physical wall. But once Bannister broke through to the other side - and this is the really interesting part - one person after another not only kept breaking the four-minute barrier, but also the mile record itself. Of the 22 mile record-holders in the last century, Bannister held the record for the shortest length of time, 46 days.

Roger Bannister's achievement reminds me that records give way. So company leadership that seems invincible, may not be. Those leaders get overtaken. And what it takes may well be what Roger Bannister described as the ability to take more out of yourself than you ever thought you had.

In this day and age, or in any day and age, what is the basic essence of an entrepreneur?

I would say that the basic essence of an entrepreneur can be classified into three primary channels.

Individuals, generally speaking, become entrepreneurs because they want the freedom to guide their own destiny. They want to be able to direct work the way they want to do it and not because somebody else told them to do it that way. They want to have a sense of purpose and contribution. And, last but certainly not least, they want to create economic value and well-being. And there is nothing wrong with any of these three channels.

With what mindset does one start a company?

If you want to be an entrepreneur but do not have the courage to dream, if you do not start an enterprise with the goal and the hope of leaving behind a legacy but are only focused on the economic benefit, then I believe you can still succeed, but there will be an emptiness. There will be an emptiness because all human beings have two sides, the emotional side as well as the economic side.

So, in the context of the courage to dream, I will talk about the companies that I started.

We didn't start off by saying that our revenues should be this or our profits should be that. We started off by saying we were going to change the way people live. In addition to wanting to change the way people live, we established certain imperatives.

In 1986, one of the imperatives we established was that we were going to be a totally virtual company. There would be no paper correspondence; it would be 100% email. In April 2001, you might say, "What's the big deal?" In 1986, this was unheard of. There was no Internet or intranet. We had put together a wide-area network. Intranet is a fancy word for a wide-area network. We put this network together ourselves and established an e-culture.

Part of that culture was that talent could live where they wanted to live. We went to Bangalore, India in 1988. We were the first company ever to do that.

It's not that we did great things; that's not why I am telling you this. I am telling you this because when you start something you want to do something nobody has done. You want to be able to innovate. You want to be able to look back and see some footprints in the sand and know that those footprints are yours and nobody else's.

Is it possible to aspire to spiritual and intellectual achievement while pursuing entrepreneurial success? Is it mutually exclusive to care and to lead? A lot of people will tell you that you can't care if you want to lead, because you will lose.

I absolutely reject that. Let me provide a truthful picture. John Steinbeck wrote in "Cannery Row":

"The things we admire in mankind - kindness, generosity, openness, honesty, understanding and feeling are perceived as the concomitants of failure in our system..."

"Those traits we detest, sharpness, greed, acquisitiveness, meanness, egotism, and self-interest are the traits of success.

While men admire the quality of the first, they love the product of the second."

And if you think about it, never were words more truly written.

As you look back, what is it that gives you the greatest satisfaction?

I will give you an answer and nothing in the answer is financial in nature. One of the elements that gives me great satisfaction is that there are 37 companies that are run by people who worked with me. I have an enormous feeling of pride and pleasure in having been able to help young people grow, to contribute by mentoring young people.

What is your definition of leadership?

The true power of running a company, the true power of growing any enterprise is 5 percent technology and 95 percent psychology. With all this technology, you run the risk of becoming a robot. Leadership is not robotics. Leadership is human. Leadership is looking people in the eye, pressing the flesh, getting them excited, caring about their families.

> *The true power of growing any enterprise is 5 percent technology and 95 percent psychology.*

What has been the key to your success?

At the end of the day I believe that there are two elements that have driven me and continue to drive me throughout my professional career. One element is intensity and passion; the second is caring for people and leaving behind a legacy of caring. At the end of the day nobody can take that away from me.

I believe these kinds of feelings don't come from business school. These are fundamentals that spring from the heart. These get inculcated in your early life. I have received a lot of strength from my family, especially my wife and two sons. When you are out there fighting in the streets in a hand-to-hand combat, you need to have a feeling of unconditional family love and support. That has enabled me to work at a pace and an intensity that would be difficult to do otherwise.

Who are your mentors and why?

My mentors are Dr. Martin Luther King, Mahatma Gandhi and General Rommel. As far as King and Gandhi are concerned, they had the courage and vision to look at the world not as it is but as it should be. If you look at Gandhi taking on the British Empire in the 1920's, it is unbelievable. If you look at Dr. Martin Luther King in 1963 taking on the white establishment, it is amazing. That is the kind of mindset that is required if you are going to succeed. People like King and Gandhi have changed the landscape of the world. They have left behind a legacy that is eternal. They went into uncharted waters and they went with courage.

Rommel was a genius in the art of war. He was extremely courageous and a highly principled person. So I take the intensity, passion and vision that King and Gandhi had and couple it with the tactical brilliance and the principled nature of Rommel and that's what I have tried to shape my life around.

Prakash Bhalerao

Ambit Design Systems

Angel Investing

Dr. Prakash Bhalerao is a well-known angel investor and venture capitalist in the Bay Area. He has helped start over fifteen successful companies and serves on the boards of a number of Bay Area high tech startups.

Bhalerao graduated from an engineering school in Indore, India. He holds a MS degree in electrical engineering and a MBA.

Raj Baronia, CEO of IndoLink and I met with Bhalerao at his residence in Cupertino Hills, CA. Dr. Bhalerao was in rapid-fire mode and his thoughts were communicated to us within a crisp hour.

Bhalerao discussed the key elements required to build a successful company. He gave us an excellent definition of a successful entrepreneur and shared his views on the Silicon Valley technological revolution and compared it with the cultural Renaissance period in Italy, four hundred years ago.

"An Entrepreneur is one who creates a direction out of confusion."

You sold Ambit Design Systems for $260 million. This is the third high tech company you have successfully helped to build and sell. What motivates you to do this? Why do you keep coming back? .

Retirement isn't yet an option. After selling my first company, I tried the retirement lifestyle for several weeks but I realized quickly that this did not work for me. I also see tremendous future opportunities in enterprises that address the needs of baby boomers, a huge market comprising millions of individuals who are now starting to think about their own retirements. It is not time yet for me to retire.

You have been very successful with the companies in which you have been involved. What are the key elements in building a company and leading it to success? What do you look for when you invest in an idea or a company?

In a simple form I look at four things: the opportunity, the market, the product and the team. You have to find a massive opportunity --- something really big. Then you have to look for an area in which there is currently confusion surrounding the opportunity. The next step is to have a "killer" product idea for addressing the opportunity and then to execute this by assembling a great "can-do" team that can tackle the opportunity.

For example, take a look at the Internet. People know it is scalable; scale it to the rest of the world and then look at the size of the opportunity you can create. Now look at the state of confusion in the market – there is chaos. Now the question is can you create a difference with your idea?

The other very important thing is having a good team. I saw a proposal from some people which had to do with the timber industry. It was an interesting B-to-B timber project proposal and I was intrigued with the idea. Then I looked at the team's background. One was an engineer from Oracle, the other was a chemical engineer. I began to wonder how these guys were going to pull off a project in the timber industry without having any real knowledge of the industry itself.

You need to have a great idea backed by a great team coupled with great confusion. Part of it also has to do with wealth creation. It is a positive feedback loop. You go through the four areas and constantly churn and refine the concept. This is how you start the company. Then you have to convince the VCs.

Let me give you an example. You tell one hundred people that there is life on Mars. Five people will believe you without question because you are their guru or mentor. Another five will believe you because it is what they've always believed themselves. Twenty people will be "Doubting Thomases" and you must win them over by the power of your argument. If you can do that, the remaining 70 people will believe anything the first thirty tell them is right. So you should always focus on capturing the first thirty percent of the market. The other seventy percent will follow along like sheep.

What are some reasons for you not to invest in a company?

Sometimes it may be because the idea was not ready. Maybe the entrepreneur was not ready to listen to what we were saying. Sometimes I have rejected the plans even though the idea was good, the market was great, the team was terrific. Sometimes I can just sense that these guys will be very difficult to deal with. An additional X-million dollars to my net worth isn't going to change my lifestyle. Why do I need the headache? I'd rather work with people I am comfortable with.

What should an entrepreneur's focus be when starting out?

> *Never, ever develop a company with the hope that you are going to get acquired.*

One thing I emphasize is the reason, the vision for the company. Never, ever develop a company with the hope that you are going to get acquired. This makes no sense. The only thing you should concentrate on is how you are going to be the number one player in the market and how your are going to achieve the highest valuation. This is the focus you must have. Never think: When I have a product I am going to sell this company to Broadcom or Cisco. You will end up making wrong decisions. Look at the example of Sabeer Bhatia, founder of Hotmail. I can bet he didn't start the company thinking that Microsoft would someday acquire it. I can point out examples of a lot of other successful companies. Out of all the companies that got the highest valuations in their market segments, 99.9% were potential leaders in their large market segments. Unfortunately this does not seem to be the case these days. A lot of companies are being started with the only vision being that the Ciscos or Alcatels will acquire them. That's the mindset for many people and they will end up paying a huge price. I do not agree with this mindset and do not support it.

You talked about the team as being a very important component to success. What is your ideal team? What is it comprised of?

An ideal team comprises a unique domain of expertise in various technologies. A team should also contain a very good marketing person to do product marketing. You need an experienced finance person or an angel. That's all you are looking for in the initial stage. That's all you need at the beginning. When the technology is proven and as you move forward there will be a few customers who partner with you and endorse your product, give you feedback that your product is genuine. This is where the marketing individual comes into the picture. As you move forward, you have to start looking at other aspects such as distribution channels, worldwide relationships and so on, depending on what challenges the company faces. You will need appropriate people in manufacturing and distribution who have managed international operations. At some point you will need a legal team and HR team. You have to identify the people you will need at the various stages and bring them in as needed, to complete the team.

What defines an entrepreneur? What sets him apart from the crowd?

An entrepreneur is one who creates a direction out of confusion. He can continuously analyze the risks and adjust to them. The risks are different when you start up a company, when you have 10 or 100 or 1000 people. Risks shift. The first risk is concerned with the technology. Then you prove the technology. Now the risk involves the product, the business itself. A true entrepreneur is like a mind reader or seer who can guess what is coming next, what you will want six months from now. The true entrepreneur continually analyzes and creates direction out of confusion.

You learn as you grow. Entrepreneurship blossoms when you leave your cocoon and venture out. It is the state of mind that gets shaped and changed. For example, look at all the Indian Freedom Fighters; most of them are foreign-returned. Why did people come from outside and create this revolution? As a matter of fact, if you look back on Indian history, the pioneers have always traveled outside their areas and from their experience they became enlightened. To me, NRI (non-resident Indian) is not an attitude or an image; it is the state of mind. It is the ability to look at a much wider perspective than what we would typically see, access it, and focus the learning into one particular area.

> *Entrepreneurship blossoms when you leave your cocoon and venture out.*

Why the Silicon Valley? Why is it the home of so many successful entrepreneurs? What is so special here? Can we replicate this in other parts of the world and spread the wealth around?

Let me paint a picture of the time we are in. We may think that what we are doing is new and innovative, but essentially we are repeating some of the things that were done four or five centuries ago.

If you go back about four or five hundred years, the world's best sculptors, painters, musicians, composers and scientists came together within a hundred mile perimeter and rose to fame during the Renaissance period.

Now we are in a high tech Renaissance, while that was a cultural one. There were certain events that took place in that geographical area around that time that sowed the seeds and those seeds grew into the success of the so called cultural entrepreneurs. It did not mean that people elsewhere had fewer capabilities or less intellect. But why did only those within that hundred-mile perimeter rise to fame? If we find out the answer to this question we will find out the reason for the high tech renaissance occurring in the Valley now. I will give you my perspective. Something made that period famous; it lasted for a while and then it dwindled. The reasons for why it lasted and why it dwindled are probably the same reasons that apply to the high-tech renaissance. I know for sure that we are in a similar renaissance period. There are very few networking company I know of that has gone under. There are only a handful of electronic design automation companies that have gone under. They get acquired or have an IPO and make their share of money. Why is this so? I think it has to do with two things that are fueling this renaissance period in the Valley. The first has to do with the education infrastructure here; the second has to do with the defense industry. Look at the educational strength in terms of the number of universities that are set up here, and the amount of investment the government has made in conjunction with the universities in developing war technologies. Technology came out of defense research. This national investment went on big time 25 years ago. Look at NASA and ARPAnet. These were the critical roots here that are having an effect now. So we are in a renaissance here. When it will disappear? I don't know. So it is very difficult to replicate this in India or anywhere else. Looking back on my own situation, had I come to this country and lived in Kansas, I would have been successful but would not have achieved the type of success that has to do with power, fame and dollars. They would not have come together as easily as they have come together here in this area.

If the Silicon Valley is the home of many young entrepreneurs, it is also home to as many investors. Angels and corporations are two examples of the many types of investors. How do they differ? What is the importance of each?

Let me begin with angels. "Angel" is a term for wealthy individuals who invest. Using this broad definition, I think California now has more angels than there are in heaven! Angel funding can be secured early in a company's life. Angels come in many shapes and sizes. Sleeping angels, who just give you the money and then go to sleep, have no idea about the progress taking place in the company. They only wake up when they smell an exit through an acquisition or an IPO. Blessing angels are those who give you the money, get on your board and "bless" your steps along the way. Lastly - the answer to your prayers – are the angels who both give you the money and actively help in making your company grow.

The second major category, "corporate funding", refers to investments that come from corporations. Ideally, these are major players in whatever industry the startup or early-stage company is in, and ideally they are also major clients of the young company. This is the approach that I used with great success in assembling $21 million for Ambit in its early years. Besides raising funds from venture capital firms and from two principal financial investors, Chancellor and J.W. Seligman, the initial corporate investors in Ambit included Cadence Design Systems, LSI Logic, and Sumitomo Corporation. While corporate funding is difficult to obtain, it is the best funding source as it increases the perceived value of the young company, brings added valuation and gives you some breathing space, as corporate investors tend to leave you alone if you so choose.

Looking at all your ventures, what is the key strategy that defines your management style?

I believe in the concept of finding the right people for a company's management and staff, and then leaving them alone.

Along your path of success, who has been your mentor?

I think at different times different people have been my mentors. In the area of business there are a couple of people whom I have observed quite closely. A person who taught me a lot is James Cudmore, who was one of the early founders of DEC, the company I joined while I was finishing my Ph.D. He was instrumental in shaping my thinking. I met Jim at a meeting and we hit it off. He was an experienced individual who could help me think things through. That's exactly what VCs do. A second person who comes to mind is in the Bay Area, the CEO of LSI Logic, and a well known personality in the

Silicon industry, Will Corrigan. I met him when I was running a semiconductor group at DEC. I like his way of handling situations, his method of analyzing things. Every once in a while when I had questions I would approach him. These men helped people build leadership and managerial skills. They would collect real data on people and identify how they could help you become better managers. There are also some teachers back home in India whom I admired very much. These teachers went way beyond the call of duty.

What one skill that you correlate to India has been important to your success?

I think it is resourcefulness. It is the capacity not to get bogged down by an obstacle, always being able to figure out a way to get around it. It's one of the best attributes of the Indian mentality. We Indians tend to creatively take advantage in such situations. I think that resourcefulness is what is needed in business. You run into problems and you have to find creative solutions. This resourcefulness is a very valuable tool.

What drives you? What motivates you?

> *Don't take no for an answer. Persistence and tenacity always pay off.*

It has always been intellectual stimulation. After a certain point, when you have made a certain amount of money, making more is not going to make any difference, unless your habits are outrageous. It is the intellectual stimulation, being around people, being around issues and problems that really challenge you, which is the single most driving factor. Different people have different appetites for fame; I don't particularly care to be famous. It is not who I am. What I really enjoy is that I have been fortunate to be able to work with so many interesting and dynamic people. Nowadays, when I see a business plan my preference is to go with someone I have known who has helped to make me successful in the past. This person will be my first preference, and I will be a help to him in any way possible. It's my way of returning a favor. Call it Dharma or Karma.

Any advice to the entrepreneur?

Don't take no for an answer. Persistence and tenacity always pay off.

Rafiq Dossani

Stanford University

The Venture Capital Ecosystem

Dr. Rafiq Dossani is a consulting professor and senior research scholar at the Asia/Pacific Research Center (A/PARC), responsible for developing and directing the South Asia Initiative. His research interests include financial, technological, and energy sector reform in India. He is currently undertaking a project on the upgrading of information technology in Indian startups and on the institutional phasing-in of power sector reform in Andhra Pradesh. Dr. Dossani serves as an advisor to India's Securities and Exchange Board in the area of venture capital reform. He is on the advisory board of two venture capital companies, Garage.com and East Gate Capital.

Dr. Dossani earlier worked for the Robert Fleming Investment Banking group, first as CEO of its India operations and later as head of its San Francisco operations. He was also the chairman and CEO of a stock brokerage firm on the OTCEI exchange in India, deputy editor of the Business India Weekly, and a professor of finance at Pennsylvania State University. Dr. Dossani holds a B.A. in economics from St. Stephen's College in New Delhi, India, an M.B.A. from the Indian Institute of Management in Calcutta, India, and a Ph.D in finance from Northwestern University.

This interview took place at Stanford University in Palo Alto, California. We talked over a cup of coffee. The focus, of course, was the world of venture capital.

In our interview, Dr. Dossani discusses the types of VCs associated with the various phases of the startup world, the startup financial strategies, mind-set, risks, and various exit strategies. We conclude with a discussion on how we can foster the VC concept in India.

"At the point of investment, all prospects look exciting."

From the viewpoint of a startup, how should they develop their idea?

Every founder starts by thinking of a business that will create value and great wealth for himself. He typically develops his ideas in collaboration with a small team. From the viewpoint of a venture capitalist, the team is important, but still peripheral to the individual founder. There is a view that great teams can be built around a great founder, but not the reverse. Venture capitalists are also worried that a great team, at the early stage, won't last long because good people tend to leave to start their own outfits. Among Indian founders there is the advantage that because of their strong networks they tend to have ready-made, dedicated teams who will stay together long enough to realize value. Venture capitalists in Silicon Valley recognize this as an advantage. On the other hand, Indian founders have not had very much experience with working in teams and often do not do it well. For example, the tendency is to be too individualistic, even when one is a team leader. This is not unique to Indians but is probably true of most Asians. By this time, venture capitalists in Silicon Valley have become aware of these unique qualities of Indian founding teams and are willing to work with them to bring in the balancing components.

What sorts of balancing components are needed in addition to a great idea?

Developing an idea usually means going to a venture capitalist, since no one else is willing to fund a startup. Of course there are various kinds of venture capitalists. At the very early stage there is the angel investor, usually a wealthy person who has been an entrepreneur and is clever about understanding the prospects of the technology idea being presented to him. This sort of association between the angel and the founders is particularly strong in the Indian community and has helped many startups get off the ground with a speed and direction that would not otherwise have been possible.

How long should the founder rely on angel financing?

Angels do not usually have the depth of contacts or industry knowledge to carry the entrepreneur beyond the stage when his ideas have reached the point of developing a business plan. Nor do they have the financial muscle to fund product demonstration and development. Broadly, one can identify the cycles of the business as shown on the following table (Figure 1) and the kind of venture capital, risks, and associated returns.

Product Stage	Seed	Startup	Proto-type	Market Testing	Exit Strategy - IPO/Buyout etc.
Time Frame	1-2 mo	3-12 mo	3-18 mo	3-12 mo	3 mo
Source of Finance	Angel	Early VC	Early VC	Mature VC	Late Stage VC
Post-stage probability of success	10%	20%	35%	50%	75%
Firm Valuation	$1-5m	$5-10m	$10-20m	$10m-50m	$100m+
Share held by VCs	10%	20%	25-35%	25-35%	0%
Burn Rate/mo	$10K	$50-100K	$150-500K	$250K-1.5m	
Return Expected	100x	50x	25x	20x	

Figure 1: Venture Capital Matrix

Returning to the question of balancing components supplied by the VC, you can see from the table how it will work. At the seed stage, the founders need the ability to argue through a good idea with an angel and develop a business plan. But is it really a good plan, given the state of the industry and competition? This knowledge and the ability to use it come at the startup stage when the business plan is exposed to the formal venture capitalists. They will be able to gauge whether the technology is disruptive or merely incremental and what the firm's value should be at that stage. At this point, the angels become passive investors and the baton is handed to the organized VC firms. Even within this group there are different kinds of VCs. Some are focused on being able to organize a good environment and provide support services such as legal support, recruitment and accounting support, and the like. Others have connections in Asia for making prototypes or to do software engineering work efficiently. So in addition to being able to evaluate technology and provide finance, early stage VCs usually provide some other support services. For example, Kleiner Perkins is famed for being able to help build the right team. Then there are Taiwanese VC firms who specialize in providing prototype manufacturing support in Taiwan, Indian VC firms who provide software engineers in India, and so on.

The early-stage VCs can take the firm up to the stage where it needs clients to test-market its product. This requires access to clients, but it is also the time when the firm needs to get itself known to people such as analysts, journalists, investment bankers and vendors. At this point, the technology has probably been proven on a small scale but needs to be tested in the market for scalability and robustness. This becomes the domain of late-stage or mature VCs and strategic corporate investors who can provide this kind of support. Such VCs also need to be able to introduce the firm to the world at large, so they should have those sorts of contacts. Because marketing is the single most expensive part of the firm, the funding at this stage is significantly larger.

You have said the startup should have a solid founder. What should the rest of the team look like?

In the early days it should be as technically sound as possible. Given the low expected shelf life of a startup, the venture capitalist feels it is important that short-run cash flow be minimized. When the probability of success per venture is only twenty or thirty percent, the venture capitalist expects that he will lose out on most of his investments. Of course he hopes to more than offset this by investing more heavily in the better prospects, but this is a process of discovery. At the point of investment, all prospects look exciting. It is only after the prototype is developed that one reaches a stage where the prospects look firmer. This is also the reason that venture capitalists stage their investments against benchmarks.

So the founding team will have to be tight. It will not usually be allowed to have such bells and whistles as a CFO or a marketing officer. Those things come later, when the product is in beta or test-market stage.

This is also the reason that early-stage venture capitalists rarely look at revenue models but focus on expenditure budgets. There is another reason for this apart from trying to minimize one's losses. To give you an example, suppose that someone came to a venture capitalist saying that he had an idea for reducing the cost of wireless connectivity from $1,000 per line to $200 by using a software-based solution in order to replace today's hardware-based solutions. In return, the quality of service would be perhaps ten percent lower as measured, let's say, by latency. After studying the idea, suppose that the venture capitalist thought this was a good prospect. Suppose the idea indeed succeeded. Who would adopt the idea? A large telecommunications utility might not rush in because it cannot afford to lower quality of service. VOIP suppliers might use it, but how much could they afford to pay, if anything?

The point I am making is that forecasting revenue is nearly impossible when technology is disruptive. You do not know who will adopt the technology, when it will be adopted and how much people will pay for it. For example, no one could have predicted, when Hotmail was developed, that web-based e-mail would always be a free service. Knowing that in advance would have prevented the development of the technology in the first place! If Sabeer Bhatia had known that his invention would generate nearly zero revenue, would he have bothered to develop Hotmail? On the contrary, he would probably have pursued his initial idea of a corporate intranet, which would have been a great loss to mankind!

So if forecasting revenue at the stage of developing a product is impossible, no VC firm should give credence to revenue forecasts. Their hope is that the product will be of immense value when it is finally developed, but given that the chances of that happening so are minimal, it makes sense to be tight on costs. A good VC firm will ask its portfolio firms to submit an expense sheet, or the "burn rate", every month, or even every week, and scrutinize it closely for avoidable expenditure.

If the startup team is so small, does that not put a burden on the CEO?

It does, unfortunately. I have seen many good teams slow down product development during the period when they are raising funds. This is because the CEO is the main person who can raise money because he represents the key technical talent in the team. He has to make every presentation; VCs will not agree to listen to a presentation without the CEO making it. Since fund-raising can take anywhere up to 6 months, it means that the CEO really has a heavy burden to bear. In addition, the CEO is usually responsible for keeping a lid on expenditure and for recruitment as well. He or she is usually a 100-hour a week person for this reason. Hopefully it will all work out, but as you can see, it needs a special person to lead a startup.

You seem to be implying that a startup should have a tight, focused mindset and design its financial strategy accordingly. Does this always make sense?

That is generally the case. Venture capitalists strongly prefer that their portfolio companies be focused on a single product. They think that if a multi-product strategy is valuable, then so should a single-product; so why not see if it works with a single product and expand later? For the startup, this is not always an easy strategy to follow. There are times when the market is strong or the product being developed has a strong following- for example, dot-coms in 1999 and fiber optics in 2000. The temptation is to take in too much money so that there is some sense of financial ease within the firm as to its strategies. For example, the firm might believe that it can better recruit good people by telling them that it has a solid financial cushion, that it could develop its products faster by spending more money. With too much money also comes the temptation to diversify too much. For example, it was common in 1999 for cash-flush dotcoms to pour a lot of money down the drain by acquiring "synergistic" startups! My view is that such thinking confuses the marginal positive impact of a little more money with the big, adverse impact of too much money. Let me give an example. Suppose there is a startup whose budget is three million dollars over the next year, to be spent roughly equally on people and equipment, with the objective of developing its prototype within this period. This might be the typical case in Silicon Valley. Suppose that the firm raises three million dollars and then finds at the end of the year that the market has soured generally, making it difficult to raise additional money even though its prototype is ready on schedule. This is a typical situation in which the CEO would feel that his decision to raise only three million was a mistake. I have come across many such cases. The reality is probably quite different. Suppose that the firm had raised six million instead of three million. My experience is that throwing in more money rarely speeds up prototype development. There are several reasons for this. More money may not be as efficiently spent. Also, the key to development is good people and the cost of good people does not change dramatically. If it cost $150,000 to recruit someone in average times, it will cost maybe twenty percent more to recruit them in boom times and twenty percent less in bad times. The difference in getting the right people is, perhaps, twenty percent, for which it does not make sense to raise a lot more money than you need in the early stages and incur the cost of heavy dilution.

On the other hand, it is important to have adequate money at the marketing stage. Many a CEO has told me when times were rough that if he had raised adequate money at earlier stages he would not be having such a tough time spending on marketing. But the response to that is that venture capitalists would never fund a company to the marketing stage when the prototype itself has not been developed. This would be too risky a strategy for the venture capitalist.

So a startup will have to take the risk that, even with a good prototype, it may not have the funds for marketing because of an adverse change in the environment. Many dotcoms, for example, failed at the stage of marketing throughout the year 2000 in the absence of adequate marketing funds when their venture capitalists pulled the plug on them. Looking at the environment in 2001, this made perfect sense for VCs to do. Even long-established dotcoms have struggled. So, if the startup dotcom had raised excess funds in 1999, when the environment was favorable, it would have merely meant it would have had a greater fall a few months later than it did. What let dotcoms down was not venture capitalists but the consumers, who did not embrace specialized dotcoms the way that they were expected to do. On the other hand, products with a promising market, at least until proven otherwise by the facts, have continued to raise enough money even in a generally adverse environment. Valuations may be lower than expected but so are salaries, rentals and other costs. By the way, here's a prediction: I think dot coms are set to recover in 2002 and beyond as consumer expectations are matched by improved service by dotcom firms. Unlike countries like India, where dotcoms failed in 2000 because there were not enough Internet users, in the U.S. the problem was that the quality of service provided was not as good as the brick-and-mortar experience. That will change over the next few years as firms improve logistics and technology.

There is another reason I have not yet discussed for why a single-product strategy is hard to adopt. Suppose a startup wants to develop a technology for data mining. If successful, it could either license that technology or develop products around it, such as CRM products. The startup might feel that licensing will not generate much revenue relative to developing products. This is where the venture capitalist has an important role to play. Developing products may not be the startup's strength, leading to inferior products; yet developing the technology alone may not have much value. I have seen several firms fail to get funding despite superior ideas because of their inability to resolve this issue in their discussion with venture capitalists.

Prior to an IPO many Indian CEOs tend to replace themselves. Why?

Many CEOs need to replace themselves once beta testing begins. The reason is that the value of the firm and most of its expenditure at that point lie in marketing, providing responsive service and rapid back-end fixes of problems. The initial CEO perhaps does not have the qualities necessary to effectively deal with these issues, so at that point he should bow out. This is a big thing, considering the Indian tradition of hanging on to the "big boss" title forever or until the kids grow up and take over. Of course, the perceived weakness of Indian CEOs, when it came to marketing, was often a problem of the stock market's perceptions rather than of the intrinsic qualities of the Indian CEO. The stock market in the early days up to, perhaps early 1999, had a perception that Indians were not as focused on stock market value as the more mainline Americans. I believe that this perception has changed, largely because of the great number of Indians who succeeded and were found to be personable as well as comfortable with the requirements of high finance. Hence, Indians, or more generally South Asians (given Wall Street's inability to distinguish among South Asians) are now well accepted in the investment community. Other Asian communities have lagged behind Indians in this respect, probably due to their difficulties with the English language.

Does the IPO continue to be a sensible exit strategy in today's changed environment?

Exit usually implies an IPO or an acquisition. Depending on the market, IPOs may be more difficult to do. Acquisitions don't usually slow down with the market, although the valuations change dramatically. But it does not really matter to the acquiring company. If Cisco bought a startup for five billion dollars in return for one percent of its shares in early 2000 (when its market capitalization was five hundred billion dollars) and if it buys a startup in early 2001 of the same quality for 2.5 billion and again issues one percent of its shares (because its market capitalization is 250 billion), Cisco is unaffected. This is because the startup costs it one percent of its equity each time. That is why acquisitions are not much affected by slowdowns in the stock markets. Sure, the acquired firm's shareholders lose, provided they are able to exit immediately. If they hold on, the valuation of the acquisition depends on how Cisco's share price performs; so again, it does not matter much.

Does India have the environment for a successful VC industry?

The Indian VC environment is very nascent. Between 1988 and 1999 a total of only 350 million dollars was invested in Indian startups through venture capital funds, of which less than fifteen percent was in high technology. So there was a lot of reform in 1999 and 2000 and new laws were passed to improve the supply of capital. The exuberant markets of 1999 and 2000 certainly helped; in 2000, over 700 million was invested in a single year alone! Most of that money went into dotcom companies that have since crashed. Interestingly, very little went into global plays, either dotcoms or those more infrastructure-oriented. It puzzled me in 1999 and 2000 as to why India's entrepreneurs were so focused on the tiny markets of India when they had the talent, as judged by their brethren in Silicon Valley, to look at bigger plays. I later understood this puzzle when I met several hundred of them during two recent visits and looked closely at their business plans. The problem is the absence of good mentors. Though technically skilled, the founders did not know which markets to enter. Instead of thinking about how to improve the quality of data mining software, for example, they thought instead about how to sell steel products over the Internet. This is because their advisors and angel financiers in India were familiar with selling steel and had never used data mining products. Even the formal venture capitalists came out of largely financial backgrounds and were unfamiliar with technology. So even though the supply of capital is much improved, the problem of a lack of good ideas remains.

How can this problem get resolved?

It will obviously take time. Silicon Valley itself took decades to develop its present startup culture. In India we do not have the presence of a cadre of successful entrepreneurs who have developed technology startups and can now use their knowledge in combination with their wealth in order to fund newcomers. In India the successful IT companies are large firms focused on providing software services. This requires project management skills using proven tools. For a startup to be successful you need someone within such a firm to say, "Aha! Here is a CRM tool that I can improve with my new approach." This is already available since India has a strong culture of startups. The problem is that the potential entrepreneur has no one with whom he can knowledgeably discuss his idea. VC firms in India are essentially financiers whose chief role is to provide the right amount of finance at the right time, which is insufficient.

The solution is, for a time, to marry Silicon Valley VCs with Indian VC firms. The former bring the advisory services on products and the latter have the local presence to identify smart people. What is needed is that an Indian VC firm should have an alliance with some successful entrepreneurs in Silicon Valley who should also operate an incubator in Silicon Valley to allow the Indian entrepreneurs to develop their ideas in a more global environment. Thus, the Indian VC firm will identify an entrepreneur for his ideas and, together with the Silicon Valley VC, they can agree to finance his project. The entrepreneur's project would hopefully be one of global scope, for which he may need to develop his team both in India and Silicon Valley. The Silicon Valley VC would provide a physical location for the Indian firm to begin its global development. It would also later introduce the firm to later stage VCs and help in marketing.

In the interim, organizations like TiE can also play an important role. For instance, charter members of TiE USA who travel to India should spend at least one day of each trip mentoring startups. In return, they should have the option of investing in them. Once a cadre of successful Indian entrepreneurs is built up within India, the process will be self-sustaining. Of course, there are still some rules that need to be changed, such as allowing Indian venture capital firms to invest overseas, but on the legal and regulatory front, eighty percent of the work has been done.

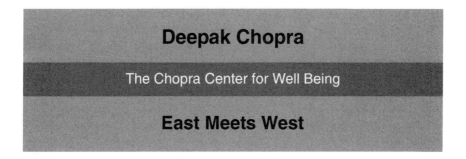

Deepak Chopra

The Chopra Center for Well Being

East Meets West

Deepak Chopra, M.D. is an internationally acclaimed leader in the field of mind and body medicine. He is widely recognized for his role in bringing time-honored Eastern principles to the Western world. Time Magazine heralds Chopra as one of the top 100 heroes and icons of the century - "the poet-prophet of alternative medicine." In 1995 he joined the distinguished company of South African President Nelson Mandela, Congresswoman Barbara Jordan, business author Tom Peters and radio personality Garrison Keillor as a recipient of the Toastmasters International Top Five Outstanding Speakers award.

Deepak Chopra continues to transform our understanding of the meaning of health, using the ancient healing methods of Ayur-Veda, which emphasizes meditation, herbal medicine, yoga and massage. His best-selling books include *Ageless Body, Timeless Mind*; *Quantum Healing*; *Perfect Health*; *The Seven Spiritual Laws of Success*; and *The Path to Love*. Formerly the Chief of Staff at Boston Regional Medical Center, Dr. Chopra built a successful endocrinology practice in Boston in the 1980's.

Raghu Batta and I conducted this interview via telephone.

Deepak Chopra is a master at simplifying and organizing difficult concepts into information that is easily understood. He was very generous and willing to share the wisdom and knowledge that he has gained in the process of amalgamating the various disciplines of medicine. We talked at length about Eastern and Western values and what role they play in the entrepreneurial world. He discussed the reasons behind the rise and success of Indian entrepreneurship. Finally, Dr. Chopra commented on elements such as leadership, education and knowledge, trust and ethics, and risk that are fundamental requirements in order for entrepreneurs to be truly successful.

> *"If you can sing your song, not worrying who listens and what they think, you're going to be extremely successful."*

Recently there has been a tremendous rise in Indian entrepreneurship in the West. To what do you attribute this?

Knowing the Indian mind, I think Indians - particularly those who have immigrated to the West- were of very good educational background. Indians are by nature adventurous, willing to relinquish the known and step into the unknown. They are also very ambitious and hardworking. All these attributes lead to a natural self-selection process in the whole area of entrepreneurship.

I think Indian families are very close knit, so they do not get distracted by fractured relationships in their families. The successful ones are not usually adversely affected by extremely unhealthy lifestyles or habits. But I think even more important is the fact that they have a tight family structure, a code of values and ethics. They have a great desire to succeed, a great desire to be recognized, to be acknowledged for what they are and who they are. These are the unique characteristics I've observed. By the way, this seems to hold true to some extent in Chinese-American families as well.

I used to teach at Harvard Medical School, and I noticed that the Asian population of children in Boston was less than 0.1 percent, yet at Harvard Medical School, probably ten to fifteen percent of the kids were of Indian or South East Asian origin. Their parents worked very hard and made lots of sacrifices in order to send them to medical school. The children in turn acknowledged that they were responsible and aware of the sacrifices that were being made by the family. I think perhaps Indian families may even overdo it, constantly discussing the schools their children are attending. You won't find that as part of normal cocktail conversations amongst other ethnic groups.

Would you sum this up as being "culture capital"?

Yes, I would say "culture capital" for sure. I would also say "creative capital" because there's a lot of creativity in the Indian-Americans.

When in India, we're not able to gain this momentum and be innovative. It is only when we come here that we see this kind of innovation and momentum. Can you comment on this?

There are two reasons for this. First, those who come are more adventurous, more willing to relinquish their environment and the comforts of the known and step into the unknown. So you have the selection process right there. Secondly, the environment in the U.S. is very supportive of that kind of entrepreneurship. It is very supportive of creativity and recognizes deservedness. The lack of that support has been very frustrating to people in India. I know of people who have done exceedingly well in this country and then have gone back to India with a great passion, a great dedication and a great sense of patriotism and nationalism. After a while they get extremely frustrated and then return to the U.S., even though they had the intention and the desire to be in India. But I think that is changing; the more I go back to India, I find there is a new feeling of freedom, a new sense of excitement and a new sense of self-worth. Thanks to the contributions of the Indians who left earlier, there is a strong acknowledgement of what Indians can contribute in terms of their creativity, their hard work and their brainpower. We're hearing a lot about that and it has resulted in the enhancement of self-esteem in India. I think what you're seeing here is having a fallout effect in India. In fact I would not be surprised if India emerges as major economic power in the world. That will probably eradicate its previous inferiority complex that has put all the attention on nuclear weapons and military involvement.

Along those lines, you make an interesting point about visiting India recently and noticing a strong sense of identity. Indians have been accused in the past of having ethnic identity but very little racial identity. Over the course of your visits in the past several years, are you starting to see a sense of national identity and self-worth? We think some of that can be attributed to economic prosperity and progress, right?

Right. And it's good that Indians are transcending their narrow boundaries to acquire a national identity. It should go even beyond that; we should have an international identity. I personally think, as Rabindranath Tagore said, "Nationalism is a form of sophisticated tribalism." I think Indians should be proud of their culture and not necessarily of whether they come from Hyderabad, Bangalore or New Delhi.

Let's switch gears to the West. When the East is coupled with the West, or Silicon Valley or the Boston area, it results in a phenomenal synergy for entrepreneurship. What does the West bring to the table?

The West brings a supportive and nurturing environment. It also brings something you won't see in Japan or many Asian countries, where there is an overt discrimination against foreign elements. If you compare the West with the rest of the world, it is not that overtly discriminatory. It's more tolerant, and there is an understanding that America is truly a melting pot. Its great strength lies in its diversity. The environment lends itself to creativity, vision, risk-taking and entrepreneurship because there is a deep understanding within the person who comes here that if you are here, you have it in you to go all the way; you can realize your dream. I think that is the main thing that the West brings. The other thing it brings, by default, is a complacency in those who have already made it. If you're complacent then you are not a good competitor.

Now switching to the negatives, what would you say are the limitations of the East in stimulating entrepreneurship and what would be your proposal to overcome them?

I see the possibility of a gradual erosion of our cultural identity and values and a loosening of both our social and family structure. I hope that as we step into the next generation we maintain a sense of cultural pride. The one thing that destroys anybody and has destroyed the American sense of well-being is lack of family values. This is a huge strength that India has in general, that families are so supportive and values are so strong that it keeps them vibrant, loving and secure. You know, my kids bring their friends home and everybody's got stepbrothers and stepsisters and stepparents and after a while you don't know who's who.

Dr. Chopra, if you look at the life cycle of an Indian - when he's born his family starts planning for his school; when he's in his teens the family starts planning for his college - there is a strong focus on education. Then when he has grown up and it's time for his marriage, his parents help in that process too. When the bride and groom meet they tend to say "yes" almost immediately. If you correlate each one of these events to a skill corresponding to entrepreneurship - for example, comparing saving to strategic planning, get-

ting married to risk-taking - you see an entrepreneurial mindset. What are your comments on this analogy?

The further West you go the more liberating it gets.

You have to have a delicate balance. I think it can be overdone, in which case it becomes imprisoning; the kids of the second generation are already rebelling against that. You can become a prisoner of the culture and then the culture becomes a huge burden. On the other hand, as you show in your examples, it certainly allows you to have a more structured life and in many ways entrepreneurship gets built right into your genes. I mean there's no question that the whole concept of dharma exists in India. For everybody in the family there is a sort of family dharma; businessmen's children become businessmen and physicians' children are more likely to become physicians. A lot of that is breaking down here right now and in some ways it is quite healthy. As I said, when you come to the U.S. you begin in Boston, which is conservative, and end up in California, which is the ultimate frontier. The further West you go the more liberating it gets. I travel a lot in Europe and I find that Europe is in many cases stagnating because of its culture. It's a prisoner of the past. So I think that while it is important that our cultural values aren't deeply eroded, we need a healthy balance between our heritage and our ability to embrace the practices of freedom that we have available here. This would lead to a balanced culture.

One of the interesting points you made earlier relates to cultural pride. A common problem that we have experienced in discussions with our friends is understanding what is really meant by the wisdom of the East, which you have spent many years studying. Even though most of us were educated in India, we find this to be a difficult question

Some time ago I came up with my own definitions of the difference between wisdom, knowledge, information, data and meaninglessness.

I think wisdom is basically knowledge that nurtures the ecosystem and its ongoing evolution without having to articulate it. That's a big part of the Indian concept of duty, of dharma, of connectedness, of family values and of social values. The rituals that we have around Diwali, for example, are methods of drawing our attention and intentions into the wisdom, which is the knowingness of our interdependence, a knowingness of interrelationship and inseparability as part of a larger ecosystem. Whether that ecosystem is the biosphere or the social system doesn't matter. This is ingrained in us Indians and, as I said, even the religious rituals are methods of drawing our attention and intentions toward the meaning, context, purpose and relationships of our lives. It's so deeply embedded that you don't have to articulate it; you are an expression of it. Hopefully, that will not disappear, because we still see strong families here. It manifests itself in the ways we deal with each other and society in general.

Given the history of our culture and wisdom, which dates back 5000 years, one of the interesting paradoxes is that modern Indian society is probably not as trusting and trustworthy as some of the western nations. For example, when we came here to study for graduate school we were astonished by the fact that the professor would just hand you a take-home exam. In Japan none of the bicycles are locked at the station. Even here in the U.S. they always give you the benefit of the doubt; when they look at your resume they assume it is truthful and correct.

Obviously there are no simple answers to that, but here are some possible scenarios. First of all, Indians have been subject to foreign invasions for a long, long time, and India is one country which has never militarily invaded another country in the past six thousand years. It's the only country about which you can say that. Indians have been subject to invasion time after time and by and large they've absorbed the different cultures and have been receptive to them. That lends a lot of richness to the Indian culture. I think two things have eroded a sense of trust. One is the subjugation that India has suffered at the hands of the British and the lack of pride that resulted from that. That lasted for 200 years. The generation immediately following independence basically became obsessed with proving itself. This was actually an overblown reaction to a perceived sense of inferiority from the past. Lack of trust also stems from a lack of economic power, from poverty. Everyone is trying to get the maximum that they can get. As India grows in economic power I think you will see that distrust abating.

In our research we have categorized the "East meets West" region into the 4 Cs: Intellectual Capital, Venture Capital, Support Capital and Culture capital. These are the core ingredients that make up the chemistry of the Silicon Valley and the Boston Area. As an expert in this domain, could you validate our theorem?

I think that's very well put. What you say is logical and makes perfect sense. I'll tell you where I come from personally regarding the secret of entrepreneurship. I think it's very important not to confuse money with wealth. Money is a symbol with which you measure somebody's value and how they contribute to society. If you are aware of that then you know that wealth is ultimately structured in your awareness, in your culture. You can therefore generate it through the appropriate transactions that are in the realm of relationships and you are not confused about it. You know, as soon as you start substituting the symbol for the reality you will start eating the menu instead of the dinner, and then you're in trouble! I think Indians recognize that instinctively; they are very good at fostering and nurturing relationships, networking, not being afraid to ask or offer favors, because they recognize that this is what ultimately creates the matrix out of which this symbol which one calls the "dollar" is generated. Money originates from a bartering system and Indians are great barterers. They've now carried it out to a new level of sophistication.

Dr. Chopra, as you can see, the web is globalizing the market. The need to replicate the East meets West scenario becomes of paramount importance.

Yes, it does. On the other hand, it's going to be spontaneous in its evolution, in that it's already begun to happen and will accelerate as we start directing our attention toward what creates this wonderful alliance and what creates the matrix. So I don't think we have to worry that it won't happen; it's going to happen as part of the evolutionary process. I just came back from attending the Global Forum 2000, hosted by Mikhail Gorbachev, and it's so obvious that all national boundaries will soon be broken down. Information technology (IT) is going to lead to a knowledge-based society and I hope ultimately into a wisdom-based society. If that happens, you don't have to worry about Indians; they know how to go for it.

Any comments on how to replicate this scenario in a global manner?

It's like learning how to ride a bike. If I can learn to ride a bike, anyone else can learn to ride a bike. So I think what you're doing is very good. That's the replication process. Look at what is happening in Silicon Valley; use it as a model; understand what the principles are and then apply those principles. There is one thing I see in Silicon Valley right now which is very gratifying and which has not been, by the way, a trait that Indians have had in the past. I believe that if Indians have lacked one thing in the past, it is philanthropy, it is generosity, a sense of selflessness and charity. Now I see that changing. Perhaps we needed a certain amount of success and a certain amount of affluence for this to happen. I see Silicon Valley entrepreneurs like Kanwal Rekhi and Guru Deshpande who are very selfless people. They are very interested in helping others. That is such a gratifying thing to see, that they feel it is their duty to help. They've made enough for themselves so they are no longer totally self-absorbed. I think that this particular trait in Indians is an emerging one that we should be so proud of. Let us hope that it continues.

We are going to switch gears here. What are your comments on entrepreneurship and leadership?

Let's look at the word LEADER as an acronym:

L = Look and listen, with the heart, with the mind and with the soul.

E = Empower yourself and those who you work with.

A = Awareness. Ask: Who am I and what do I want? Who are you and what do you want?

D =Doing. Be action-oriented.

E =Enter higher states of awareness such as creativity, vision, and intuition.

R = Responsibility. Walk your talk.

S = Synchro-destiny.

What are your comments on education and knowledge?

I think education is a very important thing that we can impart to our children. But education must not be just knowledge-based, it has to be wisdom-based. The one thing that's lacking in our educational system is education about insight, about imagination, about intuition, about creativity and vision and a sense of the sacred. This is lacking everywhere in the world. It was something that was once a part of the Indian culture in "gurukulas" and in Shantiniketan, started by Rabindranath Tagore. Now it's an idea which needs to be resurrected, really resurrected. There is knowledge about the world and there is knowledge about oneself. And the knowledge about oneself is about very basic, fundamental things: Who am I? What do I want? What's my role? Is there meaning and purpose to my existence? What are the mechanics of insight, imagination, intention, intuition, understanding, knowingness, creativity and vision?

Your comments on risk-taking?

If you do not take risks you are doomed to eternal senility. You never make any progress. You have to take risks; you have to make mistakes; you have to learn by mistakes and you have to learn not to make the same mistakes over again. But if you stop making mistakes and you never move, you'll stagnate. And if you stagnate, you die. So risk is a very, very important component. But it must be risk with sobriety, risk with awareness, risk with alertness. Good or bad results don't matter; you start afresh every time. You learn from the bad results and you start all over again. With good results you learn too. There is a saying attributed to Lord Shiva, the first yogi: "I use memories but I do not allow memories to use me." Using memories is a form of creativity, while allowing memories to use you is self-victimization.

Your comments on trust and ethics?

In Vedanta teachings, the purpose of a business is to serve society, and making money is a by-product of that service.

Ethics are very important because one must pay attention to the ethical nature of all transactions, all business transactions. In Vedanta, they say the purpose of a business is to serve society. If you go to business school here, the first thing you are told is that the purpose of a business is to make money. In Vedanta teachings, the purpose of a business is to serve society and making money is a by-product of that service. If you have that inner attitude, you're going to be very successful.

On the other hand, if you sacrifice your ethics and your honesty and your truthfulness in your transactions, sooner or later the law of karma will destroy you. No matter how successful you are you can't escape the cosmic credit and debit accountant. The accounting is far more precise, far more accurate than anything you will see in your bank statement. You should be aware of that. And I think that should be part of our teaching, as it once was. That's why successful businessmen were successful. Trust comes from experience. You can't tell somebody to be trustworthy if their experience belies that. In order to get trust you have to be trustworthy and you must create an environment of trust in your organization. Once you do that you can go a step forward.

This brings us to the next logical question: what are the habits of successful people?

I can only talk about this from personal experience and personal observation. It depends on how you define success. If you define it in purely material terms then the habits of successful people are: number one, they are hardworking; two, they have driving ambition; three, they make exacting plans; four, they are obsessed with success; five, they have a heart attack or a fractured relationship or become prone to addictive behavior. So if you are defining success in purely materialistic terms, then those are the habits and you're asking for trouble!

If you mean by success to grasp the meaning or purpose of life, it means the progressive realization of your goals which are worthy; it means the expansion of happiness, the ability to feel joy and spread it to others, it means having a sense of connection with the creative power of the universe. You know how to get in touch with your inner silence and are not easily swayed by the good or bad opinions of others. And even though you are responsive to feedback, you are not swayed by criticism or praise. You are detached from outcome even though you have an intended outcome. You are focused in the present. You believe in giving and receiving. You know that every action you take and every choice you make has consequences, and you have the insight and the vision to see the effect of those choices in the long run.

In order to take care of yourself, in other words, you stay physically and emotionally healthy. You don't abuse your body through toxic relationships or toxic habits or toxic food or toxic substances or toxic environments. Finally, you know that you have a unique ability to express yourself, that you can sing your song. In one of Rumi Sufi's poems he says, "I want to sing like birds, sing not worrying who listens and what they think." If you can sing your song, not worrying who listens and what they think, you're going to be extremely successful.

You have a phenomenal stage presence. You are a charismatic speaker. Did it come naturally to you, or did you develop it?

When I was in school in India, in St. Columbus, I was very interested in debating and I used to represent my school in All-India debates. I won many prizes in the national and international debating contests in school, college and medical school. I was very involved in that. I thought debating was an essential skill with which one could dissect a problem to its ultimate logic and that it didn't matter which side you were on. You were trained to examine every subject in great detail and then prove your point. So I was brought up with that kind of tradition in school and college and medical school. And then when I became a physician I was very fond of teaching in medical school. I always taught using the Socratic method. I taught for a while at Harvard, Boston University and Tufts Medical School as a medical instructor and as an assistant clinical professor at Boston Medical School. I didn't believe in didactic teaching. I would ask my students: If you were God, how would you design a protein molecule? Within 2 hours the students would collectively design a protein molecule as God would have designed it. I was just shocked that everybody had that ability, and even if they didn't have it by themselves, if you got them together they certainly could have come up with what God would have come up with. It was amazing for me to discover that. After that I just started using that technique in all my classes and I found that I didn't really have to teach anything. Everybody, if given an opportunity, has infinite potential and it just needs to be unlocked.

You started the Chopra Center for Well-Being in 1995. What was the need, speaking from an entrepreneur's standpoint?

The center was initially established so that I could have a place that expressed what was in my books. Otherwise, everything that I said would just be theoretical, and I wanted a place where I could put it into practical terms. So the center has many activities. We see patients; we do workshops. People come here for learning, for self-empowerment, for training, for mind/body workshops. There are CEOs and politicians who come from all over the world and there is something we offer to just about everyone who comes here. My goal was to make the center a practical expression of what was contained in my books.

What skills do you attribute to your upbringing?

I grew up in India listening to stories from the Mahabharata and Ramayana and the great Puranas, told by my grandmother. As a child, I somehow had this vision that these Gods and Goddesses were not external beings but that you could actually imagine being one of them. Later, I understood that these great mythical deities were basically states of potentiality that one could manifest. I grew up with that belief and I actually teach that now to everybody. I think India's great contribution to the world is its living mythology. You go to India and you see that when the Ramayana is being shown on television everything comes to a standstill. It's vibrant, alive, living mythology. I think mythology, when absorbed and imbibed into consciousness, with a deep understanding that mythical beings are symbols of states of energy, of information and of awareness in your own consciousness, can really empower people.

Dr. Chopra, what makes you tick? What is your driving force?

I think the main thing is that I really enjoy myself and I have a passion for what I do. There's something new around the corner for me every time I open my eyes.

About the Author

Gurmeet is a Silicon Valley engineer and author. He has authored several acclaimed books on Business and Quality Management and has extensive management experience from Matsushita and Apple Computer. He currently works in operations management at a Silicon Valley startup. Gurmeet lives with his wife in the heart of Silicon Valley, CA.